THE PATH TO *Liberation*

WHISPERS OF AMMA

Swami Amritachitswarupananda Puri

The Path to Liberation-Whispers of Amma
Swami Amritachitswarupananda Puri

Published by:
Amrita Books
Amrita Enterprises Private Limited
Vallikavu, Clappana P.O.,
Kollam 690 525, Kerala, India

First Edition September 2025

Design: Arun Raj • Typesetting & Layout: Chandrasekaran K
(Amrita Office of Communication – AOC)

For more information contact:
Email: info@amritabooks.in
Website: www.amritabooks.com

Ashram Website:
www.amritapuri.org
www.amma.org
www.embracingtheworld.org

CONTENTS

FOREWORD

Om Shri Guru Charan Kamalebhyo Namah

With folded hands, I bow to Amma, the eternal guiding light, whose boundless compassion has poured forth as these sacred "Whispers." This book, The Path to Liberation – Whispers of Amma, is not merely a text but a living transmission of wisdom, meant to guide sincere seekers step by step toward the ultimate truth of the Self.

Amma reminds us at the very outset: "Without Sādhana Chatuṣṭaya Sampatti, one cannot know Brahman." These fourfold qualifications — discernment , dispassion, discipline of mind, and longing for liberation — are the very foundation of Vedantic pursuit. Without them, even the most profound teachings remain only as concepts; with them, the Truth reveals itself in the heart of the seeker.

This book unfolds the journey systematically, beginning with external actions and practices, gradually moving inward through knowledge, discernment, and self-inquiry, and culminating in the abiding light of Self-knowledge. Here when the word ignorance is mentioned, it should be taken as the ignorance of the indwelling Paramamatman (The Supreme Consciousness) Each chapter is like a step on a sacred pilgrimage:

External actions and practices prepare the ground through purity of conduct.

Moving towards knowledge and discerning between the real and the illusionary.

Internal realization of "I am"-ness as separate from the body and mind dawns

The more one rests in this "I am" Beingness, the more clarity and peace one experiences

Dissolution of ego unveils the unchanging substratum of existence.

Final realization and freedom reveal the Atman's true nature as limitless Consciousness.

With this realization of oneness, the free being lives as pure Awareness, free from bondage and untouched by duality.

The clarity with which Amma's teachings are expressed here makes this book both practical and profound. It is not merely philosophy to be admired but a living guide to be practiced, step by step, in one's own life.

Dear reader, approach these pages not with the curiosity of the intellect alone, but with the humility of the heart. Amma may be known for her extensive charitable work around the world but in reality she is the walking, talking and acting Shruti (scripture) Amma's teachings of spirituality comes from direct Self knowledge.

Let these whispers become your inner compass. May Amma's grace flow through every word, leading you to the peace, freedom, and bliss that is your true nature.

Lokāḥ Samastāḥ Sukhino Bhavantu — May all beings everywhere be happy and free.

With reverence and gratitude,

Shripad Roy Hegde
USA

PREFACE

This book, The Path to Liberation—Whispers of Amma, emerges from the living stream of Amma's teachings, flowing with clarity, compassion, and truth. It is not written as a mere intellectual exercise, but as a companion for seekers walking the inner journey. The chapters trace a gradual unfolding—from external practices, to the dawning of knowledge, to the final recognition of the Self as ever free. The material in this book is repetitive by design, intended to reinforce sravana,mananam and nidhidyasana so that the seeker gains conviction and is grounded is their True Nature. Each section invites reflection, self-inquiry, and transformation, resonating with Amma's guidance that practice and realization must go hand in hand. The wisdom offered here is universal, transcending boundaries of religion or culture, rooted in the eternal call of the Self. It is written in the spirit of service, to share Amma's message that liberation is not far away, but the very nature of who we are. May the reader approach these pages with openness, humility, and faith, and discover light in the midst of life's uncertainties. May Amma lead us into the radiant Light of Immortality.

Swami Amritachitswarupananda Puri
Amritapuri

INTRODUCTION

**“ True peace comes not from accumulating more,
but from letting go. When we renounce the ego
and surrender to love, we experience
the unity that is our true nature. ”
— Amma**

The Path to Liberation — Whispers of Amma was born from a simple intention: to place Amma’s living wisdom in the hands and hearts of sincere seekers. In an age overflowing with information yet starved of stillness, these pages offer not arguments but pointers—gentle, compassionate whispers that turn the mind inward.

This is not a book of abstract speculation. It is meant as a companion for the journey from restlessness to repose, from ego-centered striving to effortless being. The inspiration behind it is Amma herself—her ability to express the highest Advaitic truth in a language the heart immediately understands.

The work weaves together themes of self-inquiry, devotion, service, and surrender—leading us from outer practices to inner recognition, from knowledge about the Self to direct recognition as the Self. The essential teachings of Advaita Vedānta shine throughout: the Ātman is not separate from Brahman; the individual self is one with the universal reality. Alongside this, Amma’s compassion brings practical guidance on karma yoga, bhakti, steadiness of mind, and the dissolving of doership. The book does not claim to provide the destination; it only offers lamps along the way, always pointing the reader back to the Self within.

This book will meet readers differently according to their readiness.

- Seekers weary of endless cycles of striving and disappointment will find here a quiet reassurance.
- Students of Vedānta may discover Amma's heart-language softening intellectual concepts into lived clarity.
- New readers, even without prior exposure to these teachings, may feel a natural resonance in the simplicity of Amma's words.

For anyone who has ever paused between two thoughts and glimpsed a stillness that needs no improvement—this book is already yours.

My own journey into Amma's teachings began during my student years, when I first met her. From those early encounters, it became clear that Amma's teaching is never apart from love-in-action. This book arises out of that experience—of service, study, silence, and gratitude taking the form of words.

I invite you to approach these pages not as a novel to be consumed, but as a pilgrimage to be walked. A few pages at a time are enough. Let one whisper linger through your day. Pause often, close your eyes, and allow the words to dissolve into silence. Read reflectively, asking: "What is this pointing to within me—right now?" Carry a pointer into daily life—whether as an act of service, a pause before reacting, or a few moments of self-inquiry. Above all, approach with gentleness. Spiritual preparation grows not by force, but through patient tending—and grace responds to such tending.

This book stands humbly within the lineage of Advaita Vedānta—the Upaniṣads, the Bhagavad Gītā, the works of Śaṅkara, and the unbroken Guru-paramparā. It bows to Śruti (revelation) and Smṛti (tradition), while carrying Amma's fragrance of compassion as method, simplicity as gateway, and love as proof. To teachers seen and unseen, to the countless hands of the Ashram, to villagers who taught me service, and above all to Amma—my pranāms. Any clarity here belongs to them; any obscurity is mine.

If this book has come into your hands, perhaps you were already listening. Perhaps something within you is ready to exchange endless becoming for simple being—to shift from "my way" to the way of truth, and to test in your own experience whether wholeness is not attained but recognized. No promise is made of sudden ecstasy, but gentler gifts await: a calmer mind, a warmer heart, a lighter step, and—when the time ripens—the recognition that the Self has always been free. Bondage was only an appearance born of not-knowing; freedom is your very nature.

So let us begin—not to gather more, but to lay aside what is unnecessary. Walk these pages as you would walk to a temple: with humility, curiosity, and love. If even one whisper turns you inward today, the book has already fulfilled its purpose.

Welcome to the path that returns you to where you have never left.

Swami Amritachitswarupananda Puri
Amritapuri
9-9-25

CHAPTER-1

External Actions and Practices

Service, Devotion, and Knowledge

"Knowledge, devotion, and selfless service are paths to purify the heart and mind. Through them, we clear away the clouds of ignorance and come to recognize the true Self, ever-present and divine." Amma

These paths work in harmony to lead seekers toward an awareness of their divine nature. Throughout human history, humanity's understanding of God has shifted from more primitive conceptions to the sophisticated spiritual insights of today. While the concept of God has evolved, the core attributes—omniscience, omnipotence, and omnipresence—have remained. The idea of Ishwara, God the manifest divine, continues to represent this presence in a personal and relatable way.

As one matures, particularly through Advaita Vedanta, a deeper, non-dualistic understanding teaches that the divine is not separate from creation but appears so due to ignorance of Brahman, the ultimate reality. The misconception of God as an external entity fades with realization, revealing that the divine essence is intrinsic to each being. This transformative understanding reorients the spiritual quest from seeking externally to realizing the divinity within.

Through devotion, service, and self-inquiry, individuals begin to see that their essence—the Atma—is not distinct but identical with Brahman. As they engage in acts of devotion and selfless service, the sense of separation dissolves, replaced by the recognition that they are of the divine whole. This realization of oneness shifts the relationship with God from one of external worship to an internal journey, where the individual essence is realized as divine.

Amma embodies this understanding in her devotional singing, especially through bhajans. When Amma sings, her deep connection to Ishwara, the personified divine, is palpable. Bhajans transcend mere music, becoming a medium through which Amma channels her yearning for the divine so that the listeners dissolve the separation between themselves and God. Thus, those present are invited into this sacred space, where the divine essence becomes tangible, not as something distant but as an intimate part of their own being.

In these moments, Amma serves as a bridge, guiding others to experience the divine within themselves. Her devotion becomes a powerful reminder that seeking God externally is unnecessary; the divine already resides within. This experience mirrors the teachings of Advaita Vedanta, where the Self and the divine are recognized as one. Through Amma's devotion, the spiritual path transforms from a quest to find God to an inner realization that the divine has always been present within.

Amma also stands as a living embodiment of the Guru lineage, reflecting the core teaching of Advaita Vedanta: "Tat Tvam Asi"—Thou art That. This fundamental truth emphasizes that the Self and Brahman are one, and devotion, while important, is a preparatory step toward realizing this ultimate oneness. Amma teaches that discipline, discernment, and devotion are vital for clearing the mind and heart, leading the seeker to self-realization.

Amma emphasizes the importance of developing dispassion toward worldly distractions and anchoring oneself in the wisdom of the Upanishads. Through control of mind and sense, the cessation of worldly interest, forbearance, faith, patience, and an unwavering aspiration for self-realization, one can progress on the spiritual path. Selfless service purifies the heart, and meditation deepens one's connection to the divine. Listening to teachings, contemplating their meaning, and meditating moves seekers beyond intellectual understanding to the direct recognition of the Self.

Atma Jnana, or Self-knowledge, refers to the higher wisdom that transcends the ordinary mind and senses. It is an all-encompassing awareness that sustains the functions of the Indriyas (senses) and the entire experience of life. In the non-dual framework, Atma Jnana is not merely intellectual knowledge but the recognition of the Self (Atma) as the all-pervading reality. This wisdom, rooted in the understanding of the true nature of the Self, becomes the foundation for spiritual practices and meditation. The deities (Devatas), symbolic representations of the divine forces in the universe, are said to revere Atma Jnana, as it embodies the essence of divine wisdom that governs all actions and experiences. It becomes both the object of meditation (Dhyeyam) and the means to attain meditation (Dhyanam), guiding the seeker toward the realization of the Self and the universe.

When one meditates on Atma Jnana with Shraddha (faith) and Samadhanam (steadfast concentration), they align themselves with the underlying consciousness that sustains everything. In this state, they are no longer bound by the dualities of success or failure, merit or sin, because their identification shifts from the body and mind to the Atma, the unchanging, infinite reality. This shift allows the individual to transcend the limitations of the senses and intellect, recognizing the Atma as the true and only Self. In this profound realization, the meditator, the process of meditation, and the object of meditation all merge into one: the Atma or Brahman, the ultimate reality. By meditating on the Self as the true essence of all existence, the seeker transcends dualities and limitations, realizing the oneness of existence and the eternal nature of the Self. This realization of Atma Jnana leads to liberation, where the meditator is no longer swayed by the illusions of the world but remains rooted in the unchanging reality of their divine nature.

Ultimately, Amma's teachings aim to guide individuals to the goal of life—self-realization. Thus devotion, discipline, and wisdom offer a comprehensive path that prepares seekers for the ultimate truth—recognizing their oneness with Brahman. Through Amma's guidance, seekers learn to transcend the ups and downs of life, realize the illusions of the mind, and experience the divine essence that resides within. So, through selfless service, deep spiritual practice, and unwavering faith, one can reach the pinnacle of human existence—Self-realization.

Yoga Leads Self-Knowledge

"Keep the body and mind healthy, for they are instruments in service. When we serve the Guru with sincerity and devotion, grace flows naturally, guiding us toward spiritual growth and inner peace." Amma

Amma reminds us that the body and mind are not just tools for worldly achievements; they are essential instruments in the spiritual journey. Yoga, in its many forms, helps to maintain the balance of body and mind, preparing the individual for higher spiritual practices. By keeping ourselves physically and mentally fit, we become more capable of engaging in service and devotion, opening ourselves up to receive the grace of the Guru, which in turn propels us toward Self-knowledge.

All living beings, as well as inanimate objects, rely on food (Annam) for survival and sustenance. Food nourishes not only the physical body but also supports the mind, allowing the individual to function in the world. The ability to navigate the three states of consciousness—waking, dreaming, and deep sleep—depends on the clarity and health of the intellect (Buddhi). This intellect is what enables us to understand and interpret the world around us. However, it is only through Self-knowledge (Atma Jnana) that one can truly grasp the ultimate nature of reality. Knowledge (Jnanam) is the key that unlocks the deeper truths of existence, helping us move beyond the surface level of experience.

For many, direct realization of this deeper truth may not be immediately accessible. Not everyone is ready to dive into the vastness of Self-knowledge without some preliminary preparation. For those who are not yet capable of directly grasping the nature of Brahman, devotional practices (Upasana) offer a path toward gradual spiritual development. Upasana helps to purify the mind and heart, making the individual more receptive to higher truths. These practices serve as stepping stones, allowing seekers to cultivate devotion, discipline, and focus, all of which prepare them for the deeper realization of the Self.

Yoga, in this context, plays a crucial role in leading one to Self-knowledge. Through physical postures, breathing exercises, and meditation, the practitioner attains a state of mental clarity and inner peace. This peace is essential for engaging in higher practices of devotion and self-inquiry. As the mind becomes calm and focused, the individual becomes more capable of understanding the teachings of the Guru and the scriptures. By aligning the body, mind, and spirit, yoga serves as a foundation for deeper spiritual growth, helping one move closer to the realization of the Self.

The journey toward Self-knowledge is gradual and requires both effort and grace. While practices like yoga and Upasana help prepare the seeker, it is ultimately the grace of the Guru that guides the individual toward true realization. As Amma teaches, when one serves the Guru with sincerity and devotion, grace flows naturally. This grace not only strengthens the individual's practice but also acts as a catalyst for spiritual growth. Through devotion, service, and sincere effort, the seeker becomes attuned to the divine presence within, allowing Self-knowledge to blossom naturally.

In essence, the path to Self-knowledge is a holistic one, combining physical, mental, and spiritual practices. Yoga helps maintain the health of the body and mind, Upasana deepens devotion, and the teachings of the Guru illuminate the way. Each aspect of the path serves a specific purpose, gradually leading the seeker toward the ultimate goal of realizing their true divine nature. Through consistent practice and the Guru's grace, the individual moves closer to understanding the eternal truth of existence, experiencing the profound peace and joy that comes with Self-realization

Effort Earns Grace

"Sincere effort and dedicated study open the heart to grace. When we strive with devotion and focus on the path, the grace of the Divine flows naturally, guiding us toward the light of truth." Amma

The essential relationship between personal effort and divine grace. While grace may seem like a gift bestowed upon us, it often arises as a result of sincere dedication and discipline. The more one engages in spiritual practices with devotion and focus, the more receptive they become to the transformative energy of grace. In this way, effort and grace are intimately connected, each reinforcing the other on the journey to Self-realization.

The individual being, known as Purusha, plays a pivotal role in the spiritual process and the unfolding of creation. Purusha possesses the unique capacity for both knowledge and action, two elements essential for navigating life and understanding deeper spiritual truths. The capacity to act and learn enables the individual to engage with the world meaningfully, while also providing the tools necessary for self-reflection and spiritual growth. Through effort in acquiring knowledge and participating in purposeful action,

Purusha advances along the path toward enlightenment, experiencing the natural flow of grace along the way.

In this context, the scriptures (Sruti) serve as a guiding light for Purusha, offering profound wisdom that leads to higher understanding. The Sruti, which includes sacred texts like the Vedas and Upanishads, is a source of eternal truths that can aid individuals in their spiritual evolution. However, to benefit from these teachings, one must approach them with reverence and an open heart. The ability to discern and follow the guidance of the scriptures is what elevates Purusha beyond mere existence, allowing for deeper spiritual development. Ignoring these teachings, on the other hand, leaves one disconnected from higher wisdom, reducing them to a life lived without deeper meaning or purpose.

Those who reject or ignore the wisdom of the scriptures are compared to animals, as they lack the appreciation and capacity to benefit from the guidance that these sacred texts provide. This comparison reflects the idea that spiritual growth requires more than mere survival or physical existence—it requires effort, discernment, and a willingness to evolve. The teachings of the Sruti offer the roadmap to navigate the illusions of the world and to recognize the deeper truths that lie beyond surface appearances. Without the wisdom of the scriptures, one risks remaining entangled in ignorance, unable to access the grace that comes with spiritual effort.

Understanding the unity between Brahman, the ultimate reality, and one's true self (swarupam) is central to spiritual progress. This understanding comes through reflection on the interplay between illusion (adhyasam) and our true nature (tadhyathmam). The world of illusion may cloud our understanding, making it difficult to see the truth of our oneness with Brahman. However, with sincere effort and guidance from the scriptures, Purusha can pierce through the veil of illusion and realize the underlying unity of existence. This realization is a key step on the path to Self-knowledge, where grace flows naturally as a result of dedicated effort.

The process of spiritual growth is a balance between effort and grace. As individuals engage in practices such as meditation, self-inquiry, and service, they are actively cultivating the conditions for grace to manifest in their lives. By embracing the knowledge provided by the scriptures and adhering to the path laid out by these sacred texts, Purusha aligns with the divine flow, making it easier for grace to enter. This relationship between effort and grace is cyclical—grace strengthens the individual's resolve, and their efforts continue to draw more grace, propelling them further along the spiritual journey.

Ultimately, it is through the harmonious interplay of effort, knowledge, and grace that one attains a deeper understanding of life and existence. The individual's effort opens the door to grace, and grace, in turn, provides the clarity and strength needed to continue on the path of spiritual growth. By following the teachings of the scriptures and striving sincerely with devotion, one can transcend the limitations of illusion and realize their oneness with Brahman. This realization is the culmination of both personal effort and divine grace, leading to the ultimate goal of Self-realization.

Unlocking Wisdom

"True austerity lies in the focused concentration of both mind and senses, guiding us to the realization of Brahman. It is through this deep inner discipline that we access the highest virtue and awaken to the divine within." Amma

This wisdom from Amma beautifully aligns with the Vedantic emphasis on self-inquiry and disciplined meditation as paths to realize the unchanging nature of the Self. In Vedanta, the journey to Self-realization involves not only intellectual understanding but also the deep inner work of aligning the mind and senses, shedding distractions, and focusing solely on the truth of our existence. Through such austerity, we transcend the illusions of the world and access the infinite, ever-present Brahman within.

Atma, often referred to as the inner Self, is the ultimate reality underlying the individual and is identical with Brahman, the Absolute. In Vedanta, the Atma is the unchanging essence that remains constant despite the various states of waking, dreaming, and deep sleep. It is beyond doubt because it is the foundation of all experience. The Atma is the subject of every perception, thought, and feeling, yet it cannot be perceived as an object. This is because the knower (Atma) cannot be the known, making it distinct from anything we can conceptualize or observe. Despite this, the Atma is ever-present and vital for all forms of existence.

The Atma, being the basis of all proofs, underlies every aspect of existence and is the foundation of all cognition. Without the Atma, there could be no experience, no perception, and no thought. However, it cannot be demonstrated through logical proofs or empirical means. Its existence is self-evident, as it is the very essence of consciousness itself. Just as a person cannot see their own eyes without a mirror, the Atma cannot be "known" in the usual sense because it is the knower of everything. The Atma remains elusive to the mind because it transcends all intellectual categories and is beyond dualistic thinking.

Although the Atma cannot be grasped by the mind or proven through external means, it can be experienced directly. This experience of the Atma is described as a realization, where one recognizes that their true nature is not limited to the body-mind complex but is instead the infinite, unchanging consciousness that is one with Brahman. This direct experience leads to liberation (moksha) as it reveals the underlying unity of all existence. In this realization, the individual self (jiva) is seen as a reflection of the Atma, which is always present, untouched by the changing phenomena of the world.

A central focus in Vedantic philosophy is the true nature of the Self, which is often misunderstood as undergoing change or possessing worldly attributes. One common objection is the belief that the Self undergoes transformation upon entering creation. However, Vedanta, supported by the teachings of the Vedas and the insights of spiritual masters like Amma, clarifies that the concept of "entry" into creation is metaphorical. As described in the Taittiriya Upanishad, the Self remains unchanged in its essence when it "enters" the world. This entry refers to the Self manifesting through various forms in the empirical world, yet its true nature remains unaltered, untouched by the limitations of name and form.

Another misconception arises from the belief that entry into creation involves a change in the attributes of the Self, as suggested by statements such as "Let me enter in the form of this individual soul and evolve name and form." Vedanta counters this by reminding us of the core teaching from the Chandogya Upanishad: Tat Tvam Asi—Thou art That. This declaration of non-duality affirms that the individual self, despite appearing limited and conditioned by the body and mind, is in essence the same as Brahman. The perception that the Self takes on different attributes upon entering creation is part of maya, the illusion that obscures the true nature of the Self. In reality, the Self remains in its pure, unchanging state, and the individual soul is merely a reflection of this eternal truth.

The practice of meditation in Vedanta plays a vital role in dispelling these illusions. It is not about superimposing qualities onto the individual self or undoing changes that are believed to have occurred. Rather, meditation serves as a tool to remove ignorance, allowing the seeker to realize the oneness of the individual self with the universal Self—Brahman. There has never been an actual transformation of the Self, only the mistaken belief that such a change has taken place. Through disciplined meditation, we awaken to the reality that the Self has always been Brahman, free from any modifications or worldly limitations.

In response to the objection that the individual soul's worldly experiences represent the true state of the Self, Vedanta offers clarity. According to the Brihadaranyaka Upanishad, the Self, as the eternal perceiver, cannot be perceived as an object within the world. The individual soul's experience of the waking, dreaming, and deep sleep states is limited by ignorance. The true Self, however, remains unaffected by these transient states. It witnesses all experiences yet remains beyond them, untouched by the attributes of the empirical world. The worldly state of the individual soul is a projection of ignorance, not the reality of the Self.

Another objection suggests that the Self possesses worldly attributes such as fear and sorrow, as these emotions are often experienced by the individual soul. Yet, Vedanta asserts that while the Self may witness fear and sorrow, these are not inherent qualities of the Self. If fear and sorrow were essential attributes of the Self, they would be inseparable from it, just as heat is inseparable from fire. However, the Self, as the eternal witness, observes these emotions without being affected by them. This distinction demonstrates that fear and sorrow are phenomena perceived by the mind within the context of worldly existence, not qualities that belong to the true, unchanging Self.

Amma's teachings further illuminate this Vedantic wisdom by emphasizing the importance of inner discipline and austerity in realizing the truth of the Self. Just as Vedanta advocates for self-inquiry and meditation to dissolve ignorance, Amma teaches that true austerity lies in the focused concentration of the mind and senses. This concentration is not just an outward discipline but an inner alignment that allows us to transcend the distractions of the world and experience the divine truth within. By practicing such inner discipline, we access the highest virtue and unlock the grace that guides us toward the realization of Brahman.

The unity between personal effort and grace is a recurring theme in both Amma's teachings and Vedantic philosophy. Effort in the form of self-discipline, meditation, and devotion prepares the mind to receive grace, which in turn deepens the seeker's understanding and accelerates their spiritual progress. This interplay between effort and grace is essential in moving beyond the illusions of worldly existence and recognizing the unchanging nature of the Self. Through sustained effort, one creates the conditions for the revelation of the Self, while grace gently guides the seeker toward the ultimate realization of oneness with Brahman.

Ultimately, both Amma's teachings and the Vedantic tradition guide us toward the same profound truth: the Self is unchanging, eternal, and identical with Brahman. The practice of focused concentration, inner discipline, and meditation helps us dissolve the illusions that cloud our perception, revealing the divine truth that has always been present within us. As we align our minds and senses with this truth, we awaken to the realization that there is no separation between the individual self and the universal Self. This awakening is the culmination of both disciplined effort and the grace that flows naturally when we strive with sincerity on the spiritual path.

Eliminating Distractions

"Contemplation on the teachings deepens understanding, clearing away doubts and leading to the realization of the Self. Through self-inquiry and the purification of the mind, we move closer to the supreme bliss where the mind is no longer bound by external distractions." Amma

This wisdom emphasizes that the journey toward self-realization is not merely intellectual but deeply experiential. The mind must be disciplined, purified, and freed from distractions to experience the profound truth of the Self. By contemplating the teachings of the Guru and scriptures and engaging in self-inquiry, the seeker clears the mental obstacles that obscure their true nature. As the mind becomes purified, it rests naturally in the bliss of the Self, free from the disturbances of the external world.

In Advaita Vedanta, the path to self-realization begins with shravanam (listening to the teachings). However, merely hearing the teachings may not be enough for many seekers, as mental impurities or doubts often prevent full comprehension of the truth. For this reason, mananam (contemplation) or vicharanam (reflection) plays a critical role. After listening to the scriptures, the seeker must engage in deep reflection to internalize the teachings, resolve doubts, and understand their true meaning. This process of continuous contemplation is essential for eliminating ignorance and attaining certainty about the Self's nature.

The role of mananam in Advaita Vedanta is to transform intellectual understanding into direct realization. During this process, the seeker repeatedly reflects upon what they have heard during shravanam, using contemplation to deepen their understanding. This continuous internalization clears away misunderstandings and deepens the realization of the Self. By resolving doubts, the seeker moves toward nirathisaya jnanam—knowledge that is free from doubt and absolutely certain. Only when the seeker has achieved this unwavering understanding does the journey progress toward the realization of supreme bliss.

Once the state of paramanandam (supreme bliss) is recognized through this deep contemplation, the mind naturally becomes absorbed in that bliss. The mind no longer seeks external activities or intellectual inquiry, as it has found fulfillment in the realization of the Self. When mananam has achieved its purpose—revealing the oneness of the Self with Brahman—further contemplation becomes unnecessary. The mind, now resting in supreme bliss, transcends the need for inquiry and reflection. This is the culmination of vicharam (inquiry), where the seeker has fully realized the unchanging reality of their true nature.

However, the process of mananam requires a certain level of chittasuddhi (purification of the mind). Through mananam, the jigjnasu is able to eliminate doubts, clarify understanding, and purify the mind. By continuously reflecting on the teachings, the seeker resolves uncertainties that obscure their knowledge of the Self. This process of deep contemplation not only clears away intellectual misunderstandings but also purifies subtle mental impurities that cannot be removed through physical actions alone. As the mind becomes purified, it becomes more receptive to the higher knowledge of Advaita Vedanta, enabling the seeker to move closer to self-realization.

Purification of the mind through mananam is essential for receiving higher knowledge. A pure mind is free from distractions, allowing the seeker to fully assimilate the teachings and realize the profound truths of non-duality. Without chittasuddhi, the mind remains entangled in doubts and misunderstandings, hindering the realization of the Self. As the mind becomes purified, it naturally aligns with the deeper understanding of its non-dual nature, allowing the seeker to recognize the oneness of the individual self with Brahman.

This process of inquiry and purification also involves investigating the layers of identification that cover the Self, known as the pancha kosas (five sheaths). These sheaths progressively veil the true nature of the Self, from the gross physical body to the subtler mental and intellectual layers. As the seeker progresses in their inquiry, they begin to negate these layers one by one, realizing that the Self is beyond all such coverings. The mind, often the source of anxieties and distractions, is seen as a sheath that obscures the blissful, unchanging reality of the Self. By transcending identification with the mental sheath, the seeker moves closer to realizing their true nature.

One of the practices that aids in this process of inquiry is manasa japa (mental repetition of a mantra). The repetition of a mantra serves as a direct connection to atma chaitanyam (consciousness), helping the seeker shift their identification from the mental sheath to the deeper, blissful essence of the Self. Through sustained repetition and meditation, the mantra reveals the non-dual truth of the Self, dissolving the mental fluctuations that sustain duality. This practice helps the seeker experience the eternal, unchanging bliss of the Self, beyond the distractions of the mind.

Amma emphasizes that true understanding comes from realizing that the all-knowing is none other than the knowing-being of the Self. This realization fosters a deep sense of peace and unity with all existence, as the seeker comes to understand that their true Self is not separate from the supreme reality. By recognizing the manomaya purusha (the self identified with the mental sheath) as none other than the paramamaya purusha (the supreme reality) and ananda swarupa (the essence of bliss), the seeker dissolves fear and attains inner peace. This insight arises from realizing that the true Self transcends the limitations and fluctuations of the mind.

Two essential tools for attaining knowledge in Advaita Vedanta are shraddha (faith) and samadhanam (single-pointed focus). Shraddha is not blind belief but a deep conviction in the teachings of the scriptures, the words of the Guru, and one's own inner capacity to realize the Self. It provides the foundation for all spiritual inquiry, giving the seeker the confidence to trust in the process of self-inquiry. As Amma often teaches, shraddhavan labhate jnanam—the one with faith attains knowledge. This faith allows the seeker to persist through doubts and obstacles, knowing that the truth lies beyond the limitations of the mind and body.

Samadhanam, on the other hand, is the tranquility or single-pointed focus that arises from a mind undisturbed by distractions. In Advaita Vedanta, this calm focus is essential because it allows the mind to transcend dualistic thoughts and realize the unity of all existence. When the mind is steady and focused, it becomes a tool for realizing the Self. This state of inner tranquility helps the seeker dissolve the mental fluctuations that sustain the illusion of duality, enabling them to rest in the oneness of the Self.

Ultimately, through the purification of the mind, deep contemplation, and unwavering faith, the seeker attains self-knowledge and realizes the supreme bliss of the Self. By eliminating distractions and focusing inward through self-inquiry, the mind becomes free from external disturbances, allowing the seeker to experience the unchanging reality of the Self. This realization of oneness with the supreme reality leads to the culmination of spiritual inquiry, where the mind, having fulfilled its purpose, rests in the bliss of the Self, beyond the need for further contemplation.

Being as Pure Knowing

"True realization comes when we transcend distinctions and see the Self in all beings, recognizing that the same essence flows through everyone. By knowing Brahman as infinite, unchanging, and blissful, we move through the world seeing everything as an expression of the one Self." Amma

This profound insight highlights the essence of Advaita Vedanta, where the ultimate goal is to dissolve all notions of separateness and recognize the universal Self in every living being. The journey to this realization involves discarding all illusions created by ignorance and understanding the true, undivided nature of reality. By realizing Brahman, the seeker moves through life with a deep sense of unity, perceiving all experiences and forms as manifestations of the one infinite Self.

In the attainment of identity with the Self of all, the process begins with a progressive realization of the different layers of the self. At first, the seeker identifies with the physical body, known as the annamaya kosa (the self made of food). As spiritual inquiry deepens, this identification shifts to subtler layers, such as the mind and intellect. Each of these layers is ultimately recognized as illusory and temporary, created by ignorance. The true Self is not confined by the physical or mental realms, and by peeling away these layers, the seeker moves closer to realizing the blissful, unchanging nature of Brahman.

The realization of Brahman is the final step in this journey. Brahman is described as infinite, unchangeable, birthless, immortal, fearless, and non-dual. It is beyond the limitations of individual identities and forms. The knowledge of Brahman dissolves all misconceptions of separation, revealing that there is no true distinction between the individual self and the universal Self. This understanding leads to the profound realization that the entire universe is a manifestation of Brahman, and every being is an expression of this same eternal reality.

Once the seeker attains this realization, they move through the world with the understanding that everything they perceive is the Self. There is no longer any separation between themselves and the world. The limitations of individual identity, such as fear, desire, or attachment, fall away. The realized being experiences a state of freedom, where they can fulfill their desires effortlessly and interact with the world without being bound by it. This freedom comes from the knowledge that everything in the universe, including food, forms, and experiences, is part of the same undivided Self.

In this state of realization, the enlightened person "sings or proclaims the sama, equlaness," which symbolizes the unity of all things with Brahman. This song of unity is not just a literal chant but a metaphor for the realization of non-difference between the Self and the world. The realized being understands that Brahman is not separate from anything, and this knowledge infuses their every action and interaction. It is a proclamation of the ultimate truth of non-duality (Advaita), where the distinctions of the physical world no longer obscure the underlying oneness of existence.

As they move through life, those who have realized the Self naturally share this knowledge with others, not through teaching alone but through their very presence. The state of absolute contentment and peace that they experience becomes a living example for others to follow. Having found fulfillment within, they no longer seek it from external sources. This inner fulfillment becomes the result of their knowledge and is shared with the world simply by being, as their existence itself becomes a beacon of the unity and peace that comes from knowing Brahman.

In this state, being and knowing are no longer separate. To fully realize the Self is to exist in pure knowing—an undivided awareness that transcends all duality. The seeker becomes the knower and the known simultaneously, as they realize that the true nature of all existence is consciousness itself. This pure knowing is the essence of Brahman, and to dwell in it is to live in the blissful awareness of the eternal, unchanging truth. In this state, all actions become spontaneous expressions of the Self, free from the limitations of individual identity.

This understanding bridges the gap between the mental and spiritual realms. When the seeker recognizes the true nature of the Self as paramamaya purusha (the supreme reality), the fluctuations of the mind no longer disturb their inner peace. Fear, sorrow, and desire are seen as passing phenomena, while the Self remains as the constant, blissful awareness beneath all experience. This realization allows the seeker to rest in their natural state of being, where they are no longer influenced by the ups and downs of the mind or the external world.

Ultimately, the journey toward self-realization leads to a state where all distinctions dissolve, and the seeker becomes one with the infinite, unchanging Brahman. This state of being is not a withdrawal from the world but an active participation in it, seeing everything as a manifestation of the Self. The enlightened being moves through life with a deep sense of unity, compassion, and joy, understanding that the same essence flows through all beings. In this state, the realized person fulfills Amma's teaching: they see the Self in all, recognize Brahman as the source of everything, and live in the pure bliss of knowing that all is one.

The Role of Knowledge and Action

"True knowledge awakens the heart, guiding every action with wisdom and compassion. When action is rooted in love and selflessness, it leads to liberation, not bondage." Amma

This profound wisdom highlights the action is necessary in life, the key lies in performing it with awareness, free from attachment to outcomes. When action flows from a heart awakened by true knowledge, it becomes a means of liberation rather than a source of bondage. This principle resonates deeply with the teachings of the Vedas, which emphasize that knowledge is the ultimate path to liberation, while action, when performed selflessly, serves as a tool to purify the mind and heart.

The Vedas, as the foundation of Vedantic philosophy, provide guidance on the ultimate objectives of human life, including liberation from the cycle of birth and death. The Sruti, or revealed texts, emphasize that the root cause of suffering and worldly existence is ignorance, the misunderstanding of the true nature of the Self. Liberation, according to the Vedas, is not attained through mere ritualistic actions but through the removal of ignorance by awakening true knowledge. This knowledge reveals the eternal, unchanging reality of the Self, which is beyond the fluctuations of the material world.

A central teaching of the Vedas is that ignorance acts as a veil, obscuring the true nature of the Self. This ignorance creates the illusion of separation, causing individuals to perceive objects and desires as external to themselves. The perception of duality leads to craving, which in turn drives people to act out of desire. These actions, rooted in attachment, perpetuate the cycle of samsara, the continuous cycle of birth, death, and rebirth, and bind the individual to worldly suffering.

The Vedas also teach that through the consistent performance of prescribed duties, one can gradually purify the mind and heart. These actions, when done with the right attitude—without attachment to their outcomes—begin to cleanse the impurities that prevent the emergence of true knowledge. The purification of the mind is essential because it creates the conditions for knowledge to arise naturally.

As the mind is purified and knowledge begins to dawn, the darkness of ignorance is dispelled. This emerging knowledge leads to a profound realization of the true nature of the Self. In this realization, the individual recognizes that their essence is not separate from the infinite, unchanging reality of Brahman. This realization brings about the cessation of worldly attachments and desires, as the individual no longer identifies with the transient, external world. Instead, they become anchored in the knowledge of their true, eternal nature.

Selfless action, or karma yoga, is a vital aspect of this process. By performing duties without attachment to their outcomes, individuals align their actions with the highest spiritual truths. Such actions are done not for personal gain but for the welfare of others and in service to the divine. This type of action purifies the doer, helping them transcend the ego and paving the way for the realization of knowledge. As Amma teaches, when action is rooted in love and selflessness, it leads to liberation.

Once the knowledge of the Self is realized, the individual's relationship with action changes fundamentally. They continue to act in the world, but these actions are no longer driven by personal desires or attachments. Instead, they are expressions of the underlying unity of all existence. The realized being sees no separation between themselves and others and performs actions out of compassion, wisdom, and love. Such actions are free from the binding effects of karma, as they are performed with the understanding that the Self is unchanging and eternal.

So, knowledge is the key to liberation; action plays an essential role in purifying the mind and preparing the individual for that realization. When both knowledge and action are rooted in selflessness and guided by wisdom, they lead to the highest state of freedom. As the Vedas and Amma's teachings both affirm, the ultimate goal is to transcend the ignorance that binds us to the cycle of desire and action and awaken to the eternal, blissful nature of the Self.

Transcending Karma, Realizing Self

"Karma is the path through which we learn, but knowledge is the light that frees us. Only by transcending the attachments to actions can we realize the divine within." Amma

When we are attached to the outcomes of our actions, we remain entangled in the cycle of desire, attachment, and suffering. Liberation comes when we transcend these attachments, allowing us to recognize the divine essence within ourselves, which has always been present.

In the context of liberation, the realization of Brahman—the ultimate reality—brings profound insight into the nature of existence. Brahman is not separate from us or the universe;

it pervades all things, both living and non-living. Liberation is not a distant goal to be attained through external efforts but an inner realization of our oneness with Brahman. When we understand that everything, including ourselves, is an expression of Brahman, we see that there is no separate self to reach. The Upanishads and the Bhagavad Gita emphasize this unity, teaching that the individual self and Brahman are one and the same.

Thus, liberation is the recognition of our inherent nature as Brahman. It is not something we must seek outside of ourselves; rather, it is the dissolution of ignorance and the realization that we are already one with the infinite reality. By transcending the attachments and desires that arise from karma, we shift from identifying with the individual ego to understanding our true nature as Brahman. This realization frees us from the limitations of worldly actions, allowing us to live in the eternal truth of our oneness with the divine.

For example, Sruti says, “Having created the world, He entered into it.” (Tai. II. vi. 1) This highlights the idea that Brahman is not separate from creation but is both within and beyond it. Another teaching, “Know the individual soul also to be myself,” (G. XIII. 2) reinforces this non-duality, showing that we are not separate from the divine. In this way, the idea of reaching a separate place or attaining something external is irrelevant when we speak of liberation. It is simply the recognition that we are already Brahman.

The teachings also emphasize that liberation does not involve physical or external achievements. It is the recognition that our true nature is Brahman, and this is something we can’t gain through outward effort. Rather, it’s an inner realization that comes through understanding. Scriptures explain this idea by saying, “One only without a second,” (Ch. VI. ii. 1) which means there is no reality other than Brahman.

In liberation, one no longer perceives differences. The Upanishads teach, "Where one does not see anything different," (Ch. VII. xxiv. 1): meaning that in the state of realization, one sees only unity, not separation or multiplicity. Another scripture asks, "What will one see there and with what?" (Bṛ. II. iv. 14; IV. v. 15) suggesting that in the realization of Brahman, there is no duality to perceive—everything is one.

The relationship between knowledge and action is an important theme in these teachings. The knowledge of Brahman leads to the understanding of oneness, where all distinctions dissolve, including the sense of agency or "doer-ship" that is tied to actions. On the other hand, action (karma) involves doing something with a sense of individual responsibility and attachment to the results. This perpetuates the perception of duality.

It's explained that knowledge and action cannot exist together in the ultimate sense. Knowledge leads to oneness and unity, while action keeps us in the realm of duality. Therefore, once knowledge of the Self is attained, action becomes unnecessary. Just as a thing seen through the eyes of someone who is ill changes once they are healed, so too does the way we perceive the world change once ignorance is removed. The enlightened individual no longer experiences the world with the same delusions or misunderstandings.

Several texts reinforce this idea. They say things like, "When there is duality, one smells, one sees, etc." (Br. II. iv. 14) This means that duality creates sensory experiences and perceptions, but these are limited. In contrast, one text states, "He goes from death to death who sees differences," (Ka. II. i. 10; Bṛ. IV. iv. 19) meaning that those who perceive separation remain bound by the cycle of birth and death.

Additionally, the Upanishads explain "And that, in which one perceives a second, is limited" (Ch. VII. xxiv. 1) therefore, perceiving any kind of "second" entity or separation is a sign of limitation and ignorance. True reality is limitless and non-dual. The perception of duality, rooted in ignorance, is false. When knowledge reveals the oneness of Brahman, the illusion of duality dissolves. As a result, the scriptures argue that liberation comes not from a combination of knowledge and action but solely from the realization of Brahman through knowledge.

Many scriptures highlight the importance of unity and non-duality. The passage states, "While he who worships another god (thinking), He is one and I am another (does not know)" (Br. I. iv. 10); "For whenever this one (i.e., the aspirant) makes the slightest difference in It, (he is smitten with fear)" (Tai. II. vii. 1). And truth belongs to unity, according to such Vedic texts as: "It should be realized in one form only" (Bṛ. IV. iv. 20), "One without a second" (Ch. VI. ii. 1), "All this is but Brahman" (Mu. II. ii. 11), "All this is but the Self" (Ch. VII. xxv. 2).
emphasizing that all of existence is one, and there is no real separation between the individual and the divine. Any perception of difference is a result of ignorance.

These teachings also clarify that karma (action) and knowledge are opposed to one another. Karma requires the perception of difference—there must be someone to act and something to act upon. In contrast, knowledge reveals the unity of all things in Brahman. For example, one scripture explains that worshiping another god, thinking, "He is one and I am another," is rooted in ignorance. When even the slightest difference is perceived, it leads to fear and suffering.

Once the unity of Brahman is realized, all distinctions dissolve, and the false perception of duality fades away. The

Upanishads consistently teach that truth resides in unity, and when this truth is fully understood, the compulsion for action and the need for it naturally fall away. Actions driven by desires and attachments are no longer necessary because the seeker has recognized their oneness with the infinite, unchanging Brahman. The scriptures serve as a guide on this journey, helping individuals uncover their true nature beyond the layers of illusion. Upon realizing this knowledge, the individual transcends the realm of desires, duties, and actions, resting peacefully in the awareness of their essential nature—Brahman.

Amma's teachings beautifully reflect this ancient wisdom. She reminds us that karma, while a teacher, must eventually be transcended through the light of knowledge. "Karma is the path through which we learn, but knowledge is the light that frees us." Once we have transcended attachments and desires, we rest in the divine awareness within, realizing that we have always been one with Brahman. This realization brings peace, freedom, and liberation, as the soul rests eternally in the unity of all existence, beyond the confines of action and duality.

Humility and Surrender

"Humility and surrender are the doorways to true knowledge. Without them, the mind remains clouded by ego. When we bow down in surrender, the heart opens, and the light of wisdom flows effortlessly." Amma

This wisdom reveals a fundamental truth about the spiritual journey: without humility and surrender, the mind remains trapped in its own illusions, blocking the emergence of deeper understanding. Humility allows the ego to dissolve, creating space for the divine presence to enter and illuminate the heart. Surrender, in turn, is the act of letting go of control, allowing God's grace and wisdom to flow into our lives. Only when the heart is open through humility and surrender can true knowledge take root.

Contrary to the belief that knowledge arises solely from the removal of obstacles, it is essential to recognize that many other factors contribute to its emergence. While it is true that clearing away distractions and mental impurities is necessary, other elements, such as God's grace, the practice of austerity, and various spiritual disciplines, play significant roles in the process. These practices are not merely supplementary but are integral to preparing the mind and heart for the reception of knowledge. Without God's grace, even the most diligent seeker might struggle to attain the profound understanding that leads to self-realization.

Practices like non-violence (ahimsa) and value-based education are not just moral guidelines but are deeply connected to the purification of the mind and heart. By practicing non-injury toward others and maintaining self-control, the seeker cultivates an environment in which the mind becomes still, and the heart becomes open to receiving knowledge. These virtues help to purify the ego and remove the barriers that obstruct spiritual progress. Ahimsa, in particular, teaches compassion and empathy, allowing the seeker to align more closely with the divine nature within themselves and others.

In addition to moral virtues, the Vedic tradition emphasizes three essential processes that lead directly to knowledge: hearing (shravanam), contemplating (mananam), and meditating (nididhyasanam). Hearing involves actively listening to the teachings of the scriptures and the wisdom imparted by the Guru. This first step introduces the seeker to the foundational truths of the Self and the nature of existence. However, merely hearing the teachings is not enough. The seeker must also engage in contemplation, reflecting deeply on these truths to understand their deeper meaning. Finally, through meditation, these teachings are internalized, allowing the seeker to experience them directly.

Each stage of life—whether the student, householder, or renunciant stage—also provides unique opportunities for spiritual growth. In the student stage, one learns discipline, focus, and begins to understand the importance of knowledge. The householder stage presents the challenge of balancing worldly responsibilities while seeking spiritual growth, offering a dynamic environment for practicing detachment. Finally, the renunciant stage focuses entirely on self-realization, allowing the seeker to dedicate themselves fully to spiritual practice. Regardless of the stage of life, all individuals can strive toward knowledge and liberation.

Despite the importance of these practices and stages, it is knowledge—jnana—that ultimately opens the door to liberation. Knowledge dispels the darkness of ignorance, which is the root cause of suffering and bondage in the material world. While virtues like non-violence, self-control, and the different stages of life help prepare the mind and body, it is the realization of the ultimate truth, Brahman, that frees us from the cycle of birth and death. Knowledge is the key that unlocks the truth of our divine nature.

Amma's teaching that "humility and surrender are the doorways to true knowledge" emphasizes that without these qualities, even the pursuit of knowledge can be hindered by the ego. A seeker must approach the teachings with humility, recognizing that their current understanding is limited, and surrender to the higher power of divine grace. This surrender is not a passive act but an active decision to release the attachment to personal will and open oneself to the will of the divine. In this way, the heart becomes a vessel for wisdom to flow effortlessly.

The practice of austerity (tapas) is also crucial in deepening the seeker's journey toward knowledge. Through self-discipline, fasting, and other spiritual practices, the seeker purifies the body and mind, making them more receptive to spiritual truths. Austerity helps remove the distractions and attachments that prevent the mind from settling into its natural state of stillness. When the mind is purified through such practices, it becomes a clearer reflection of the divine, allowing wisdom to emerge naturally.

God's grace, as Amma frequently reminds us, is the ultimate factor in the attainment of knowledge. While personal effort is important, it is divine grace that truly lifts the veil of ignorance and reveals the eternal truth. Surrendering to this grace is an act of profound humility, acknowledging that the ego alone cannot lead to enlightenment. By opening oneself to grace, the seeker allows divine wisdom to flood the heart, bringing with it the realization of the Self.

In conclusion, while spiritual practices such as austerity, non-violence, and the stages of life play an important role in preparing the seeker for self-realization, it is humility, surrender, and knowledge that lead to liberation. Knowledge is the light that dispels ignorance, but it can only emerge in a heart that is purified and open. As Amma teaches, by bowing down in humility and surrender, the heart opens, and wisdom flows effortlessly, guiding the seeker toward the realization of the ultimate truth—Brahman. Through this knowledge, the individual transcends the limitations of the ego and attains liberation, resting in the awareness of their true divine nature.

Wisdom Blossoms in Renunciation

"Karma purifies the mind, but true wisdom comes through renunciation. When we let go of attachment to the fruits of our actions, the light of knowledge shines, revealing the Divine within." Amma

Karma, or action, is a fundamental concept in spiritual practice, but it is not limited to specific rituals like fire sacrifices (Agnihotra). In Amma's teachings, karma is understood as a wide spectrum of disciplines and practices that lead to the purification of the mind. These include celibacy, austerity, truthfulness, control of the senses, non-violence, concentration, and meditation. Each of these actions serves to purify the individual, creating the right conditions for spiritual knowledge to emerge. By cultivating these virtues, one purifies the mind and prepares it to receive the light of knowledge that reveals the divine within.

Amma's statement aligns with the ancient wisdom of the Upanishads, which emphasize the importance of concentration and meditation in realizing the ultimate reality, Brahman. The Upanishads state that one should seek to know Brahman through deep focus and sustained meditation. Concentration and meditation, therefore, play a pivotal role in helping individuals discover the true essence of everything. As the mind becomes still, it can penetrate beyond the illusions of the world and perceive the underlying reality of Brahman, leading to the realization of one's true nature.

Interestingly, spiritual knowledge can arise even before one enters the householder stage of life, suggesting that the effects of spiritual practices performed in past lives can carry forward into the present. When an individual has already gained the knowledge that karma aims to cultivate, the necessity of performing specific worldly duties, such as rituals or seeking material achievements, becomes irrelevant. The spiritual maturity acquired in past lives allows one to bypass certain stages of worldly life and focus directly on the pursuit of enlightenment.

Traditionally, family life, with its focus on duties like raising children and achieving worldly success, serves as a means to attain temporary goals such as prosperity in this life, honor in the afterlife, or ascension to higher spiritual realms. However, for someone who has realized the eternal truth of the Self, these temporary goals lose their appeal. The desires for wealth, progeny, and worldly honor become irrelevant once the seeker understands that true fulfillment lies in the eternal realm of the Self, not in the fleeting achievements of the world.

Even for individuals who have embraced family responsibilities, the rise of knowledge eventually leads to the cessation of karma. As spiritual wisdom deepens, worldly actions no longer seem necessary, and renunciation naturally follows. Amma emphasizes that when one understands the impermanence of worldly achievements, renunciation is not a forced action but a spontaneous result of spiritual maturity. This mirrors ancient teachings, where many individuals renounced their worldly life to focus solely on spiritual growth and realization of the Self.

A person who develops detachment from worldly pursuits often benefits from spiritual progress made in previous lives. This explains why some individuals are born with an inherent dispassion for material success and a natural inclination toward spiritual enlightenment. The Vedas, while emphasizing karma, do not contradict the pursuit of knowledge. In fact, the performance of karmas such as fire rituals and celibacy in past lives can create a favorable environment for spiritual knowledge to arise in the current life.

Amma's teachings, in alignment with the Vedic tradition, remind us that for those who have cultivated spiritual detachment, it is often beneficial to transition to stages of life more conducive to enlightenment. Renunciation or a life focused on spiritual pursuits helps foster further progress toward self-realization. These stages encourage introspection, detachment, and the focused pursuit of spiritual knowledge, allowing the seeker to move closer to the ultimate goal of enlightenment.

The Vedas place great emphasis on karma, as it provides a path for individuals with strong desires for worldly outcomes such as offspring, honor, and ascension to higher realms. However, as Amma points out, these karmas also serve as stepping stones to enlightenment. By engaging in the prescribed actions with detachment from their fruits, the individual purifies their mind and heart, preparing themselves for the emergence of knowledge that transcends worldly desires.

Ultimately, while karma is emphasized as a necessary step on the path to enlightenment, the ultimate goal remains the realization of the Self. As Amma teaches, true wisdom blossoms when one renounces attachment to the fruits of their actions. This renunciation allows the light of knowledge to shine, revealing the divine essence within. The practices of karma, while essential, are only the means to an end—preparing the seeker for the final realization of the oneness of the Self and Brahman, the absolute reality.

In conclusion, Amma's words guide us to understand that karma, while purifying the mind, is only part of the spiritual journey. True wisdom emerges when we let go of the attachment to results, allowing the light of knowledge to reveal the divine within. Through practices of self-discipline, concentration, and meditation, we prepare ourselves for this realization. However, it is through renunciation—whether of desires, attachments, or even worldly responsibilities—that the final wisdom of non-duality blossoms, leading us to the realization that we are none other than the eternal Self, Brahman.

CHAPTER-2

Moving Toward Knowledge and Discerning the Illusion

Awareness

"True knowledge arises when we realize that the Self is both the knower and the knowledge. In this understanding, we see that Jnanam is none other than Ishwara, the divine consciousness that pervades all."
Amma

The common misconception many people fall into is thinking, "I have awareness," as if awareness were an object that belongs to someone. This creates a false sense of ownership and leads to the belief that awareness can come and go. This misunderstanding implies that awareness is impermanent and dependent on external conditions, which contradicts the true nature of awareness. When we identify awareness as something we possess, we reduce it to the level of an action or experience that relies on a doer or external circumstance. This perspective limits the understanding of awareness and misrepresents its connection to Brahman, the ultimate reality.

In reality, awareness is not something we "have" or "do." It is not subject to time or circumstance. Awareness is our essential nature, constant and unchanging, and recognizing this truth is the key to spiritual awakening. When we view awareness as separate from the Self, we fall into the trap of associating it with actions like seeing or thinking, as if awareness depended on an active subject. Brahman, as the source of all existence, is beyond these limitations. Trying to understand Brahman through the lens of action, as if knowledge were just another experience or event, leads to impermanence and dependence, missing the essence of what Brahman truly is.

In Vedantic philosophy, the concept of Aham refers to the fundamental sense of "I" or I-awareness that every individual experiences. It is this awareness that forms the core of our identity and shapes our sense of self. However, this "I" is understood to exist on two distinct levels: the lower self and the higher Self. The lower self is the ego or Ahamkara, the aspect of the individual that identifies with the body, mind, and external world. It is rooted in the illusion of separateness and individuality, leading to attachment, desire, and suffering. On the other hand, the higher Self, also referred to as the pure Self or Suddha Atman, is the true essence of one's being. It is beyond the ego and exists as pure consciousness, untainted by the illusions of the material world.

The lower self, known as Ahamkara, is the aspect of the "I" that is entangled in the material world and the physical body. It is the ego-consciousness that identifies with personal experiences, desires, and emotions. This identification with the body and mind gives rise to the sense of individuality, creating the illusion that the self is separate from others and from the ultimate reality (Brahman). Ahamkara is the source of ego-driven behaviors, attachments, and suffering, as it operates under the belief that the individual is independent and autonomous. This "I" is conditioned by ignorance (avidya), and it is through spiritual practice and self-inquiry that one can transcend this limited identification.

In contrast to the lower self, the higher Self represents the pure, unconditioned "I", which is identical to Brahman, the ultimate reality. This Suddha Atman is the true nature of every individual, untouched by the limitations of the body-mind complex. It is the pure consciousness that exists beyond the dualities of subject and object, time and space. While the lower self is bound by the illusions of the material world, the higher Self is infinite and eternal, embodying Sat-Chit-Ananda—existence, consciousness, and bliss. Realizing this higher Self is the goal of spiritual practice in Vedanta, where one transcends the ego and attains liberation (moksha) by recognizing that the true "I" is not the individual ego but the universal consciousness that pervades all existence.

The relationship between the mind, the senses, and awareness further illustrates the distinction between the doer and the Self. The mind and external objects are lifeless on their own, mere combinations of basic elements. However, when the mind engages with external objects through the senses, we become conscious of experiences, like feeling heat or sensing light. This awareness is not a result of the mind's activities; rather, it arises from the presence of consciousness, which is our true nature. Like a magnet bringing life to a piece of iron, the mind only appears conscious because of the underlying constant awareness of the Self.

Brahman, the ultimate reality, cannot be fully understood through intellectual efforts or words alone. If we reduce Brahman to knowledge understood as action, we misunderstand its infinite and formless nature. Just as external objects and the mind depend on something deeper to be perceived, our understanding of Brahman and awareness must move beyond the surface meaning of words. Brahman cannot be defined in terms of doing or experiencing. It is the foundation of all that exists, much like how a painting relies on the wall it's painted on. This underlying essence, which is constant and unchanging, is the Self.

Amma's teachings encourage us to recognize that knowledge is not separate from the Self. Knowledge, or awareness, is the inherent nature of the Self, and wherever there is knowledge, it reflects the presence of the Self. The Self is not an agent of action, nor does it depend on external objects to exist. It is both the knower and the knowledge, the constant source of all perception and experience. When we move beyond the literal interpretations of words, we can understand that the Self is not something to be attained or owned but is ever-present, always aware.

The greatest error comes when we treat knowledge as something we "do" or "have." This leads to a mistaken view of knowledge as an impermanent or dependent phenomenon, subject to change based on circumstances. In truth, knowledge, or awareness, is the constant, unchanging essence of the Self. It is not something that can be lost, gained, or modified. As Amma's teachings reveal, the Self is the ever-present, unchanging awareness that pervades all of existence, and understanding this brings us closer to the realization of our true nature.

To free ourselves from these misconceptions, it is crucial to understand that awareness is not an object or property of the mind, nor is it dependent on sensory experiences. Awareness is our intrinsic nature, the very essence of who we are. By recognizing this truth, we overcome the flawed perception that awareness is a transient phenomenon. This realization is the key to understanding the non-dual nature of Brahman, where awareness and existence are one and the same, eternal and unchanging.

In the pursuit of true knowledge, we must go beyond intellectual understanding and move towards direct experience of the Self. Meditation and spiritual practices help us quiet the mind and detach from the external world, allowing the recognition that awareness is not something we possess but something we are. This shift in perspective leads to a profound realization: we are not separate from awareness or Brahman; we are the very embodiment of it. This understanding is the essence of non-duality, where the knower and the knowledge are one.

The Self, as Amma teaches, is both the knower and the knowledge, inseparable from the divine consciousness that pervades everything. When we grasp this truth, we see that Ishwara, or God, is not a separate entity but the manifestation of the same awareness that is our true nature.

This realization dissolves the boundaries between the individual self and the universal consciousness, leading to the understanding that all is one.

In conclusion, the realization of true knowledge is the recognition that we are awareness itself, not possessors of awareness. As Amma beautifully expresses, the Self is both the knower and the knowledge, and in this realization, we understand that Jnanam, or knowledge, is none other than Ishwara. By transcending the mistaken notion of awareness as an object, we come to know the Self as the eternal, unchanging essence of all existence. This is the highest wisdom and the key to spiritual liberation.

Contemplation Reveals Truth

"True knowledge is always direct, for the Self is self-luminous and ever-present. Through listening, reflection, and deep contemplation, the veil of doubt is lifted, allowing the radiant truth of our own existence to be fully realized." Amma

Jnanam (knowledge) is referred to as aparoksha (direct) because it involves the immediate realization of the truth, particularly in relation to the Self (Atma). In contrast, when knowledge is derived through teachings or logic, it is known as paroksha jnanam (indirect knowledge). The key difference between these two lies in the way the knowledge is experienced—direct knowledge means the object of knowledge is known immediately, while indirect knowledge remains conceptual.

The Atma is inherently self-luminous, meaning it does not rely on anything external for its existence or knowledge. It is the very source of all awareness, and as such, does not need external validation to be known. Amma's teaching beautifully reflects this truth, emphasizing that the Self is always present and self-revealing, waiting to be realized through direct, inner contemplation. The act of listening to teachings is valuable, but it serves as a stepping stone toward direct realization.

When we hear about the Self as Sat-Chit-Ananda (existence-consciousness-bliss), this can lead to the possibility of aparoksha jnanam—the direct realization of our true nature. This realization is not abstract or theoretical; it is the immediate understanding that the Self is the very essence of one's being, not something external or distant. Amma's wisdom guides us toward this direct experience, reminding us that true knowledge cannot remain second-hand—it must be lived and realized in the present moment.

However, even after this initial glimpse of aparoksha jnanam, there can still be lingering obstacles that cloud the mind. Ignorance (ajnanam), doubt (samsaya), and false knowledge (viparyaya) may persist, preventing the clarity of full realization. These obstacles can coexist with the knowledge of the Self, creating confusion and misunderstanding, and requiring further contemplation to dissolve fully. Amma teaches that through deep reflection and inquiry, the remaining veils of ignorance can be lifted.

The importance of contemplation and reflection cannot be overstated in this process. Shravanam (listening to teachings), mananam (reflecting on the teachings), and nididhyasanam (deep meditation) are essential practices on the path to clearing these obstacles. While indirect knowledge (paroksha) might lead us to the door of realization, it is only through direct experience (aparoksha) that we can fully grasp the truth of our own existence. Contemplation is the key to lifting the veil that obscures the radiant truth.

Amma emphasizes that the Self is ever-present, and knowledge of the Self is immediate and direct once the veils of doubt are lifted. However, the journey toward full realization is not always instantaneous. The remnants of false identification with the body-mind complex may persist even after the initial awakening. In such cases, it is essential to continue contemplating the teachings, thereby reinforcing the understanding of the Self's ever-luminous presence.

The Self does not require external effort to exist; it simply is, much like how the sun shines regardless of whether it is obscured by clouds. The obstacles of ignorance and doubt act like those clouds, veiling the light of the Self. But with persistent inquiry and reflection, these clouds begin to part, revealing the direct, self-evident truth that the Atma has always been present and fully realized. Amma's wisdom reminds us that true knowledge is not something to be gained, but something to be recognized as always present.

As we continue to reflect and meditate on the teachings, the experience of oneness deepens. This deep contemplation leads to the eradication of viparyaya—the misconceptions or false knowledge that arise due to ignorance. Once this false knowledge is dissolved, the Self shines without obstruction, and the clarity of direct realization becomes firmly established. The process is gradual but transformative, as layers of misunderstanding fall away, revealing the pure essence of existence.

In this process, the role of a Guru or teacher is invaluable. The teachings serve as a mirror, helping us see the truth more clearly, but the realization itself must be direct and personal. Through deep contemplation, we gradually align our intellectual understanding with the direct experience of the Self. Amma's teachings serve as a guiding light in this journey, emphasizing that the Self is not something to be reached but something to be uncovered within.

Amma's analogy of lifting the veil of doubt resonates deeply with this process. Just as the sun remains unchanged behind the clouds, the Self is ever-luminous, waiting to be recognized once the clouds of ignorance are cleared. It is through this direct, self-luminous knowledge that we realize the eternal truth of our existence. The journey from indirect knowledge to direct realization is one of peeling away layers of falsehood until only the truth remains.

Finally, aparoksha jnanam brings about a profound shift in perception. Once the veil of ignorance is lifted, we no longer see the world through the lens of separation. The realization of the Self as pure awareness brings with it the understanding that all distinctions—between self and other, subject and object—are merely illusions. What remains is the experience of oneness, where the individual ego dissolves into the infinite consciousness of Brahman.

In conclusion, Amma's teaching that "true knowledge is always direct" points to the profound truth that the Self is not an external concept to be understood but an inner reality to be realized. The distinction between indirect (paroksha) and direct (aparoksha) knowledge emphasizes the importance of going beyond mere intellectual understanding to experience the Self directly. Through listening, reflection, and deep contemplation, the veils of ignorance are lifted, revealing the radiant truth of our own existence as the Self, which is always present, self-luminous, and free.

The Infinite Light of Awareness

"The true fruit of self-knowledge is the removal of all doubt and the firm conviction of one's divine nature. Just as light needs no other source to reveal itself, the Atma shines with its own inherent luminosity, dispelling all ignorance." Amma

Atma Vidhya, or the knowledge of the Self, ultimately leads to a profound realization that dispels all doubts and brings a firm conviction in one's divine nature. This self-knowledge is not an intellectual understanding alone, but a direct experience (pratyaksham) of the truth. It removes all uncertainty (samsayam) about one's true essence, revealing the Atma as the eternal and unchanging reality. The journey of Atma Vidhya is one of dissolving ignorance (avidya), which keeps us bound to limited identities of the body and mind. Once this ignorance is removed, the clarity of the Self shines without question.

Just as light does not need another light to recognize its presence, the Atma is inherently self-luminous. It does not rely on external validation to prove its existence. The Atma, by its own nature, shines and reveals the truth of one's being. The realization of this truth does not require further confirmation because the Self is immutable. When the light of Atma Vidhya arises, it dispels the darkness of ignorance, much like the dawn naturally removes the night. This process is entirely self-contained, and there is no need for external evidence to support the realization of the Self.

The attachments to the body, mind, and ego—the false notions of "I" and "mine"—are rooted in ignorance. Through the practice of vidhya (knowledge), these misconceptions are removed. These false identifications create a sense of duality, leading to separation between oneself and others, between the individual and the divine. Once these attachments are dissolved, the inherent luminosity of the Atma shines forth, revealing the true nature of the Self as pure consciousness, free from any limitation. This is the state of being untainted by the fluctuations of the mind and the illusions of the material world.

As ignorance fades away, the seeker realizes that the Atma is not confined to the limited identity of an individual self, bound by the transient world of forms. Instead, the Atma is the infinite, undivided reality—Brahman. This understanding is not conceptual but experiential. Through direct experience, the seeker sees that they are not separate from the absolute reality but are, in fact, that very essence. This realization brings a sense of ultimate freedom and peace, for the individual no longer feels constrained by the body, mind, or the dualities of the world.

The illumination of the Atma brings unshakable certainty about one's true nature. No longer does the individual question their identity or purpose. The falsehoods that arose from ignorance—such as the belief that one is the body-mind complex—disappear completely. What remains is the undeniable truth that the Self is infinite, blissful, and complete. This knowledge brings ananda (bliss) and purnam (completeness), qualities that are the natural state of the realized Self. The seeker no longer searches for fulfillment outside, for they realize they are already whole.

In the same way that light effortlessly shines and reveals everything around it, the Atma effortlessly illuminates the truth of one's being. The process of self-realization is not about acquiring something new but about recognizing what has always been there. The light of awareness has always been shining within, but ignorance obscured it. Once that ignorance is removed, the Atma's inherent luminosity becomes evident. There is no need for further seeking or questioning; the realization itself is self-sufficient and complete.

Through the knowledge of the Self, one transcends the limitations of the material world. The sense of duality, which creates the illusion of separation between the individual and the divine, is dissolved. The seeker realizes that there is no separation between themselves and Ishwara, the divine consciousness. In this understanding, all experiences of limitation and suffering fall away, and the individual abides in the awareness of their true nature—eternal, limitless, and full of bliss.

In conclusion, the journey of Atma Vidhya leads to the realization that the Self is both the knower and the knowledge. Through the removal of ignorance and the firm conviction in one's divine nature, the Atma reveals itself as the infinite light of awareness, dispelling all doubts and bringing the ultimate freedom and peace of self-realization. The seeker comes to know that their true nature is pure consciousness, ever-present and free, and in this knowledge, they find eternal bliss and completeness.

Action Prepares, Knowledge Liberates

"Sadhana is essential for preparing the mind to receive true knowledge, but liberation itself is eternal and beyond action. When we realize our true nature through teachings like 'Tat Twam Asi,' fear dissolves, and we rest in the peace of non-duality." Amma

In Advaita Vedanta, sadhana, or spiritual practice, serves as an essential foundation in preparing the mind for the realization of true knowledge. Spiritual qualifications like viveka (discernment) and vairagya (dispassion) must be developed through sadhana for knowledge to arise. The purpose of these qualifications is to cleanse the mind and refine one's perception, enabling the individual to grasp the non-dual truth. Through actions like karma (selfless action) and upasana (worship), the seeker cultivates the readiness for jnana (knowledge). However, while actions may prepare the seeker, they do not directly lead to moksham (liberation), which is inherent and eternal.

Liberation, according to Advaita, is not something created or attained through karma. It is already present as the true nature of the Self (Atma), and the role of sadhana is to remove the ignorance (avidya) that veils this realization. The teachings of mahavakyas (great statements) like "Tat

Twam Asi" ("You are That") serve as pointers to this truth. These statements guide the seeker toward realizing that the individual self (jiva) is not separate from the ultimate reality, Brahman. The direct experience of this knowledge is what liberates, not the accumulation of good deeds or rituals.

Once this non-dual truth is realized, the notion of separation between the individual self and the universe dissolves. In this state of realization, the seeker understands that there is no distinct "I" apart from the universal Brahman. The individual experiences abhaya prathishta, or fearlessness, because all duality—which gives rise to fear—disappears. Fear, after all, is rooted in the idea of being separate, vulnerable, and threatened by an external world. In non-duality, there is no "other" to be feared; only oneness exists.

Moksham, therefore, is not something that requires ongoing effort through rituals or worship. It is the direct realization of one's already liberated nature. Just as the sun does not need to be created—it only needs the clouds to be removed to shine—liberation is simply the removal of ignorance.

The peace that comes from non-dual realization is unlike any temporary peace offered by worldly actions or achievements. It is the realization that the Self is infinite, unchanging, and eternal. The jiva, having identified with the transient body and mind, experiences fear, desire, and suffering in a world of duality. But through self-knowledge, these limiting identifications fall away, leaving the individual established in the reality of the undivided Brahman.

This establishment in knowledge is not a mental construct or a temporary state of bliss. It is the recognition that one has always been free. The illusion of bondage was simply the result of ignorance, and once that ignorance is dispelled through knowledge, the seeker recognizes the truth of their eternal nature. In this realization, there is no need for further effort or action because there is no longer a sense of lack or incompleteness.

Liberation, or moksham, is often described as a state of "resting" in Advaita. This does not imply inactivity, but rather the absence of the restless seeking that characterizes worldly life. Before realizing the truth, individuals engage in actions hoping to attain happiness, security, and fulfillment. However, once the realization of the Self dawns, the seeker understands that these qualities are not external achievements but intrinsic aspects of their true nature.

In conclusion, the teachings of Advaita Vedanta emphasize that sadhana is crucial for preparing the mind, but knowledge alone leads to liberation. The realization that "You are That" dissolves the false notions of separation and fear, allowing the individual to rest in the peace of non-duality. Moksham is not something attained through action, but the direct experience of one's already liberated nature. Through knowledge, fear vanishes, and the seeker abides in the eternal truth of the Self.

Transcendental Knowledge

"The Atma is pure existence and consciousness. It is the eternal, unchanging presence that underlies all life, illuminating the truth of who we are." — Amma

In Vedantic teachings, the Jiva is the embodied Self where there is a mistaken identification of each for the other. This misidentification results in the illusion of separateness, giving rise to the phenomenal ego. As Amma states, "The Atma is pure existence and consciousness." The Jiva is a complex entity, consisting of the mind-body organism and a reflection of consciousness. Although consciousness (Atma) is pure and unchanging, it is mistakenly qualified by the internal organs of the body and mind, creating the illusion of individuality. This reflection of consciousness within the Jiva is known as Cidabhāsa. It is through this complex that the Jiva operates in the world, perceiving itself as a distinct entity while still being, at its core, identical with Brahman.

Amma's teaching, "The Atma is the eternal, unchanging presence that underlies all life," resonates with the understanding that while the Jiva experiences individuality, it is rooted in the same eternal consciousness. The Jiva, being a product of ignorance (avidya), falsely identifies with the body, mind, and ego. This creates the appearance of many individuals, though in reality, all Jivas share the same substratum - the Atma. The illusion of separateness is maintained by the two aspects of avidya, namely avarana (concealment) and viksepa (projection). These aspects hide the true nature of the Self and project the false notion of duality, causing the Jiva to see itself as separate from the universe.

Jnana (knowledge) is the key to dispelling the illusion of separateness. As Amma points out, "True knowledge is always direct, for the Self is immutable and ever-present." In Vedanta, Jnana is viewed as a modification of the mind, inspired by the witness self (Sakshi). The mind undergoes changes or modifications (vritti), but the element of consciousness that illuminates these modifications remains eternal. Jnana is the process through which the Jiva shifts from identifying with the body-mind complex to recognizing its true nature as Atma. This knowledge can be either mediate or immediate, depending on whether the Self is directly realized or understood conceptually.

In Vedanta, knowledge can be either mediate or immediate. Mediate knowledge refers to knowledge that is gained through inference, hearsay, or external sources. It is the knowledge of objects that are not directly experienced but understood conceptually. For instance, when one infers the presence of fire from seeing smoke, that is mediate knowledge. In contrast, immediate knowledge is the direct perception of an object without any mediation. It is the immediate and direct experience of the reality, such as seeing fire directly rather than inferring its presence.

In the context of Jnana, immediate knowledge occurs when both the "that" and the "what" of an object are revealed simultaneously. For immediate knowledge to take place, certain conditions must be fulfilled: the object must be directly knowable (yogya), the object must exist at the time of perception, and there must be an intimate relation between the subject (the knower) and the object (the known). When these conditions are met, the Jiva can experience direct knowledge, bypassing the limitations of the mind and conceptual thought.

Sakshi-jnana is considered the highest form of knowledge because it arises directly from the Sakshi, or witness consciousness. The Sakshi is the pure awareness that observes all mental modifications without being affected by them. Sakshi-jnana is immediate, direct, and self-luminous, meaning it does not require any external validation or proof. It is the realization of the Self as the ultimate reality, beyond the body-mind complex.

This form of knowledge is crucial for the Jiva's liberation because it allows the individual to see beyond the illusion of separateness. Sakshi-jnana reveals the underlying unity of all existence, showing that the Jiva is not separate from Brahman but is, in fact, identical with it. This realization dissolves the ego and the false identification with the body and mind, leading to the state of moksha (liberation).

In contrast to Sakshi-jnana, Vritti-jnana arises from the modifications of the mind. It is the knowledge that is contingent upon thought and perception, making it indirect and mediated. While Vritti-jnana can lead to important insights and understandings, it is limited by the mind's capacity to comprehend reality. The mind, being influenced by past experiences, desires, and attachments, often distorts the truth, creating a veil of illusion. Therefore, Vritti-jnana is not as reliable as Sakshi-jnana, which is free from mental distortions.

However, Vritti-jnana is still valuable in the spiritual journey. It serves as a preliminary form of knowledge that prepares the Jiva for the higher realization of Sakshi-jnana. Through contemplation, reflection, and meditation, the Jiva can refine its Vritti-jnana, gradually removing the distortions of the mind and moving closer to the direct experience of the Self. This process is essential for breaking free from the cycle of samsara and attaining liberation.

Immediate knowledge is essential for the Jiva's liberation because it allows for the direct experience of the Self, free from the limitations of the mind. In immediate knowledge, the intimate relationship between the knower and the known is established, allowing the Jiva to perceive the Self without any conceptual mediation. This direct knowledge is transformative, as it dissolves the illusion of separateness and reveals the unity of the Self and Brahman.

For immediate knowledge to occur, the object of knowledge (in this case, the Self) must be directly knowable, existent at the time of perception, and intimately related to the knower. In the case of the Self, these conditions are always fulfilled because the Self is ever-present, eternal, and self-luminous. Therefore, the Jiva has the potential to attain immediate knowledge at any moment, provided the veil of ignorance is lifted through right knowledge (Jnana).

Jnana is the key to overcoming the ignorance that binds the Jiva to the cycle of samsara. Ignorance, or avidya, creates the false identification of the Self with the body, mind, and ego, leading to the illusion of separateness. This ignorance is the root cause of all suffering, as it perpetuates the belief in duality and prevents the Jiva from realizing its true nature as Atman. Through the cultivation of Jnana, the Jiva can gradually dissolve this ignorance, leading to the direct experience of Sakshi-jnana.

The process of attaining Jnana involves shravanam (listening to teachings), mananam (reflecting on those teachings), and nididhyasanam (meditation). These practices help to refine the Jiva's Vritti-jnana, removing the distortions created by the mind and preparing the individual for the higher realization of Sakshi-jnana. Once the Jiva attains this direct knowledge, the veil of ignorance is lifted, and the Jiva realizes its oneness with Brahman, leading to moksha.

The journey toward realizing Brahman is not one that can be achieved through intellect alone. Paramartha Vigjnanam, or transcendental knowledge, is required to perceive the true nature of Brahman, and the Guru plays a vital role in guiding the seeker toward this realization. As Amma's wisdom teaches, the Guru helps the seeker move beyond the illusion of duality, leading them to the direct realization of the Self. Through the Guru's presence and teachings, the seeker learns to see past the transient world of names and forms, recognizing that Brahman is the unchanging reality behind all appearances.

As the seeker deepens their understanding of Jnana, they begin to transcend the illusions of duality. Amma's teaching, "The realization of Brahman brings an end to all seeking," encapsulates this process. Once the Jiva recognizes that the Atma and Brahman are one, the false identification with the body and mind dissolves, and the ego, which is the source of separateness, falls away. This leads to the experience of non-duality (Advaita), where the distinctions between the self and the universe vanish. The Jiva experiences the world not as a collection of separate entities, but as a manifestation of the same infinite consciousness.

Through meditation and self-inquiry, the Jiva can deepen its experience of Sakshi-jnana. As Amma points out, "The mind, which is ordinarily scattered and restless, becomes disciplined and focused." Meditation allows the seeker to turn inward, detaching from the transient world of forms and recognizing the unchanging reality of Brahman. This inner concentration creates a space where the Jiva can directly experience non-duality, dissolving the limitations of the ego and resting in the knowledge that all of existence is one.

The realization of Brahman as the ultimate reality is the goal of Jnana and leads to the liberation of the Jiva. Amma's teaching, "The Atma shines with its own inherent luminosity," reflects the direct experience of liberation, where the Jiva no longer seeks external objects or desires, having realized that the ultimate fulfillment is found within. In this state, the Jiva is no longer bound by the limitations of time, space, or individuality. The illusion of separateness falls away, revealing the boundless, infinite nature of the Self. The Jiva recognizes that it has always been one with Brahman, and liberation is not a distant goal but the realization of the Self's eternal truth.

In conclusion, the Jiva's journey from ignorance to liberation is guided by the light of Jnana and the teachings of the Guru. As Amma states, "The Atma is pure existence and consciousness." By recognizing the Atma as the self-luminous reality that underlies all life, the Jiva transcends the illusions of separateness and duality. Through Sakshi-jnana, the Jiva realizes its oneness with Brahman, experiencing the world not as a collection of distinct entities, but as a manifestation of the same infinite consciousness. In this state of non-dual awareness, the Jiva rests in the eternal peace of its true nature, liberated from the cycles of samsara, and fully aligned with the unchanging truth of Brahman.

Freedom from Ignorance

"The purpose of the scriptures is to guide us toward the realization of our true nature, beyond the dualities of duty and desire. Once the knowledge of the Self is attained, the need for actions and obligations dissolves, as we rest in the supreme truth." Amma

In spiritual teachings, the primary role of the scriptures is to lead us toward the realization of our true nature. These teachings are consistent, as their ultimate goal is to liberate individuals from ignorance and guide them toward the realization of the Self. Just as fire cannot simultaneously possess both heat and cold, scriptures cannot prescribe contradictory actions, such as advocating attachment to duties while also preaching detachment. The realization of the Self eliminates the need for further action or obligation, as one is established in the supreme truth of oneness with Brahman.

Scriptures serve as a guide for matters that are not self-evident, particularly when it comes to the realization of the Self. Scriptures serve to illuminate this higher knowledge and direct individuals toward self-realization, rather than fostering new desires or attachments.

There is no contradiction within the teachings of the scriptures. Just as fire cannot possess coldness or the sun cannot harbor darkness, the teachings on the Self remain logically consistent.

Avidya operates through two aspects: avarana (concealment) and viksepa (projection). Avarana hides the true nature of reality, preventing individuals from perceiving their true Self, which is identical with Brahman, the Absolute. Viksepa projects false notions of reality, creating the illusion of duality and separateness that characterizes the experience of the world. These two functions of avidya work together to obscure the truth and perpetuate the cycle of illusion, leading individuals to identify with the body, mind, and ego rather than realizing their oneness with Brahman.

The locus of avidya can be understood in two ways: either as residing in the individual self (jiva) or in the Absolute (Brahman). In the individual, avidya is the ignorance that veils one's understanding of their true nature, keeping them bound to the cycle of birth, death, and rebirth (samsara). In the broader cosmic sense, avidya is said to be rooted in Brahman, not in a literal sense, but as the medium through which Brahman's true nature is concealed from the perspective of the illusory world. Ultimately, avidya is dispelled through jñana (right knowledge), allowing one to transcend illusion and realize the Self as Brahman, leading to liberation (moksha).

The role of the scriptures is to guide individuals to the realization of the Self, which is synonymous with realizing their innate divinity. The knowledge imparted by the scriptures leads to an understanding that one is not the body or mind but the eternal, unchanging Self. Once this realization occurs, it is illogical for the scriptures to impose further actions or obligations that contradict this newfound awareness. The individual who realizes their oneness with Brahman is beyond the dualities of virtue and vice, pleasure and pain, as they are no longer motivated by desires that drive actions.

In the realm of self-realization, prescribed duties (karma) lose their significance. Before attaining knowledge of the Self, actions are often motivated by the desire to achieve something positive or avoid something negative. However, after the realization of the Self, the individual transcends this dualistic thinking. They recognize that their true nature is already complete, and therefore, there is no need for actions driven by a sense of incompleteness. This understanding brings liberation from the cycle of karma and the endless pursuit of desires.

Amma's teachings emphasize that the knowledge of the Self dissolves the need for any further prescribed duties. Once an individual realizes their true nature as the Atma, they are no longer bound by societal or religious expectations to perform certain actions. They are free from the obligations that once seemed essential because they now operate from a space of inner completeness and peace. The realization that "I am the Self" liberates them from the motivations that drive most human actions.

This liberation from duty and desire does not mean that the realized individual becomes inactive. Rather, their actions are no longer driven by personal desires or the pursuit of outcomes. They act spontaneously and selflessly, in alignment with the natural flow of life. This state of being is characterized by a deep sense of peace and fulfillment, as the individual recognizes that they are not separate from the world but an integral part of the universal Self.

The scriptures play a crucial role in this process of self-realization, but once their purpose is fulfilled, they are no longer needed. Just as a raft is used to cross a river and then left behind, the teachings of the scriptures serve their purpose by guiding the individual to the realization of the Self.

Ultimately, Amma's teachings remind us that the purpose of the scriptures is to guide us toward the realization of our true nature, beyond the dualities of pleasure and pain. Once the knowledge of the Self is attained, the need for actions and obligations dissolves, and we rest in the supreme truth of our own being. This realization brings freedom from ignorance and the liberation that comes from knowing that we are the infinite, eternal Self.

Ego: The Eclipse of Truth

"Ignorance arises from identifying with the ego and body, but true knowledge reveals the Self as beyond all forms. Just as day and night don't affect the sun, the Self remains untouched by ignorance, shining in its eternal light." Amma

Ahamkāra, often referred to as "I"-ness or egoism, represents the concept of individuality and the notion of a separate self. In Vedantic philosophy, Ahamkāra is known as the "I-maker," as it creates the sense of a distinct personal identity. It is the part of the antahkarana (inner instrument) that forms the ego and gives rise to the feeling of self-assertion. This aspect of the mind is responsible for the notion of "I" and "mine," leading to identification with the body, mind, and sensory experiences. As the source of self-centeredness, Ahamkāra forms the basis of the ego's attachment to worldly objects and desires, perpetuating the illusion of separateness from the ultimate reality, Brahman.

In Advaita philosophy, the idea of superimposition is used to explain how illusion arises and why human beings mistake themselves for something they are not. Superimposition means attributing the qualities of one thing to another. A simple example is mistaking a rope for a snake in dim light. The rope is real, but the snake is falsely imagined. In the same way, human beings superimpose the body and the mind onto the Self, and the Self onto the body and the mind. This mistake creates the entire structure of human misunderstanding.

The first kind of error is the superimposition of the impermanent body and mind onto the Self. The Self is pure awareness—unchanging, limitless, and free. Yet, because of ignorance, we take the experiences of the body and mind to belong to this Self. A formula to understand this misconception is "I am {insert body-mind complex term here}." We say, "I am tall, I am young, I am sad, I am happy," as though awareness itself were changing and bound by conditions. But awareness is never young or old, happy or sad. These qualities belong to the body and the mind, not to the Self. By confusing them, we lose sight of our real nature.

The second kind of error is the superimposition of the Self onto the body and mind. They appear sentient only because of the Self's presence. A formula to understand this misconception is "Body/mind is {insert consciousness term here}." We say "Body is alive, the mind is thinking, senses are seeing." Here, the qualities of pure awareness are falsely attributed to the body and mind. The body appears to be alive because awareness is mistaken as its property. The mind appears conscious because awareness is wrongly attributed to it. In truth, the body is material, and the mind is an instrument. They have no awareness of their own. It is only because awareness is superimposed upon them that they seem to shine with life and intelligence.

From the time we get up till we sleep, we are living in superimposition. Because we attribute the qualities of the body and mind to the Self, we feel limited, vulnerable, and separate. Because we attribute the qualities of the Self to the body and mind, we give them a false sense of permanence and importance. Together, these mistakes weave the illusion that "I am this body" or "I am this mind," when in truth, awareness alone is what we are.

The consequence of this double superimposition is suffering. When the body is taken as the Self, its aging, illness, and death are felt as threats to one's very existence. When the mind is taken as the Self, its moods, fears, and desires dominate one's sense of reality. By identifying with what is transient, we become trapped in endless cycles of attachment, striving, and disappointment. Life becomes a struggle to preserve what can never last.

The way out is through knowledge—knowledge that is not intellectual alone, but direct recognition. By carefully observing, one sees that awareness is never actually touched by the body's conditions or the mind's fluctuations. Just as the screen remains untouched by the movie projected upon it, awareness remains free while the play of life unfolds within it. Recognizing this truth removes the confusion. The body is seen as body, the mind as mind, and the Self as Self—unchanging, luminous, and free.

This removal of superimposition is liberation. When the body is no longer mistaken for the Self, fear of death loses its hold. When the mind is no longer mistaken for the Self, its thoughts and emotions lose their power to bind. What remains is the natural clarity of being, in which one knows: I am awareness itself—limitless, whole, untouched by the rise and fall of appearances.

Amma's analogy of day and night further clarifies the relationship between ignorance and the Self. Day and night exist only for an observer on Earth; they have no intrinsic reality for the sun, which remains constant regardless of the Earth's rotation. Similarly, ignorance and knowledge are qualities that belong to the perceiver—the jnani (knower of the Self) and the ajnani (one ignorant of the Self). However, they do not affect the Self itself. The Atma is eternal, unchanging, and untouched by both knowledge and ignorance. It shines with its own light, just as the sun is unaffected by the alternation of day and night.

The identification with the body and mind is what is referred to as prathyaksha ajnanam, or immediate ignorance. This form of ignorance is directly perceived because it stems from the immediate experience of being bound to the physical body and mind. As long as one is entangled in this false identification, the true nature of the Self remains obscured. However, when prathyakshya jnanam, direct knowledge of the Self, arises, it dispels this ignorance in the same direct manner. The moment this realization occurs, the illusory nature of the ego is shattered, and the individual sees themselves as the Atma—the true, unchanging essence.

Though Atma Jnanam operates within the mind to remove ignorance, it's crucial to understand that even knowledge is a transformation of the mind (anthakarna parinamam). The mind undergoes modifications based on the knowledge it receives, and it is through these modifications that ignorance is dissolved. Despite this, the Atma itself remains beyond the mind and unaffected by these changes. The mind acts as a tool through which the veil of ignorance is lifted, but the Self is ever-present, untouched by the fluctuations of the mental realm.

The realization of the Self, however, is not merely an intellectual understanding. It is an experiential transformation that shifts one's entire perspective. The ego's eclipse over the mind and Self is like a shadow—it is not a real obstruction but an illusion that disappears when the light of knowledge shines. With the dawn of Atma Jnanam, the seeker no longer identifies with the transient body-mind complex. Instead, they rest in the awareness of the Atma, the unbounded reality that is ever-present, beyond form, and infinite in nature.

When the mind becomes free of ignorance, the direct perception of the Self leads to a profound inner freedom. Doubts and misperceptions about one's identity dissolve. This clarity brings not only intellectual understanding but a lived experience of being the Self. The ego, once seen as a real entity, is now recognized as a mere superimposition on the Self, an illusion that vanishes with true knowledge. In this state, one no longer feels confined by the limitations of individuality but experiences a sense of boundlessness and unity with all.

The Atma, like the sun, always shines in its own light, unaffected by the illusions of day and night. Even when ignorance seems to obscure it, the Self remains constant and unchanging. It is only the mind, influenced by ignorance, that experiences fluctuations. Through the guidance of Amma's teachings, one can realize that the Atma is beyond all these changes.

Thus, ego's eclipse of the truth is merely an illusion, a temporary shadow cast over the brilliance of the Self. Once this illusion is pierced by the light of Atma Jnanam, the seeker experiences liberation. They see clearly that their true nature is not bound by the physical or mental limitations they once believed in. This freedom from ignorance brings a deep sense of peace and clarity, as the seeker recognizes their oneness with the infinite, eternal reality.

In essence, Amma's teachings on the ego as the eclipse of truth guide us toward the understanding that the Self is beyond all forms and illusions. By identifying with the body and mind, we obscure the true light of the Atma. However, through the direct experience of knowledge, this eclipse is lifted, and the Self is revealed in its full glory. In this realization, the dualities of knowledge and ignorance fall away, and what remains is the ever-shining light of the Atma, untouched and eternal.

Ultimately, Amma's message is that the Self is ever-present and ever-luminous, beyond the temporary illusions of ego and ignorance. True liberation comes when we realize that the ego, like an eclipse, is not a permanent obstruction but a passing shadow that vanishes when the light of knowledge arises. This understanding allows us to rest in the eternal light of the Self, free from ignorance, and firmly rooted in the truth of our own divine nature.

Beyond Action, Only Knowing

"Both knowledge and action are essential steps on the spiritual path. Knowledge illuminates the truth, while selfless action purifies the heart. Together, they lead to the ultimate realization of oneness with the Divine." Amma

In the worldly state, individuals are often driven by desires and attachments to material objects, seeking enjoyment and fulfillment from external sources. This longing arises from the perception that the world and its objects are separate from the Self. Such desires are rooted in the illusion of duality, where external objects seem to exist independently of the observer. As long as one perceives the world through this lens, the pursuit of desires continues, and the individual remains bound by the limitations of material existence.

However, through self-knowledge, one comes to understand that the Self is all-encompassing and that no separation truly exists between the observer and the observed. When this realization dawns, the desire for external objects naturally fades, as one no longer craves what is already an inherent part of their own being. This unity of perception, where the Self is seen as non-different from everything else, leads to liberation. In this liberated state, the individual no longer seeks fulfillment through external means but finds complete satisfaction in abiding in their true nature, the Atma.

The distinction between knowledge (jnana) and action (karma) is central to this discussion. Knowledge pertains to the direct realization of the Self's oneness with all, while action involves performing tasks and seeking results within the realm of duality. Karma reinforces the perception of separateness by operating in the world of desires and outcomes, thus creating further entanglement. Therefore, liberation cannot be achieved solely through karma. Instead, it is knowledge that unveils the truth of the Self, dispelling the ignorance that causes bondage.

While knowledge is ultimately the means to liberation, karma still holds an important place in preparing an individual for this realization. Actions performed selflessly, without attachment to their outcomes, purify the heart and mind. This purification, achieved through dutiful action, helps remove the layers of ignorance and ego that obscure the truth of the Self. Such purification creates the fertile ground where knowledge can arise. In this way, action serves as a preparatory step on the spiritual path.

The Vedic scriptures emphasize this balance between knowledge and karma. While knowledge directly leads to liberation, the karmas prescribed by the scriptures—such as rituals, service, and selfless actions—play a significant role in the initial stages of spiritual growth. These actions cleanse the individual of accumulated impurities and sins, making them more receptive to the truth of the Self. Therefore, karma is not in conflict with knowledge; instead, it supports and facilitates the emergence of knowledge.

Amma's teachings highlight that selfless actions, performed with devotion and without expectation of reward, serve to purify the heart. This purification process helps prepare the individual for the higher stages of spiritual evolution. While karma is necessary in the beginning, it is knowledge that ultimately liberates the individual from the cycle of birth and death.

Thus, karma and knowledge are complementary on the spiritual path. Karma purifies, while knowledge liberates.

In this journey, desires lose their hold as the seeker comes to understand the futility of pursuing external objects for fulfillment. The true fulfillment lies within, in the recognition of the Self as the ultimate reality. Once this knowledge is firmly established, the need for action diminishes, and the individual rests in the awareness of their own divine nature. This state of being transcends all dualities, and the seeker experiences the eternal peace of non-duality.

In conclusion, the highest goal of liberation is achieved through the illumination of knowledge, not through the accumulation of actions. While karma plays an essential role in purifying the heart and mind in the early stages of spiritual practice, it is knowledge that brings about the final realization of the Self. As Amma emphasizes, both knowledge and action are necessary steps on the spiritual path, but it is knowledge that ultimately leads to liberation, dissolving the illusion of separateness and revealing the oneness of the Self with the Divine.

Names and Forms

"All names and forms are fleeting, but the true nature is the essence that underlies everything. When we look beyond the surface, we realize the same divine presence exists in all beings and all things." Amma

The fleeting nature of names and forms is a central theme in spiritual traditions, particularly in Advaita Vedanta. Names and forms refer to the various objects, beings, and manifestations we see in the world. These appearances, while seemingly diverse and separate, are mere expressions of the one unchanging reality beneath them. Amma's quote beautifully encapsulates this truth, emphasizing that while the forms we perceive may change, the essence remains constant and undisturbed. The ultimate realization is that this divine essence is present in all things, even if it is masked by names and forms.

The Chandogya Upanishad explains this concept through the metaphor of clay in the famous verse Vacharambhana (Chandogya Upanishad, 6.1.5). The Upanishad illustrates that just as clay takes many forms, such as pots, vases, and statues, these forms do not alter the essential nature of the clay. In the same way, the Atma (Self) manifests in different forms in the world, but its essence remains unchanged. The forms and names we assign to these objects are like labels, useful for identification but ultimately unable to define the true nature of the underlying reality.

This metaphor reveals a profound spiritual truth. The external forms we perceive with our senses are transient. They come into existence, change, and disappear over time. However, the essence—the Atma, or pure consciousness—remains constant. Just as the clay remains unchanged despite being molded into different shapes, the true nature of reality remains unaltered by the changing forms and names of the material world.

In spiritual practice, recognizing the impermanence of names and forms is crucial to understanding the deeper reality of the Self. When we become attached to the external world, we identify with the forms and names that are bound by time and space. We begin to believe that these changing forms define us, leading to suffering when they inevitably fade or transform. Amma's teachings encourage us to look beyond the surface, to recognize that these external forms are temporary expressions of a deeper, unchanging truth.

The Chandogya Upanishad further explains that knowledge of this essential unity—of the underlying reality that transcends names and forms—leads to liberation. This knowledge is not merely intellectual; it is a direct experiential understanding that arises through self-inquiry and meditation. By contemplating the transient nature of the world and focusing on the eternal essence within, we begin to dissolve the illusion of separateness. This dissolution of duality is the key to spiritual freedom.

Amma's teachings echo this wisdom by urging us to cultivate this awareness in our daily lives. When we realize that names and forms are fleeting, we naturally begin to detach from worldly desires and attachments. This detachment is not about rejecting the world, but about seeing it as it truly is—a play of forms on the surface of the unchanging reality. In this way, we live in the world without being bound by it, recognizing that the divine presence pervades all things.

Furthermore, this understanding of names and forms leads to a deep sense of unity and compassion. When we realize that the same divine essence exists in all beings, the divisions we create between ourselves and others begin to dissolve. We no longer see others as separate entities with distinct identities but as expressions of the same infinite reality. This realization fosters a sense of oneness, where love, compassion, and service naturally arise.

Amma's emphasis on devotion, selfless service, and meditation aligns with this path of realization. Through these practices, we purify the mind and heart, allowing us to see beyond the surface of names and forms. Devotion helps us connect with the divine essence in all things, while selfless service reminds us that we are all interconnected. Meditation, meanwhile, provides the direct experience of the Self, revealing the infinite consciousness that underlies all existence.

In conclusion, understanding the transient nature of names and forms and recognizing the eternal essence that pervades everything is key to spiritual growth. Amma's teachings and the wisdom of the Chandogya Upanishad guide us toward this realization, reminding us that the ultimate truth is beyond words, forms, and concepts. When we look beyond the fleeting appearances of the world, we discover the unchanging divine presence that exists within all beings and all things, leading us to the experience of oneness and liberation.

Modulations of Sat

"Names and forms are but fleeting manifestations, mere shadows on the surface. The true essence lies beyond them, in the unchanging reality of the Self." Amma

In the state of sushupti (deep sleep), there is no awareness of names, forms, or distinctions. These elements that define our waking experience dissolve, becoming unmanifest, much like a lump of gold that has not yet been shaped into ornaments. Upon waking, the same names and forms reappear, just as gold can be shaped into different ornaments. However, these forms, whether in sleep or waking, are not independent of the underlying reality, just as the ornaments are never separate from the gold from which they are formed. In essence, names and forms are fleeting, while the unchanging reality—sat, or pure existence—remains constant.

Similarly, the world we perceive, with all its forms, time, and space, is not separate from Brahman (the ultimate reality). Time (kalam), space (desam), and the entire universe (jagath) are manifestations of Brahman, just as various ornaments are forms of gold. These forms appear distinct to us, yet their essence is the same. In Advaita Vedanta, this concept is expressed through the idea of mithya, meaning that the world is not unreal but exists dependent on Brahman, much like how ornaments depend on gold for their existence.

This understanding shifts our perception of reality. Rather than seeing the world as separate from its source, we come to realize that everything—time, space, and objects—are expressions of the same divine essence. Prapancham (creation) is a manifestation of Ishwara (God), not something apart from it. All aspects of creation are rooted in Brahman, even though they appear distinct due to our limited, conditioned perception. This realization dissolves the false distinction between creator and creation, allowing us to see the non-dual nature of existence.

Amma's quote and the Upanishadic wisdom emphasize that names and forms are like the shadows of the true essence that lies beyond them. Our attachment to these temporary forms keeps us from recognizing the unchanging reality that pervades all things. By shifting our focus from the fleeting to the eternal, we begin to see that Brahman is both the source and substance of all creation. This insight leads to a deeper understanding of the self and the universe, where all distinctions merge into the oneness of Brahman.

In the end, the world of forms, while appearing distinct, is simply a modulation of sat—pure existence. Just as different ornaments are merely expressions of the same gold, the world and its objects are expressions of Brahman. Understanding this non-dual reality is key to transcending the illusions of separation and recognizing the oneness that underlies all.

Misnomer of Names and Forms

"Names and forms are but passing waves on the ocean of consciousness, while the true essence remains ever changeless and eternal." Amma

The Aitareya Upanishad (1-1-1) begins with the profound statement that in the beginning, only the Atma (the Self) existed, and nothing else. The Atma, in its unmanifested form, alone contemplated, "Let me create the worlds." This foundational passage highlights the concept that the Atma is the source of all creation, not relying on any external force or material. It is the essence that, through sheer omniscience, manifests all worlds and forms.

As the Atman manifests in different forms, it assumes various names. The idea is akin to how water, though still water, can take the form of foam when conditions change. Despite the transformation into names and forms, the essence—Atma—remains unchanged, omnipresent, and eternal. This teaching emphasizes that the reality of the world is not separate from the Self, and thus, the world of names and forms is ultimately mithya (illusory) in its separateness from the fundamental reality.

Atma, often referred to as the inner Self, is the ultimate reality underlying the individual and is identical with Brahman, the Absolute. In Vedanta, the Atma is the unchanging essence that remains constant despite the various states of waking, dreaming, and deep sleep. It is beyond doubt because it is the foundation of all experience. The Atma is the subject of every perception, thought, and feeling, yet it cannot be perceived as an object. This is because the knower (Atma) cannot be the known, making it distinct from anything we can conceptualize or observe. Despite this, the Atma is ever-present and vital for all forms of existence.

The Atma, being the basis of all proofs, underlies every aspect of existence and is the foundation of all cognition. Without the Atma, there could be no experience, no perception, and no thought. However, it cannot be demonstrated through logical proofs or empirical means. Its existence is self-evident, as it is the very essence of consciousness itself. Just as a person cannot see their own eyes without a mirror, the Atma cannot be "known" in the usual sense because it is the knower of everything. The Atma remains elusive to the mind because it transcends all intellectual categories and is beyond dualistic thinking.

Although the Atma cannot be grasped by the mind or proven through external means, it can be experienced directly. This experience of the Atma is described as a realization, where one recognizes that their true nature is not limited to the body-mind complex but is instead the infinite, unchanging consciousness that is one with Brahman. This direct experience leads to liberation (moksha) as it reveals the underlying unity of all existence. In this realization, the individual self (jiva) is seen as a reflection of the Atma, which is always present, untouched by the changing phenomena of the world.

To explain how the Atma manifests the universe, two analogies are offered. First is the analogy of the intelligent carpenter. Just as a carpenter constructs a palace based solely on his knowledge and intention, the Atma manifests the universe through its own inherent power and wisdom. The world arises from the Atman as effortlessly as foam arises from water. In this analogy, the Atma is both the material and the efficient cause of the universe.

The second analogy likens the Atma to a skilled conjurer or magician. The Atma manifests the world through its creative power, transcending the ordinary notions of cause and effect. This conjurer analogy emphasizes the boundlessness of the Atma, capable of manifesting the universe without being subject to the material processes or limitations that we typically associate with creation.

These analogies highlight the Atma's power of manifestation—its ability to create through sheer will and knowledge rather than any physical mechanism. Like passing waves on the ocean of consciousness, names and forms arise and dissolve, while the essence—the Atma—remains eternally present, untouched, and unchanging.

The Upanishads also emphasize the distinction between superior and inferior knowledge. Superior knowledge refers to the understanding of Brahman—the ultimate reality—while inferior knowledge pertains to worldly matters and transient pursuits. It is the knowledge of Brahman that liberates the seeker from the cycle of birth and death, as it dissolves ignorance (avidya) and reveals the true nature of the Self.

To attain this knowledge, the Upanishads stress the importance of renunciation (sannyasa). Renouncing worldly attachments and desires allows the seeker to focus solely on the pursuit of Brahmajnana (knowledge of Brahman). Through this path, one transcends the limitations of material existence, realizing the eternal oneness of all.

In conclusion, names and forms are fleeting manifestations, mere waves on the ocean of consciousness. Just as foam on water does not alter the essence of the water, the world of names and forms does not alter the unchanging reality of the Atman. Realizing this, we understand that the true essence lies beyond all appearances, ever changeless and eternal. Through renunciation and the pursuit of knowledge, one reaches the highest goal—Self-realization, where all names and forms are seen as mere expressions of the one, non-dual reality.

Self as Eternal Knowledge

"The Self is pure knowledge, beyond intellect and thought. True Jñana shines with clarity, illuminating the eternal truth that is ever-present within, untouched by time or change." — Amma

In Advaita Vedanta, the term "knowledge" (Jnana) is not understood as an active process of knowing or learning, as it would be for a limited individual. Instead, when we refer to Brahman, the ultimate reality, as knowledge, we speak of its very nature as pure awareness or consciousness. This consciousness is beyond intellect, thought, or mental processes. It is the substratum of all knowing and being, an ever-present reality that underlies existence itself.

The Self, or Atma, is inherently of the same nature as Brahman—infinite and eternal. Therefore, when we say the Self is knowledge, we do not mean it gains or loses knowledge like an ordinary mind. Rather, knowledge in this sense is the eternal, changeless awareness that illumines all experiences. It is not dependent on the external world, nor does it fluctuate with time or circumstances. This is why Amma says, “True Jñana shines with clarity, illuminating the eternal truth that is ever-present within.” It points to an intrinsic, self-luminous awareness.

If we were to misunderstand Brahman as an active knower, it would imply that Brahman is subject to change. To be an agent of knowing, Brahman would have to gain or lose knowledge over time, which contradicts the essential nature of Brahman as infinite and unchanging. As Brahman is limitless, it cannot be bound by time, space, or the process of acquiring knowledge, which belongs to the realm of duality and change.

The Chandogya Upanishad clarifies this concept, emphasizing that the infinite (Brahman) is not in need of knowing anything outside of itself. In contrast, the finite, limited being requires knowledge of the external world to function. If Brahman were confined to the process of knowing, it would imply that Brahman is limited, finite, and dependent, which is contradictory to its nature as the absolute, all-pervading reality.

This understanding highlights a crucial distinction between ordinary knowledge and the true knowledge of the Self. The knowledge that belongs to the mind is subject to doubt, change, and impermanence, but the knowledge that is the Self is beyond such limitations. It is not knowledge “about” something—it is the ever-present awareness that makes all knowledge possible. It is like the light that illumines objects but remains unaffected by them.

In this context, Amma’s teaching that “The Self is pure knowledge, beyond intellect and thought” points directly to the truth that the Self is not an intellectual concept but the very essence of awareness. This knowledge is untainted by the fluctuations of thought, untouched by time, and eternally clear. It is the foundation upon which all experience rests, yet it remains unchanged by the experiences it illumines.

The Chandogya Upanishad also illustrates this concept through the metaphor of space. Just as space remains unchanged and unaffected by the objects that exist within it, so too does the Self remain unaffected by the contents of the mind or the external world. The awareness that is the Self is present in all states—waking, dreaming, and deep sleep—but it is not altered by them.

Thus, when we refer to Brahman or the Self as knowledge, we are not speaking of an active knower. Rather, we refer to the very essence of consciousness, the unchanging awareness that illumines all forms of knowledge. This awareness is complete and infinite in itself, needing nothing external to confirm or validate its existence. It is eternal, self-sufficient, and beyond all limitations of duality and thought.

The realization of this eternal knowledge is what brings liberation (moksha). When one realizes that their true nature is this unchanging awareness, untouched by the transient experiences of the world, they are freed from the cycle of birth and death. This is why the Upanishads teach that knowledge of the Self is the highest knowledge, as it reveals the eternal truth that lies at the core of existence.

In conclusion, Amma's teaching that "True Jñana shines with clarity" speaks to the self-revealing nature of the Self. This knowledge is not something that needs to be acquired or gained through effort; rather, it is the realization of what has always been present—the pure, unchanging consciousness that underlies all of life. It is this knowledge that dissolves all ignorance and reveals the Self as infinite, eternal, and beyond all limitation.

Letting Go to Realize Truth

"When we let go of the illusion of identifying with the body and mind, we uncover the boundless love within. In that love, we discover our true Self, which is infinite, eternal, and one with all." — Amma

The key to self-realization is letting go of the attachments and illusions that bind us to the body and mind. In Advaita Vedanta, it is taught that the individual soul (jiva) is inherently identical to Brahman, the ultimate reality. However, ignorance (avidya) leads the individual to mistakenly identify with the limited body and mind, believing that they are separate from the infinite. This creates a false sense of duality and keeps the individual trapped in the cycle of birth and death (samsara), preventing them from experiencing their true nature, which is one with the infinite, eternal Brahman.

A helpful analogy that illustrates this idea is the story of ten men crossing a river. Once they reached the other side, they counted themselves to make sure everyone had made it across safely. However, each man forgot to include himself in the count, leading them to believe that one of them had drowned. They became distressed, thinking that someone was missing. It wasn't until a passerby pointed out that all ten men were present that they realized their mistake. The missing person had never existed—each man had simply overlooked himself in the count.

This story parallels the individual's relationship with Brahman. Just as the ten men failed to recognize that they were all present, we often fail to recognize our true nature as Brahman. We become so focused on the external world and our physical and mental identities that we forget the infinite Self within. This forgetfulness, or ignorance, leads to the illusion of separation. We begin to identify with the non-Self—believing, "I am this body, I am this mind"—instead of recognizing that our true nature is beyond these limited identities.

When we let go of this false identification with the body and mind, we uncover the boundless love and consciousness that is our true nature. Brahman, the ultimate reality, is described as infinite consciousness, existence, and bliss (Sat-Chit-Ananda). This infinite reality is the essence of who we truly are. Amma's teaching that "in that love, we discover our true Self" refers to this moment of realization, where we no longer see ourselves as separate, limited beings but as the infinite, unchanging reality that underlies all existence.

The process of self-realization, like the story of the ten men, requires guidance or knowledge to point us in the right direction. Just as the passerby helped the men realize their mistake, the guidance of a Guru or the study of scriptures can help us see past our ignorance and understand the truth. The Upanishads, the teachings of non-duality, and the wisdom of the Guru are essential in this process, providing the knowledge that helps dispel ignorance. This knowledge allows the seeker to recognize that the Self is not the body or the mind, but the infinite Brahman.

Ignorance of our true nature creates a false sense of separateness, leading to suffering and attachment to the transient world. When we mistakenly identify with the body and mind, we are bound by the limitations of birth, death, pleasure, pain, and the fluctuations of the external world. However, when we realize that the Self is none other than Brahman, the eternal and infinite reality, this ignorance is dispelled, and we experience the peace and freedom that comes from knowing our oneness with all of existence.

Through this realization, we understand that the external world, with all its names and forms, is merely an expression of Brahman. The world appears to be separate, but in reality, it is not distinct from the infinite consciousness that pervades everything. Just as the forms made of clay are not separate from the clay itself, the world of names and forms is not separate from Brahman. When we let go of our attachment to the external world and our identification with the body and mind, we see beyond the illusion of separateness and recognize the divine essence that is present in all things.

This is the essence of Amma's teaching: when we let go of the illusion of separateness, we uncover the boundless love and unity that is our true nature. The realization that the Self is infinite, eternal, and one with all is not something that is gained or attained, but something that is uncovered. It has always been there, waiting to be recognized. In this state of realization, there is no longer a need for external validation or fulfillment, because the Self is complete and fulfilled in itself.

In conclusion, self-realization is not about becoming something new but about letting go of the illusions that prevent us from seeing the truth. By releasing the identification with the body and mind, we uncover the boundless love and infinite consciousness that is our true nature. This realization leads to a profound sense of unity and peace, where we no longer see ourselves as separate individuals but as one with the infinite Brahman, the eternal reality that underlies all existence. Through this process, we fulfill the highest goal of life, which is to realize the Self and live in the light of that truth.

Eternal Light of Oneness

"The world of dualities, like the eater and the eaten, is merely a reflection of Ishwara and holds no true reality. When ignorance is dispelled, the knower of Brahman realizes their oneness with the entire universe, free from fear, shining with the eternal light of the Self." Amma

The perception of duality, such as the relationship between the eater and the eaten, is central to the experience of the phenomenal world. These distinctions arise from the relative reality we experience through the senses, but Advaita Vedanta teaches that such dualities are not absolutely real. The world, in all its forms and distinctions, is a manifestation of maya (illusion) and exists only because of Brahman, the one unchanging reality that underlies all existence. Therefore, when one asks, "If the phenomenal existence is not real, then what is meant by saying, 'I am the eaten and the eater'?", the confusion arises from misunderstanding the relationship between the relative and the absolute.

The phenomenal world, including the dualities of eater and eaten, subject and object, is real only in a dependent sense. This means that these distinctions exist only within the realm of maya and do not possess independent reality. They exist because of Brahman, which serves as the substratum of all forms and appearances. While the distinctions may appear real to the ignorant mind, they dissolve when the light of knowledge dispels ignorance. As Amma's quote suggests, these dualities are mere reflections of Ishwara, the manifest aspect of Brahman, and hold no true reality in themselves.

In the Upanishads, the expression "I am food" illustrates this point. This statement symbolizes the realization that all aspects of existence, whether it be the eater or the eaten, are permeated by Brahman. From the perspective of maya, the roles of eater and eaten seem distinct, but in reality, they are both manifestations of the same underlying consciousness. Brahman is not only the subject (the one who eats) but also the object (the food that is eaten), and this duality exists only as an illusion created by ignorance.

The eradication of ignorance (avidya) is the key to realizing the truth of non-duality. Through Atma Jnana (Self-knowledge), one comes to understand that the distinctions between eater and eaten are illusory. The perception of separation arises from ignorance, and when this ignorance is dispelled through knowledge, the individual no longer perceives the duality. In this state of realization, there is no longer fear, no sense of otherness, and no separation. The knower of Brahman sees everything as one undivided reality.

When a person attains Brahmajnana (knowledge of Brahman), they realize their true identity as Brahman itself. In this state of realization, the individual understands that all forms, names, and experiences are manifestations of the one unchanging reality. The person no longer identifies with the limited ego or body but instead identifies with the entire universe as an expression of Brahman. The dualities that once seemed real—such as subject and object, eater and eaten—are now understood as illusory, and the individual shines with the eternal light of the Self.

This realization leads to the dissolution of all fears and attachments that arise from the perception of duality. Fear stems from the belief in separation—from the idea that one is vulnerable to external forces. However, once the individual realizes their oneness with Brahman, they understand that there is no "other" to fear. In non-duality, everything is one, and the person abides in the infinite, eternal reality, free from the limitations imposed by ignorance.

The effulgence of the person who has realized their oneness with Brahman is often compared to the radiance of the eternal sun. Just as the sun shines with its own light, illuminating everything around it, the person of knowledge radiates pure consciousness, illuminating the truth of non-duality. This effulgence symbolizes the dissolution of ignorance and the realization of the eternal, unchanging nature of the Self. In this state, the person is no longer bound by the dualities and illusions of the phenomenal world but exists in the truth of Brahman, which is free, infinite, and unconditioned.

This state of realization is described as the "eternal light of the Self," as referenced in Amma's teachings. The eternal light represents the knowledge of non-duality, which dispels the darkness of ignorance. Once this light is recognized, the person of knowledge abides in the peace and freedom of oneness, beyond the illusion of duality and separateness. They are no longer concerned with the transient roles of eater and eaten because they understand that these roles are mere appearances within the play of maya.

In conclusion, the realization of non-duality—the understanding that the eater and the eaten are not separate entities but expressions of the same reality—leads to the dissolution of fear and ignorance. The knower of Brahman sees through the illusions of the phenomenal world and recognizes the eternal, unchanging light of the Self that underlies all existence. This realization brings ultimate freedom, as the individual transcends the limitations of duality and abides in the infinite, radiant consciousness of Brahman. As Amma teaches, this knowledge allows one to shine with the eternal light of oneness, free from fear and firmly established in the truth of their divine nature.

The Unfathomable and Invisible Truth

"Ishwara is the unseen, indescribable reality guiding all existence. To truly perceive this divine presence, we must be humble, for it is in humility that the hidden becomes revealed." Amma

Ishwara (God) is understood as the Absolute (Brahman) conditioned by avidya or maya (ignorance or illusion). While Brahman, the ultimate reality, is non-dual, without attributes, and beyond distinctions, Ishwara emerges as the personalized form of Brahman that interacts with the world. This conception of Ishvara, referred to as Saguna Brahman, allows for the creation, maintenance, and dissolution of the universe within the framework of duality, though these distinctions are ultimately seen as illusory. Ishwara is not separate from Brahman but is Brahman as perceived through the lens of ignorance.

Ishwara is described as both the material and efficient cause of the universe, meaning that the world arises from and is sustained by Ishvara. Unlike in certain other philosophical systems where God may be seen only as the efficient cause (the one who designs or creates), in Advaita Vedanta, Ishwara is also the material cause, implying that the very substance of the world is none other than Ishvara. This non-dual nature of creation reflects the foundational Advaitic principle that all distinctions are ultimately unreal, and the universe is a manifestation of Brahman under the influence of maya.

Despite Ishwara's role as the creator, preserver, and destroyer of the universe, omnipotent and omniscient, these attributes are considered part of the realm of saguna (with qualities) and maya. In the highest truth (paramarthika satya), Brahman transcends even these distinctions and is nirguna (without qualities), formless, and beyond all concepts of power or knowledge. Ishvara, therefore, serves as a bridge for the individual to understand the divine in a relational way, while Advaita Vedanta ultimately encourages the realization of the formless, unconditioned Brahman as one's true Self, beyond the dualities of creator and creation.

Amma's teaching on humility plays a crucial role in accessing this hidden knowledge. To perceive the divine presence of Ishwara, the unseen guiding force of all existence, one must approach the inquiry with humility. The ego-driven pursuit of understanding creates barriers to experiencing Brahman, which is why only through the dissolution of egoic tendencies can the hidden truth be revealed. Humility, in this context, opens the heart and mind to the subtle presence of Ishwara and allows the individual to move beyond the surface-level perception of reality.

Amma's quote highlights that Ishwara, the unseen reality guiding all creation, is ever-present but beyond the grasp of the mind. In this subtle understanding, Brahman as Ishwara acts as the ultimate cause of the universe, orchestrating the cosmic cycles of creation, preservation, and dissolution. However, due to the veiling effect of Māyā, the individual perceives only the surface level of reality, where distinctions between subject and object, knower and known, persist.

Humility becomes the key to unlocking this higher perception. In the absence of ego, one can perceive that the essence of Ishwara pervades all of existence. This humility allows for the unfolding of deeper knowledge, leading to the realization that all forms, names, and distinctions are mere reflections of Māyā. When ignorance is removed through the practice of self-inquiry, meditation, and devotion, the hidden truth of Brahman as the eternal, unchanging reality is revealed.

The Chandogya Upanishad emphasizes that when the mind quiets down and the ego dissolves, the individual becomes attuned to the presence of the parame vyoman. In this state of deep inner awareness, the separation between the knower, the known, and knowledge itself fades away. The seeker comes to know that all distinctions are illusory and that Brahman alone exists as the substratum of all reality.

Ultimately, the truth that Brahman is the sole reality guiding all existence remains hidden due to the limitations of the human mind and the illusory nature of the material world. However, through humility and the removal of ignorance, the individual can transcend these limitations and come to experience the presence of Ishwara as the guiding force behind all of creation. In this realization, all dualities dissolve, and the knower merges with the known in the eternal light of oneness.

Thus, as Amma teaches, the perception of Ishwara—the divine, invisible presence guiding all existence—requires humility and a readiness to surrender the ego. In this state of openness and grace, the individual can glimpse the unfathomable truth that lies beyond the limitations of names, forms, and concepts. This understanding leads to the realization of Brahman as the all-pervading, unchanging reality, which remains hidden to those still bound by the illusions of the world.

Inseparableness is Essence

"The all-pervading Atma is the ultimate Truth, and its essence is pure love. When we recognize this, we see that love is not separate from truth—it is the very heart of existence." Amma

Atma, the Self, is the infinite and all-encompassing reality. According to Advaita Vedanta, the realization of the Atma as the ultimate Truth leads to the recognition of oneness with the universe. In this recognition, love is seen not as an emotion or an act between two separate beings but as the very fabric of existence itself. Love is inherent to the nature of Atma because Atma is indivisible, and this indivisibility manifests as pure, unconditional love. It is the expression of oneness where there is no distinction between the subject and the object, between the lover and the loved.

In non-duality, the core teaching is that separation is an illusion created by the mind. When this illusion dissolves, what remains is the indivisible reality of Atma, and the essence of that reality is pure love. As Amma explains, love is not something external that we need to seek; rather, it is the natural state of being when we recognize our true nature as Atma. This love is not limited by conditions or circumstances because it is the very ground of existence, the heart of the universe, inseparable from truth itself.

Amma's words remind us that love and truth are not separate. Truth refers to the realization of the oneness of all existence, while love is the expression of that oneness. When we recognize the all-pervading nature of Atma, we see that everything is interconnected and arises from the same source. This realization dissolves the perception of duality—the idea that there is a separate "I" and a separate "other." In this state, love becomes the fundamental experience because there is no longer any separation.

The experience of inseparability is transformative. When we recognize that love is the essence of all things, we stop seeking it outside of ourselves. We come to understand that we are already whole, already connected to everything around us. In the realization of non-duality, the search for love ends because the Self is love itself. There is no need to seek it in relationships, achievements, or external objects, for it is the core of our very being. This understanding brings a deep sense of fulfillment, peace, and joy.

Inseparableness is also reflected in how the Atma permeates everything in the universe. Just as space holds and pervades all objects without being affected by them, the Atma exists within every being, unchanged by the apparent differences and forms. This realization allows us to perceive that the same divine essence flows through all beings, and this divine essence is love. When we see others not as separate but as expressions of the same Self, love naturally arises in the heart.

Amma's teaching also points to the dissolution of egoic boundaries. The ego, which is based on the false perception of separateness, creates the illusion of needing to "acquire" love or "achieve" truth. However, once the ego dissolves, we recognize that love and truth have always been present. The barriers we perceived were illusory, and the inseparability of love and truth becomes clear. The Atma, as the foundation of all reality, is ever-present, unchanging, and full of love.

When love is understood as inseparable from truth, it transforms how we relate to the world. Instead of seeing others as separate individuals to whom we owe love or from whom we seek love, we begin to see them as manifestations of the same divine Self. This shift brings about selfless love—love that is not transactional or conditional but arises naturally from the recognition of oneness. In this state, service to others becomes an expression of love because we see others as extensions of ourselves.

This understanding also has profound implications for spiritual practice. In the path of bhakti (devotion), love for the Divine becomes the means of realizing oneness. In jnana (knowledge), truth is realized through self-inquiry and discernment. However, Amma's teaching shows that both paths ultimately lead to the same realization—that truth and love are not separate. Whether through devotion or knowledge, the seeker arrives at the same destination: the realization that the essence of existence is inseparable love and truth.

This inseparability of love and truth reveals the non-dual nature of reality. In duality, love is often seen as an emotional connection between individuals, and truth as an abstract concept to be intellectually grasped. But in non-duality, both love and truth converge into a singular experience of unity. The heart and the mind are no longer in conflict because they are expressions of the same ultimate reality. This understanding brings about a deep harmony and inner peace.

The inseparableness of Atma also leads to the recognition that love is not limited by time or space. Just as Atma transcends all temporal and spatial boundaries, so too does love. The realization of the Self as eternal and infinite means that love is also eternal and infinite. This love is not bound by conditions or the limitations of the physical world. It flows through all beings, through all of creation, constantly manifesting itself as the very essence of life.

In conclusion, Amma's teaching on inseparableness shows us that the essence of the Self is pure love. When we realize that the Atma is all-pervading and indivisible, we understand that love and truth are not separate concepts but are the very foundation of existence. By recognizing the oneness of all beings, we experience a deep, unconditioned love that flows naturally from the recognition of our true nature. In this realization, we see that love is the heart of existence, inseparable from the truth of who we are.

CHAPTER-3

Internal Realization of Oneness and Self-Realization

Inquiry into Reality

"Journey inward to the deepest Self, where the essence is intrinsic and unique. It is there that you will find the only Truth, the eternal reality that shines beyond all illusion." Amma

Amma's statement points directly to the essence of spiritual practice: turning inward to discover the true Self. This inward journey is essential because the external world, with its transient experiences, constantly distracts us from realizing our intrinsic and eternal nature. The deepest Self is where we find the truth that is beyond all illusions—unaffected by the external forms of existence. This truth, which is the essence of our being, is both intrinsic and unique.

According to Sruti (revealed scriptures), Brahman—the ultimate Reality, the ground of the universe, the Absolute, and the Divine. The term "Brahman" is derived from the root brh, which means "to expand," signifying something that is greater than the greatest. Brahman is the unchanging and eternal truth that transcends all worldly distinctions. It is often described as "that which puts an end to differences," emphasizing its role as the Absolute Reality, free from any relative distinctions or comparisons. From an acosmic viewpoint, Brahman is devoid of empirical characteristics, meaning it cannot be compared to anything similar or different from it, making it unique and beyond all forms of differentiation.

Brahman is the all-pervasive supreme principle of the universe. It is the foundational essence that underlies and sustains all existence. The nature of Brahman is expounded in the Upanishads and Vedantic philosophy, where it is described through the concept of Sat-Chit-Ananda—Existence, Consciousness, and Bliss absolute. This triadic description attempts to convey the essence of Brahman, though the ultimate reality of Brahman is beyond words and intellectual comprehension. Brahman is not limited to physical or material existence but is the very source of all things, embodying the ultimate existence (sat), pure consciousness (cit), and infinite bliss (ananda). This understanding underscores Brahman's transcendental nature and its all-encompassing presence in the universe.

Brahman is said to be indescribable in words. It transcends all human concepts, thoughts, and language, making it nirguna—beyond any attributes or qualities. While words can offer glimpses or descriptions of Brahman, they ultimately fall short of capturing its true essence. Advaita Vedanta declares Brahman as the only Truth, and everything else, including names and forms, is considered a mere appearance or illusion (maya). This is why Brahman is seen as beyond all conceptualization, and the highest understanding is one of direct experience rather than intellectual explanation.

Though Brahman is ultimately beyond attributes, other Vedantic schools recognize that it can be described through its saguna or "with attributes" aspect. While Brahman in its purest form is beyond all characteristics, words can describe its glorious attributes. In the saguna form, Brahman is seen as having qualities such as omnipotence, omniscience, and omnipresence, representing the Divine in a way that is relatable to the human mind. This form of Brahman is the source of all divine manifestations and gods in Hinduism, allowing individuals to relate to the Absolute through worship, devotion, and reverence for its many forms and qualities.

Brahman in two primary modes: as nisprapancha, the Reality beyond the universe's appearance, and saprapancha, the all-inclusive ground of the universe. In its nisprapancha form, Brahman is pure and transcendent, existing beyond all name and form. As saprapancha, Brahman is the ground from which the universe emerges and is sustained. It is described both positively, as existence (sat), knowledge (cit), bliss (ananda), and infinity (ananta), and negatively through the method of neti neti ("not this, not this"), which seeks to negate all false identifications to arrive at the truth of Brahman. This dual mode highlights the versatility of Brahman as both the source and essence of all creation while remaining beyond it.

Brahman with limiting conditions and Brahman free from all limiting conditions. When Brahman is qualified by the distinctions of name and form, it takes on a conditioned aspect, appearing as the manifold world. However, in its purest state, Brahman is free from all limiting conditions and distinctions. This unconditioned Brahman is the essence of non-duality, where the individual self (Atman) and Brahman are one and the same. The realization of this unity—where the individual transcends the limitations of ego, mind, and body—is the ultimate goal leading to liberation (moksha) and the direct experience of Brahman as the sole reality of existence.

So, Sat-Chit-Ananda—Existence, Consciousness, and Bliss—is used to describe the nature of the Self. The essence of the Self is not something that needs to be attained from outside; it is already present within us. However, due to layers of ignorance and attachment to the body and mind, this truth remains obscured. Amma's teaching reminds us that the truth of the Self can only be discovered by looking inward, not by seeking validation or answers in the external world.

The journey inward is a process of peeling away the layers of illusion. These illusions are created by identification with the ego, thoughts, emotions, and the physical body. When we identify with these layers, we forget our true nature and become trapped in the endless cycle of desires and aversions.

By turning inward, we begin to see that these layers are not who we truly are. They are merely temporary coverings that conceal the deeper reality of the Self.

As Amma says, the essence of the Self is intrinsic, meaning it is inherent and natural to our being. It is not something we need to acquire or create. Instead, it is always present, waiting to be uncovered. This intrinsic nature is also unique—distinct from anything else we experience in the external world. It is beyond time, space, and form. While the external world is constantly changing, the Self remains unchanging, unaffected by the fluctuations of the material world.

The process of self-inquiry, often described in Advaita Vedanta, involves questioning the nature of the self. This inquiry leads us to the realization that we are not the body, not the mind, and not the ego. These are all temporary aspects of our existence. The true Self is the eternal consciousness that witnesses all experiences without being affected by them. This realization brings freedom from the limitations of the body and mind and reveals the infinite nature of the Self.

Amma's emphasis on "the only Truth" points to the non-dual nature of reality. In our ordinary perception, we see the world as divided into subject and object, self and other. However, through the inward journey, we realize that this division is illusory. There is only one reality, and that is the Self. Everything we perceive as separate is actually an expression of this one truth. This is the realization of oneness, where all distinctions between the individual self and the universe dissolve.

The realization of the Self is not just an intellectual understanding but a direct, experiential knowing. When we turn inward and experience the Self, we see that it is the source of all knowledge, love, and bliss. This experience transcends the mind and intellect, as the Self is beyond thought. It is pure awareness, free from any limitations. This is the "eternal reality" that Amma speaks of, which shines with its own inherent luminosity, dispelling all illusions and doubts.

Illusions, or maya, are the false perceptions that make us believe we are separate from the divine. The world of names and forms is temporary and ever-changing, but the Self remains constant. The illusion lies in believing that the temporary is real and permanent. By turning inward and recognizing the Self, we transcend these illusions and realize that the external world is merely a play of forms on the surface of the unchanging reality.

Amma's guidance aligns with the teachings of the Upanishads, which also emphasize the inward journey to realize the truth of the Self. The Upanishadic teaching "Tat Tvam Asi" (You are That) reveals that the individual self (jiva) is none other than Brahman, the ultimate reality. The Self is not different from the divine; it is the divine. This realization dissolves all sense of separateness and brings about a profound understanding of the oneness of existence.

The practice of turning inward requires discipline and perseverance. Meditation, self-inquiry, and devotion are the tools that help us quiet the mind and focus our attention on the inner reality. When the mind becomes still, the truth of the Self is revealed. This stillness is not the absence of thought but the recognition of the consciousness that underlies all thought. In this stillness, we find the peace and bliss that is our true nature.

In conclusion, Amma's teaching encourages us to embark on the inward journey to discover the only Truth—the eternal, unchanging reality that lies beyond all illusion. This truth is the essence of who we are, intrinsic and unique. By turning inward, we realize that the Self is not separate from the divine but is the very heart of existence. This realization brings the experience of oneness, where all distinctions dissolve, and we rest in the infinite bliss of the Self.

Neti Neti

"Through the practice of Neti-Neti, we strip away all false identities—'I am not the body, not the mind, not the ego.' In this process of negation, the truth emerges: The Self (Atma) alone exists, timeless and ever-present, beyond all limitations." Amma

In Advaita Vedanta, the phrase "Not this, not this" (Neti Neti) (Brhadaranyaka Upaniṣad 2-3-6) is employed to describe Brahman, the ultimate reality, by negating all attributes that might be mistakenly applied to it. This method of elimination is used because Brahman, in its true essence, is beyond all limiting adjuncts like name, form, action, species, or qualities. In our everyday experience, we identify and describe objects through their distinguishing characteristics—such as a cow's color or horns. However, Brahman is formless and attributeless, so words and concepts cannot encapsulate it. Describing Brahman in positive terms, such as "It is like this" or "It possesses such qualities," is therefore inadequate.

While Brahman is often referred to with terms like 'Knowledge, Bliss, Brahman' (Taittiriya upanishad III. ix. 28), and 'Pure Intelligence' (Brhadaranyaka Upaniṣad II. iv. 12),these are descriptions based on superimposed attributes. These words point to aspects of Brahman as understood through our limited perspective but do not capture the essence of Brahman itself. These descriptors—though useful—are only approximate and stem from the empirical world where name, form, and action are operative. Brahman, in its pure state, is free from all adjuncts, including these superimpositions, making it impossible to describe in conventional terms. Thus, any attempt to define Brahman using positive descriptions remains incomplete.

When trying to communicate Brahman's true nature, the only effective method is through negation, as expressed in Neti Neti—"not this, not this." By removing all possible attributions and specifications, we acknowledge that Brahman transcends all categories of human thought and experience. This process of elimination highlights that Brahman is not confined by any attribute that the mind can conceive. It emphasizes that silence and the absence of all qualifying terms are the closest ways to express the absolute reality that is Brahman—an entity that is beyond all dualistic distinctions.

The practice of Neti-Neti, which translates to "not this, not that," is a powerful method of negation used in Advaita Vedanta to realize the true Self by removing all false identifications with the body, mind, and ego. Through this process, the aspirant methodically negates everything that is impermanent, transient, and limited, realizing that these things cannot be the ultimate reality. By stripping away these false identities, the aspirant arrives at the realization of the timeless and ever-present Atma, or Self, which alone exists beyond all limitations.

The essence of Neti-Neti is to reject the body, mind, emotions, thoughts, and any external identifications as "not-Self." The body, subject to birth, decay, and death, is impermanent. The mind, full of fluctuating thoughts and emotions, is ever-changing. The ego, which identifies with one's personality, successes, failures, and roles in life, is also transient. The Neti-Neti practice guides the seeker to see that these are merely coverings over the true Self, which is beyond all change, beyond the temporary nature of these aspects.

As the seeker moves deeper into this process of negation, what remains is the eternal, unchanging Self. Brahman, the ultimate reality, cannot be fully described or captured through ordinary language. No word, concept, or image can define Brahman because it exists beyond the realm of creation and destruction. The scriptures teach this through a process of negation, helping us to remove the illusions that we have constructed around our identity and to reveal the eternal truth of Brahman, which lies beyond all forms and names.

Jnanam, or knowledge, is not a simple intellectual understanding but is the very essence of Brahman. This knowledge is eternal, unchanging, and is inseparable from the Self. Brahman is not something separate from the world or from the objects it illuminates. It is the underlying reality of all that exists. The process of Neti-Neti helps us to peel away the layers of ignorance and false identifications that obscure this knowledge, allowing the truth of Brahman to shine forth in its supreme, all-encompassing nature.

The practice of Neti-Neti does not mean rejecting the world but understanding the true nature of the world as an expression of Brahman. The world, as we perceive it, is limited by time, space, and causation. It appears to be real to the senses and the mind, but through the practice of Neti-Neti, the seeker realizes that the world is mithya—an illusion or appearance that depends on Brahman for its existence. By negating the false reality of the world, the seeker comes to see that Brahman is the only reality, ever-present and all-pervasive.

The intellect (buddhi) plays a key role in this journey of realization. It is described as a cave that holds the knowledge of the Self, the knower, and the known. The intellect illuminates the objects of perception and experience, but it also has the capacity to transcend these objects and lead the seeker toward the ultimate knowledge of the Self. When purified through spiritual practice and reflection, the intellect becomes a tool for realizing the truth beyond the limitations of the mind and senses.

Through the process of Neti-Neti, the seeker comes to understand that liberation is not something to be attained in the future or through external efforts. It is the natural state of the Self, which is already free, infinite, and eternal. The attachments to the body, mind, and ego are what bind us to the cycle of birth and death. By negating these attachments, the seeker realizes their true nature as the Atma, which is beyond birth, beyond death, and beyond all limitations.

This realization brings a profound sense of peace and freedom. The dualities of the world—pleasure and pain, success and failure, life and death—lose their hold over the seeker. The knowledge that "I am not the body, not the mind, not the ego" brings the understanding that the true Self is untouched by the ups and downs of life. The Self remains ever the same, like the sun that is unaffected by the clouds that pass before it.

Amma's teaching emphasizes that the Self is timeless and ever-present, and this realization is not something that can be grasped through the mind or intellect alone. It is a direct, experiential knowing that comes when we let go of all identifications with the non-Self. The process of negation through Neti-Neti is a powerful tool for arriving at this realization, but it must be complemented by devotion, meditation, and the guidance of a realized teacher.

In conclusion, the practice of Neti-Neti leads the seeker to the recognition that the body, mind, and ego are not the true Self. By stripping away these false identities, the eternal, unchanging nature of the Atma is revealed. This Self is none other than Brahman, the ultimate reality, which is beyond all limitations and dualities. Through Amma's guidance and the practice of Neti-Neti, the seeker moves beyond the illusions of the material world and realizes the infinite, eternal truth that is the essence of all existence.

The Guru Mirrors Infinite Truth

"The Guru is a reflection of the ultimate truth, beyond personal attributes, and seeing the Guru as an individual leads to suffering. When we establish ourselves in the Self with unwavering faith, all external needs are effortlessly fulfilled through divine grace." Amma

In the spiritual journey, the role of the Guru is paramount. The Guru is not merely an individual or a teacher with a personal identity but a direct reflection of Para Brahman, the ultimate, infinite truth. When viewed through the lens of individuality, the disciple is likely to project their own biases and limitations onto the Guru, which leads to confusion, suffering, and attachment. This projection of personal likes, dislikes, and expectations obstructs the disciple's ability to see the Guru as the embodiment of the ultimate truth, beyond personal attributes. In this mistaken view, the disciple's suffering (dukham) emerges from their inability to perceive the Guru's essence, which is none other than Brahman.

Amma's teachings emphasize that the Guru, established in the hrudhaya akase (heart space), is the mirror of Para Brahman—the infinite and eternal Self that transcends the dualities of the material world. The dualistic perception, where the disciple views the Guru as a separate entity, only leads to suffering, as the disciple's karmic impressions (dosham) and ignorance (avidya) shape their understanding of the Guru. When seen from the higher perspective, the Guru is the gateway to realizing the Self, and through unwavering faith and surrender, the disciple is led towards the path of liberation.

The Guru's role is to guide the disciple toward atma nishtatha—steadfastness in the Self. This is the ultimate goal, where the individual transcends their limited ego and recognizes their true nature as Brahman, the non-dual reality. As long as the disciple sees the Guru through the lens of ego, they remain entangled in the cycle of suffering and karmic consequences. However, when the disciple surrenders to the Guru as an embodiment of the divine, they begin to dissolve their ego and align with the universal truth. The Guru, in the Advaitic tradition, is seen as purnam—complete and whole. This completeness is not tied to the Guru's individual identity but rather as a reflection of the universal Ishwara (divine). The Guru, therefore, serves as a mirror, reflecting the ultimate reality to the disciple. When the disciple surrenders to the Guru with this understanding, they are led beyond the limitations of their own ego, entering a state of oneness with the infinite. This process of surrender and self-inquiry leads the disciple to recognize that the Guru and the Self are not separate entities but expressions of the same ultimate truth.

The Guru, being rooted in Brahman, guides the disciple through the path of non-duality, leading them to the realization of their own inherent divinity. In this state, the disciple recognizes that all external needs and desires are effortlessly fulfilled through divine grace, as these desires lose their importance in the light of Self-realization.
The path to Self-realization requires atma nishtatha, or steadfastness in the Self. The key difference between a jnani (knower of the Self) and an ajnani (ignorant person) lies in their identification with the Self. A jnani is deeply rooted in the understanding that their true essence is Brahman, while an ajnani remains caught in the web of ego and individuality, mistaking external circumstances and personal identity as the core of existence.

To pursue atma nishtatha, one must turn inward and cultivate unwavering faith in the Self. This requires the discipline to move away from external pursuits, recognizing their fleeting nature. As Amma teaches, by aligning with the Self, all material and external needs are naturally fulfilled. The focus of the disciple must shift from seeking external validation or fulfillment to realizing the inner truth that they are already whole and complete. The Guru, in this journey, serves as the guide who reflects this truth back to the disciple, enabling them to dissolve their ego and embrace their divine nature.

Amma's teachings highlight the importance of faith and trust in the Guru's grace. The disciple must trust that once they establish themselves in the Self, all external desires will be effortlessly fulfilled. This does not mean that the disciple must ignore their worldly responsibilities, but rather that they recognize that true fulfillment comes from within, not from external actions or achievements. By cultivating atma nishtatha, the disciple finds that their material needs are naturally taken care of through divine grace, and they can focus their energy on their spiritual growth and self-realization.

When the disciple fully surrenders to the Guru's wisdom and aligns themselves with the divine, they begin to experience the harmony between inner spiritual alignment and outer life. The Guru's grace ensures that the disciple's path is smooth and that their spiritual needs are met. The key to this process is the disciple's faith and devotion, which allow them to transcend their ego and embrace the infinite nature of the Self.

While knowledge and discernment are crucial on the path to realization, Amma emphasizes that devotion to the Guru is equally important. Devotion softens the heart and opens the disciple to receive the Guru's grace. Through devotion, the disciple is able to surrender their ego and align more fully with the truth reflected by the Guru. In this way, devotion and knowledge work together, leading the disciple to the ultimate goal of Self-realization.

Devotion helps the disciple move beyond the intellectual understanding of non-duality and into the experiential realization of the Self. The Guru, by embodying the truth of Para Brahman, guides the disciple from mere conceptual knowledge to direct experience. In this process, the disciple comes to see that the Guru, the Self, and the universe are not separate but are all expressions of the same infinite reality.

Ultimately, the Guru is not separate from the disciple. As Amma teaches, the Guru is a mirror, reflecting the disciple's true nature back to them. The disciple's journey is one of recognizing this truth and dissolving the illusion of separation. By surrendering to the Guru's grace and wisdom, the disciple is guided to the realization that their true nature is Brahman—eternal, infinite, and beyond all dualities.

The Guru's role is to remind the disciple of their inherent divinity and to help them move beyond the limitations of ego and individuality. Through faith, devotion, and self-inquiry, the disciple is led to the understanding that the Guru and the Self are one and the same. In this realization, all suffering and duality dissolve, leaving only the eternal light of the Self, shining in its infinite glory.

In conclusion, Amma's teachings on the Guru emphasize that the Guru is not an individual to be worshipped but a reflection of the ultimate truth. By recognizing the non-dual nature of the Guru, the disciple is guided to atma nishtatha—steadfastness in the Self—which leads to liberation. The Guru's grace ensures that all external needs are fulfilled as the disciple moves toward the realization of their own divine nature. Through devotion, self-inquiry, and the guidance of the Guru, the disciple attains the ultimate goal of oneness with Brahman.

Beyond Doubt and Fear

"The Atma is ever unchanging, but ignorance clouds our perception of it. True knowledge dispels doubts, ignorance, and fear, allowing us to experience the boundless peace of the Self." Amma

The Atma, or the Self, is eternally unchanging and free from any modifications or limitations. However, due to ignorance, we fail to consciously experience the Atma's true nature. This ignorance creates a veil that leads us to falsely identify with the body, mind, and ego, obscuring the true essence of who we are. The natural state of the Atma—pure, unchanging, and ever-present—is not recognized by the individual because the mind is clouded by ignorance. This misconception leads to attachment to transient aspects of existence, creating doubts, fears, and confusion.

The path to overcoming ignorance lies in the practice of listening to teachings, reflecting on those teachings, and deep meditation. These practices are essential in cultivating self-knowledge, which gradually dispels the layers of false identification that arise from the ego and the external world. Through this process, we come to realize that our true nature is not limited by the body or mind but is the boundless Atma, the unchanging Self.

Once the seeker begins to cultivate this knowledge, the direct realization of the Atma removes three significant obstacles on the spiritual path: doubt, ignorance, and fear. These obstacles arise from the mistaken belief that the Self is tied to the physical body and mental constructs. By acquiring the knowledge of the Atma, the seeker can transcend these limitations and experience lasting peace and clarity.

Doubt is the first major obstacle that arises from ignorance. We are often confused about our true identity, wondering whether we are merely the body and mind or something greater. When the knowledge of the Atma dawns, these doubts are dissolved. The seeker no longer questions their identity, for the realization of the Self brings absolute certainty and clarity. The individual recognizes that they are not confined to the body or mind but are the unchanging, eternal Atma that transcends all dualities. This direct realization removes the doubt and confusion that previously clouded the seeker's mind.

Ignorance is the root cause of our identification with the body, mind, and external world. It is the darkness that prevents us from perceiving the true nature of the Self. Through knowledge, this ignorance is dispelled like the lifting of a veil. Just as light illuminates what was previously hidden in darkness, self-knowledge reveals the truth of the Atma, which is beyond all dualities, beyond birth and death, and beyond any form of limitation. The ignorance that once clouded the mind is removed, and the seeker is able to see the truth of their eternal and infinite nature.

Fear arises from the perception of separation. When we identify with the body and mind, we feel vulnerable and exposed to external threats, which generates fear. This fear is rooted in the belief that we are separate from the rest of existence and are subject to the uncertainties of life and death. However, once ignorance is removed and the seeker realizes their true nature as the Atma, which is eternal and unchanging, fear vanishes. In the knowledge that the Self is one with Brahman, the ultimate reality, the individual no longer experiences fear because there is no "other" to fear. The recognition of non-duality—where the Self is one with all—brings about a state of fearlessness.

The ignorance that clouds our perception of the Self is the source of all suffering. By identifying with the body and mind, we become attached to transient things, leading to desires, aversions, and fears. This cycle of attachment perpetuates our suffering, as we seek happiness in things that are inherently impermanent. However, when knowledge removes ignorance, the attachments fall away, and the seeker experiences the boundless peace of the Self. This peace is not dependent on external circumstances but is the natural state of the Atma, which is ever-present and unchanging.

The knowledge of the Self gained through spiritual practice becomes the tool for liberation. It leads to the direct experience of the unchanging Atma, which is free from the limitations imposed by ignorance. This knowledge brings about a profound transformation in the seeker's perception of reality. No longer bound by the illusions of the external world, the seeker experiences true freedom and liberation from the cycle of birth and death. The realization that the Self is eternal, infinite, and beyond all dualities brings about a state of liberation.

Fear is a natural response when we feel separate from the world around us. However, once we realize the truth of non-duality—that the Self is one with Brahman—fear dissolves. The sense of separation that generates fear no longer exists, and the individual abides in a state of oneness with the entire universe. This realization brings about a deep sense of peace and fearlessness, as the seeker understands that there is nothing external to fear. The Atma, being eternal and unchanging, is beyond any harm or threat.

The peace that arises from the knowledge of the Self is boundless and eternal. It is not a fleeting sense of calm that depends on external circumstances but a deep, unshakable peace that comes from knowing one's true nature. This peace is the natural state of the Atma, which is ever-present and unaffected by the changes in the external world. The seeker who realizes the Atma experiences this peace as their true essence, free from the disturbances of the mind and the world.

Once the seeker attains the knowledge of the Atma, they live in a state of clarity and freedom. The attachments, desires, and fears that once dominated their life fall away, and they abide in the truth of their eternal nature. This knowledge transforms the way they interact with the world, as they no longer seek fulfillment in external objects but rest in the boundless peace of the Self. The seeker becomes established in the knowledge that they are the Atma, which is beyond all limitations and dualities.

Amma's teaching that the Atma is ever-unchanging, and that ignorance clouds our perception of it, points to the transformative power of self-knowledge. By removing ignorance, doubt, and fear, we come to experience the boundless peace and freedom of the Self. The Atma, being eternal and infinite, is beyond all limitations, and through knowledge, we realize that our true nature is not confined to the body or mind but is one with the ultimate reality, Brahman.

In the Light of Stillness

"The true Self is not something to be attained externally but realized within as one's own essence. Through this understanding, we transcend the illusion of separateness and recognize that the Self and Brahman are eternally one." Amma

The nature of the Self is often misunderstood, with many mistaking temporary experiences of bliss or happiness for the realization of the true Self. This misconception arises from the belief that the Self is something that can be attained or acquired through external means, rather than something that already exists within us as our true essence. As Amma says, "The true Self is not something to be attained externally but realized within as one's own essence." The process of realizing the Self is not about transformation or movement toward something outside of oneself, but about uncovering the eternal truth that is already present within.

The objection that the Self and Brahman are non-different often leads to confusion. Critics argue that if the Self and Brahman are one, how can the individual "attain" the blissful Self? This misunderstanding stems from viewing attainment in a physical or conventional sense, where one entity moves toward or acquires another. However, the scriptures' reference to attaining the blissful Self does not imply such external acquisition. Instead, it points to enlightenment—a realization of the true nature of the Self. This realization dispels the ignorance that creates the illusion of separateness and duality, revealing the inherent oneness of the Self with Brahman.

When the scriptures speak of "attaining" the Self, they refer to an inner awakening, where the individual transcends the limitations imposed by ignorance. The blissful Self, often mistaken for the ultimate reality, is actually a limited identification based on transient experiences of happiness. This blissful state is not the supreme Self (Brahman) but a reflection of the deeper truth. The process of realization involves transcending the false identification with this blissful Self and recognizing the non-dual nature of Brahman and the Self. There is no physical movement or change; instead, it is the removal of ignorance and the direct recognition of the eternal truth that has always been present

The realization of Brahman as the true Self leads to the dissolution of misconceptions. In this state of enlightenment, the individual no longer identifies with the limited self or the body but understands that the Self is identical with Brahman, the ultimate reality. This understanding removes the illusion of duality and reveals the eternal oneness that underlies all existence. The realization is not about reaching a new state or acquiring something different, but about uncovering the truth that has always been present—the unity of the Self and Brahman, which transcends all dualities and reveals the boundless peace within.

The journey toward realizing Brahman is beautifully described in the Taittiriya Upanishad (3.1.3), which states:

In the Brihadaranyaka Upanishad (4.4.18), it is said that

prāṇasya prāṇamuta cakśuṣaścakśuruta śrotrasya śrotraṃ manaso ye mano viduḥ | te nicikyurbrahma purāṇamagryam

"Those who have known the Vital Force of the vital force, the Eye of the eye, the Ear of the ear, and the Mind of the mind, have realized the ancient, primordial Brahman." This implies that Brahman is the source of all sensory and mental activity. The senses, such as the eye and ear, and the mind itself, function only because of the pure intelligence of the Atman (Self), which is their life force. Without the light of Brahman, these faculties are inert, like pieces of wood.

Those who realize that the Self (Atman) is the mind of the mind, the essence behind all cognitive and sensory processes, understand that the Self is not an object of perception. It is the innermost reality that makes all perception possible. By recognizing this truth, one attains a deep understanding of the primordial Brahman, the eternal reality behind all existence. This knowledge dispels the ignorance that creates the illusion of separateness and reveals the true nature of the Self as one with Brahman.

In Amma's teaching, the journey inward to realize this oneness is a process of stripping away the false identifications with the body, mind, and ego. The Self, being eternal and beyond change, is not something to be sought externally. Rather, it is realized as one's own essence. As this realization deepens, the individual transcends the illusion of separateness and experiences the boundless love, peace, and unity that are the hallmarks of the Self's true nature. Through this understanding, we come to recognize that the Self and Brahman are eternally one, and this oneness is the foundation of all existence.

No Beginning, No End

"For the one who has realized their oneness with Brahman, the need for action dissolves, as all desires and limitations vanish. In the state of supreme knowledge, there is nothing left to attain, and action becomes irrelevant." Amma

When the supreme knowledge of Brahman is attained, the individual's understanding of the world and themselves shifts dramatically. As Amma beautifully states, "For the one who has realized their oneness with Brahman, the need for action dissolves, as all desires and limitations vanish. In the state of supreme knowledge, there is nothing left to attain, and action becomes irrelevant." This realization brings an end to the idea that fulfillment can be achieved through worldly action, as the knower sees that they are already complete, having merged with the ultimate reality, Brahman.

For those who have realized their oneness with Brahman, the usual motivations for action—desires, fears, or aspirations—lose their significance. Action (karma) is typically driven by a sense of lack or incompleteness, compelling individuals to act in order to gain what they perceive as missing, whether it is material wealth, happiness, or knowledge. However, once the knower realizes their identity with Brahman, they understand that they are already whole and complete. The infinite bliss and fulfillment that comes from this knowledge make the pursuit of external achievements unnecessary.

In this state of realization, the individual transcends the realm of karma. The Vedic scriptures prescribe various actions to guide individuals toward desired outcomes, such as prosperity or spiritual growth, but these prescriptions apply only to those who still have desires. For the one who has realized their oneness with Brahman, there is nothing left to attain, and therefore, no need for prescribed actions. The knower lives in a state of freedom from worldly concerns and injunctions, beyond the dualities of success and failure, gain and loss.

Furthermore, the idea of "acting" becomes irrelevant in this state of realization. The knower is no longer caught in the duality of actor and action. They simply exist, and whatever actions arise do so naturally and effortlessly, without any sense of personal involvement or attachment to outcomes. This state of being reflects the ultimate freedom and peace that comes from realizing the Self as Brahman. The realization of oneness with Brahman dissolves the illusion of separateness and with it, the need to act in order to achieve or acquire anything.

In the realized state, there is no longer a sense of personal "I" striving for fulfillment. The ego, which drives action, fades away, leaving behind the pure awareness of the Self. This awareness transcends all desires, fears, and limitations, as the individual now knows that they are infinite and eternal, beyond birth and death. The Self is complete in itself, needing nothing from the external world to feel whole or fulfilled.

Thus, in the light of supreme knowledge, action as we understand it in the worldly sense becomes unnecessary. The knower of Brahman, having realized their true nature, no longer feels the need to engage in action to fulfill desires or reach specific goals. Instead, they live in a state of natural harmony with the truth of existence, free from the dualities and limitations of the world.

Creator and Creation

"Creation and the Creator are not separate. True knowledge reveals their oneness, showing us that the essence of all creation is the same divine presence that resides within the Creator." — Amma

Creation and the Creator are often perceived as separate entities, with creation being viewed as something external to the Creator. However, as Amma says, "Creation and the Creator are not separate. True knowledge reveals their oneness, showing us that the essence of all creation is the same divine presence that resides within the Creator." This understanding points toward the non-dual nature of reality, where both creation and the Creator are simply different expressions of the same underlying truth, Brahman.

The perception of the universe as something distinct from the Self is understood to be an illusion created by ignorance. This illusion is perpetuated by the identification with the body and mind, which reinforces the sense of separateness. However, through self-inquiry and the guidance of a Guru, one can transcend this illusion and recognize the unity of all creation with the Creator.

Ultimately, this realization brings about the dissolution of duality and leads to the recognition of the Self as Brahman. The individual no longer sees themselves as separate from the universe or from the Creator. Instead, they realize that their true nature is one with the all-pervading Atman, which is the essence of both the Creator and the creation.

In conclusion, the understanding that creation and the Creator are not separate is central to the realization of non-duality. Through the principle of Mahath Tatwam, one can perceive the unity of all things and recognize that both the individual and the cosmos are expressions of the same consciousness. This realization leads to the dissolution of the illusion of separateness and reveals the oneness of the Self with all of existence, as Amma so beautifully conveys in her teachings.

Eternal Bliss

"True bliss is not found in external pleasures, but in the realization of the Self, beyond desires and attachments. This bliss is the natural state of existence and knowledge, ever-present in the one who has transcended all cravings." Amma

Eternal bliss, as described by Amma, is a state far beyond the fleeting joys we experience through external pleasures. In her words, "True bliss is not found in external pleasures, but in the realization of the Self, beyond desires and attachments. This bliss is the natural state of existence and knowledge, ever-present in the one who has transcended all cravings." This understanding of bliss, or anandam, is the pure, unchanging joy that arises not from outside circumstances but from within one's true nature.

In contrast to the happiness that comes from sensory objects (vishaya janyam), which is temporary and dependent on external factors, anandam is innate and independent. It is swabhavikam anandam—the natural state of being that manifests when one transcends desires and no longer seeks fulfillment through the external world. The one who has achieved this state is akamahathan—free from desires—and rests in the bliss of their own true self, not affected by the fluctuations of the material world.

This bliss is directly connected to the realization of Sat (existence) and Jnanam (knowledge). These two aspects—pure existence and pure knowledge—are united in the Self, and through the realization of this union, one experiences anandam. The Self is beyond duality and beyond the transient joys and sorrows of worldly life. In transcending desires, one can experience this state of bliss, which is steady, unchanging, and unaffected by external experiences.

The bliss of the Self, or Atmanandam, is distinct from any pleasure that can be attained through action, spiritual practices, or discipline (sadhana). While practices like meditation, prayer, and self-inquiry can help purify the mind and prepare it for deeper realizations, Atmanandam is not a result of effort. It is the natural state of the Self, present regardless of one's actions or experiences. This state of bliss exists beyond the duality of pleasure and pain, beyond the experiencer and the experienced, and is independent of any external stimuli.

In deep sleep, where the mind and senses are at rest, we experience a glimpse of this anandam. In that state, there are no desires, no objects of enjoyment, and no distractions. The mind is temporarily freed from its usual attachments and identifications, and in this state, the individual experiences a form of bliss. However, this experience is limited and brief compared to the enduring bliss realized through Self-knowledge. The experience in deep sleep is just a reflection of the true, continuous Atmanandam, which arises when one fully recognizes their true nature as Ananda Swarupam—the embodiment of bliss.

The key to this realization is the transcendence of desires. As long as the individual seeks happiness through external means, they remain trapped in the cycle of pleasure and pain, joy and sorrow. But once desires are subdued, the Self shines forth in its true, blissful nature. The anandam of the Self is not just a transient experience; it is a constant state that exists whether one is awake, dreaming, or in deep sleep. It is the foundation of all experience and the very essence of the Self.

Amma's teachings point to the fact that the true Self is beyond all the ups and downs of worldly life. It is not swayed by external circumstances, because it is rooted in the eternal. The joy that comes from realizing the Self is not comparable to any worldly pleasure, because it is infinite, boundless, and free from all limitations. In this state, one no longer seeks fulfillment outside, for they have found the source of all bliss within.

The realization of this blissful nature brings with it profound peace. The seeker who comes to know their true Self as Ananda Swarupam understands that they are complete, whole, and perfect. This understanding dissolves the constant search for happiness through relationships, possessions, or achievements. Instead, the individual rests in the joy of simply being, knowing that they are eternally one with the infinite Sat (existence) and Jnanam (knowledge).

As Amma teaches, this anandam is the natural state of the Self. It is not something to be attained or achieved; it is simply uncovered by letting go of desires, attachments, and false identifications. In this way, the journey to realizing eternal bliss is a journey inward, to the heart of one's own being. When all distractions are set aside, and the mind is stilled, the bliss of the Self shines forth naturally, without effort, and without end.

End of Fear

"Fear dissolves in the light of Atma Jnana, for when we realize the true Self, we are no longer bound by the illusions of the world. Liberation comes through this direct experience, freeing us from the cycles of fear and attachment." Amma

Fear is one of the most pervasive emotions experienced by individuals, but it is ultimately a product of ignorance, particularly ignorance of the true nature of the Self. As Amma teaches, “Fear dissolves in the light of Atma Jnana, for when we realize the true Self, we are no longer bound by the illusions of the world. Liberation comes through this direct experience, freeing us from the cycles of fear and attachment.” This statement captures the essence of how knowledge of the Atma (Self) leads to the dissolution of fear, which arises from misconceptions about who we are and our relationship to the world.

The root of fear lies in the belief that we are separate, limited beings. We identify with the body, mind, and ego, and therefore feel vulnerable to external threats—whether they be physical, emotional, or existential. However, once we gain Atma Jnana (Self-knowledge), this identification with the body and ego falls away, revealing the true nature of the Self as eternal, unchanging, and beyond all dualities. This understanding brings about baya nivruthi (the end of fear), as the individual no longer sees themselves as bound by worldly conditions or subject to harm.

The experience of fear is closely tied to the ignorance of avidya—the lack of knowledge about the true nature of existence. In this state of ignorance, we perceive the world through the lens of duality, seeing ourselves as distinct from others, from the world, and from Ishwara (God). This sense of separation creates vulnerability and fear, as we believe we are subject to forces beyond our control. However, the realization that the Self (Atma) and Ishwara are one and the same dissolves this duality. When we understand that the essence of God and the Self are identical, we recognize that we are not separate, but part of the infinite, non-dual reality of Brahman.

This understanding of the unity between Atma and Ishwara removes the illusion of separateness that is the root cause of fear. Once the veil of ignorance is lifted, we come to know that there is no external force to fear because we are, in essence, one with the entire cosmos. Fear, which arises from the belief in a limited, vulnerable self, is replaced by the profound peace of knowing the Atma as infinite and eternal. This is the state of moksha (liberation), where all attachments and anxieties tied to the material world dissolve.

In ignorance, individuals often mistakenly attribute fear to Ishwara, believing that divine will brings both joy and sorrow. However, the divine does not create fear; it is our misunderstanding of the divine nature that causes fear. When we see ourselves as separate from Ishwara, we project our vulnerabilities onto the divine, creating a relationship of fear rather than trust. However, through the grace of Ishwara and dedicated spiritual practice, we can purify our minds and remove the ignorance that creates this fear. This process ultimately leads to the realization that Ishwara and the Self are one, bringing about the end of fear.

Spiritual practices, including devotion, meditation, and service, are essential for purifying the mind and preparing it for the realization of non-duality. However, these practices alone are not sufficient without the knowledge of the ultimate reality. It is through the teachings of the Guru, scripture, and self-inquiry that one comes to realize the truth of non-duality. Listening to the teachings (sravana), reflecting on them (manana), and deeply meditating on the truth (nididhyasana) lead to the direct experience of Atma Jnana, which dispels the ignorance that creates fear.

The journey toward fearlessness involves recognizing that the worldly experience of fear is rooted in illusion. The perception of duality and separation from others, from the world, and from God is a result of ignorance, not reality. When we engage in spiritual practices with the aim of realizing the Self, we develop the readiness to receive the truth of non-duality, which ultimately dissolves all fear. This realization brings an end to the cycle of birth and death (samsara) and liberates the individual from the anxieties of worldly existence.

Once the truth of non-duality is realized, the individual no longer identifies with the body-mind complex and no longer fears death or suffering. The individual becomes established in the unchanging, eternal Self, which is free from all limitations. In this state, fear has no place, because there is no "other" to fear, no external threat, and no sense of vulnerability. The individual abides in the state of abhayam (fearlessness), fully immersed in the peace and bliss of the Self.

The ultimate liberation from fear is the direct experience of the unity of Atma and Brahman. In this realization, the individual transcends all illusions of separateness and duality, and with it, all fear and attachment. This is the highest state of existence, where the knower lives in the boundless peace of the Self, free from the cycles of fear and suffering that characterize worldly life. As Amma teaches, this liberation comes not from external changes but from the inner realization of the Self's eternal, unchanging nature.

Thus, the dissolution of fear is not merely a psychological or emotional shift; it is the result of a profound spiritual realization. When we see the truth of our oneness with Brahman, we are freed from the illusions of the world, and the fear that once bound us dissolves in the light of Atma Jnana. This is the ultimate freedom, the state of liberation where we rest in the boundless peace and bliss of the Self.

Freedom from Cravings

"Freedom from desires is the key to realizing the full bliss of the Self. When one is free from cravings, they naturally abide in the complete and eternal joy that is not separate from their true nature." Amma

This principle of akamahathwam (freedom from desires) is central to the spiritual practice of a Tatwa Jnani—one who has realized the true nature of the Self. Desires are what often create a sense of lack and incompleteness within the individual, but once these desires are transcended, the mind rests in its natural state of bliss (ananda), which is infinite and unbroken.

Desires lead the mind outward, chasing after fleeting experiences and pleasures. While these temporary joys may provide a momentary sense of happiness, they are not lasting, and the mind quickly returns to its state of dissatisfaction and longing. For those who have not realized the true nature of the Self, life becomes a continuous cycle of seeking fulfillment through external objects and experiences. However, a Tatwa Jnani understands that the fulfillment they seek cannot be found outside themselves. Their state of ananda is not dependent on external factors but arises from within, as an expression of their true nature.

The bliss that the Tatwa Jnani experiences is not fleeting or partial, but constant and complete. Unlike worldly pleasures, which are fragmented and limited, the bliss of the Self is boundless and eternal. This state of purnam (completeness) is the natural result of self-realization, where all cravings and desires have been transcended. The Tatwa Jnani no longer experiences the mind's constant movement between attraction and aversion. Instead, they abide in the unchanging bliss of the Self, where there is no sense of lack or incompleteness.

In this state of realization, the distinction between the experiencer and the experience dissolves. The Tatwa Jnani recognizes that the ananda they experience is not something separate from the Self. It is not an object to be attained or achieved through effort. Rather, it is the very essence of the Self. In this non-dual understanding, there is no separation between the one who experiences bliss and the bliss itself. The Tatwa Jnani abides in the state of sahaja ananda, the innate and spontaneous bliss that is not dependent on external conditions.

This realization of sahaja ananda leads to the dissolution of all dualities. The Tatwa Jnani no longer sees themselves as a separate individual seeking happiness in the external world. They realize that they are the source of all bliss, and that this bliss is not affected by the changes and fluctuations of the external world. In this state, there is no longer any desire or attachment to worldly objects, because the Tatwa Jnani knows that true fulfillment lies within, in the realization of the Self.

The state of akamahathwam is the key to experiencing this boundless and eternal bliss. When desires are transcended, the mind becomes still, and the individual is no longer driven by the need to acquire or achieve anything. This stillness of mind allows the Tatwa Jnani to fully experience the joy of their own being, without any interference from external distractions or cravings. This is the state of purnam, where the individual is complete and whole, without any sense of lack or need.

The process of realizing the Self and transcending desires involves deep self-inquiry and contemplation. Through spiritual practices such as meditation, the seeker gradually loosens their attachment to desires and external objects. As the mind becomes more purified, the seeker begins to recognize the true nature of the Self as pure ananda. This recognition leads to the dissolution of the ego and the realization that the Self is not separate from the bliss it seeks.

In this state of self-realization, the Tatwa Jnani no longer identifies with the body-mind complex. They understand that the true Self is beyond all limitations and dualities, and that it is the source of all bliss and fulfillment. This understanding brings about a profound inner peace and contentment, as the Tatwa Jnani no longer seeks anything outside themselves. They are fully established in the knowledge of their own completeness, and they experience the infinite joy of the Self in every moment.

Ultimately, the freedom from desires is what allows the Tatwa Jnani to experience the full and eternal bliss of the Self. When the mind is no longer swayed by cravings and attachments, it rests in its natural state of ananda. This state of purnam is the realization of the Self's true nature as infinite and complete. As Amma says, when one is free from cravings, they naturally abide in the eternal joy that is not separate from their true nature.

Inner Illumination of the True Self

"Ishwara resides within the heart of every being, manifesting as love, compassion, and wisdom. When we turn inward with devotion, we discover that the divine has always been within us, waiting to be realized." Amma

This points to the profound realization that the divine essence is not something external but exists within us. This inner illumination is the direct experience of the Self, or Brahman, which resides in the heart-space as pure consciousness and the ultimate reality.

The heart, in spiritual texts, is often referred to as the "supreme space," Hridayakasha. This is because it is seen as the seat of Brahman within the individual. In meditation or deep reflection, the inner space of the heart becomes the arena where one experiences the boundless consciousness of Brahman. It is not just an abstract concept but a living, direct perception that takes place in the mind, which itself is rooted in the heart. The heart-space is where the eternal witness, Brahman, manifests through the individual's consciousness.

According to the Upanishadic teachings, the space within the heart is the same as the cosmic space outside, connecting the microcosm and the macrocosm. This space, where Brahman resides, allows for a direct experience of the divine within. When we understand that the space outside, inside, and within the heart is all one and the same, it becomes clear that Brahman, the Self, is present everywhere, yet most intimately within our own heart.

The experience of Brahman within the heart is not a theoretical understanding but a direct, felt experience that arises when the mind turns inward. Brahman as the witness is always present in the mind, but it is only when the mind becomes still and free from distractions that this presence is perceived. The Vedic texts emphasize this direct experience, asserting that true knowledge of Brahman is not simply intellectual but an inner realization of the divine within the heart's space.

This direct experience of Brahman in the heart goes beyond intellectual understanding. If Brahman were only understood as something cosmic and unmanifest, like Māyā (the cosmic illusion), it would remain an abstract concept. However, through turning inward, one experiences Brahman directly in the mind, which resides in the heart. This understanding is more profound than any indirect knowledge or conceptualization of the divine.

As we come to recognize Brahman within the heart, we realize that this consciousness is the same essence of love, compassion, and wisdom that Amma speaks of. Ishwara, as the personal manifestation of Brahman, is not separate from the Self but dwells within each of us. This recognition dissolves the barriers of separation and reveals the oneness of all beings, connected through the divine presence that resides in every heart.

Through devotion and self-inquiry, the individual begins to experience this inner illumination. The heart becomes the center of one's spiritual experience, where the presence of Brahman is felt directly. This realization transforms the individual's perception of the world, as they no longer see themselves as separate from others but recognize the same divine presence in all.

The continuity of space—outer, inner, and within the heart—reflects the non-dual nature of Brahman. There is no real separation between the individual and the cosmic reality. The heart-space, where Brahman is most intimately experienced, is the gateway to understanding the oneness of existence. It is through the heart that we come to know Brahman, not as a distant, cosmic force, but as the very essence of our being.

This inner illumination is crucial for spiritual awakening. As the mind becomes purified through meditation, devotion, and self-inquiry, the light of Brahman shines forth from the heart. The individual realizes that the love, compassion, and wisdom they seek are not external but are the natural qualities of the divine Self within. This realization brings about a profound sense of peace and unity, as one comes to know that the divine presence is always there, guiding and nurturing from within.

In conclusion, the experience of Brahman as the divine presence within the heart is the ultimate realization of the Self. Through the inner journey of devotion and self-inquiry, we discover that Ishwara—the embodiment of love, compassion, and wisdom—has always been within us. This realization of oneness with the divine leads to the inner illumination that reveals the eternal truth: the Self and Brahman are one, and this truth shines brightly in the heart of every being.

Preparation for Self-Realization

"Purifying the mind is essential for the light of true knowledge to shine, as ignorance and doubts cloud our understanding of the Self. Only when the mind is clear through self-inquiry does the direct experience of the Self become fully realized, free from all illusions." Amma

The purification of the mind (chittasudhi) is the essential step in preparing for self-realization. This purification is not merely a matter of intellectual study or theoretical understanding but involves a deep cleansing of the inner faculties that have been clouded by ignorance (ajnana) and doubts (samsaya). The nature of this purification is one that removes these mental obstructions, allowing the natural light of the Self to shine forth, unimpeded by misconceptions.

The process of purifying the mind requires dedicated practice in the form of self-inquiry, self-reflection, and contemplation, referred to in Vedantic tradition as shravana (listening to the teachings), manana (reflecting upon them), and nididhyasana (deep meditation on the truth). These practices are the pathways through which the seeker can dissolve ignorance and gain clarity about the true nature of the Self. As Amma emphasizes, self-inquiry is essential because knowledge of the Self cannot be transferred from one person to another—it must arise internally, through the direct experience of one's own nature, free from the distortions of doubt and misunderstanding.

Even though the Self is ever-present and self-evident (sada

aparoksham), there remains a clear distinction between the state of the ajnani (one who is ignorant of the Self) and the jnani (one who has realized the Self). The ajnani, trapped in the illusions generated by ignorance, continues to identify with the body, mind, and ego, mistaking the external world for ultimate reality. They remain caught in the dualities of pleasure and pain, success and failure, joy and sorrow, believing in the separateness of existence and seeking fulfillment in fleeting external experiences.

In contrast, the jnani, whose mind has been purified, directly experiences the truth of the Self and lives in the state of non-duality (Advaita). For the jnani, ignorance, doubts, and false identifications have been completely eradicated. They no longer perceive the world through the lens of duality but recognize the underlying unity of all existence. As Amma explains, the jnani perceives all actions, whether deemed good or bad, as manifestations of the divine. They are not attached to outcomes and remain unaffected by the ups and downs of worldly experiences.

This realization of the Self brings about liberation (mukti)—freedom from the bondage of ignorance, doubts, and false knowledge. However, this liberation is not something that happens in the future or is attained after death; it is a present, immediate experience. The jnani realizes that they were never truly bound by anything other than ignorance, and with its dissolution, they see clearly that their true nature has always been one with Brahman, the infinite and eternal reality.

Liberation, in this sense, is the recognition that the Self has always been free, untouched by the limitations and conditions imposed by the mind and body. The illusion of separateness and duality vanishes, and the jnani abides in the eternal peace and completeness of the Self. The external world, with all its challenges and changes, no longer has the power to disturb the jnani, for their perception is anchored in the unchanging truth of non-duality.

In this state of realization, there is no longer any need for external pursuits, as the jnani has found fulfillment in the direct experience of the Self. The mind, now purified and free from cravings and attachments, rests naturally in the bliss of its true nature. The jnani experiences the world as a play of consciousness, without being swayed by desires or fears, for they know that the essence of all beings and things is none other than Brahman.

This state of self-realization is not reserved for a select few but is accessible to all who sincerely seek to purify their minds and engage in the practice of self-inquiry. The process may take time, but as the mind becomes clearer, the light of the Self gradually shines through, revealing the eternal, unchanging truth that has always been present. As Amma reminds us, it is through the purification of the mind that the illusions of separation and duality are dissolved, and the seeker comes to know their true Self, free from all limitations and bound only by the infinite love and wisdom that reside within.

Peace

"Supreme peace is realized when the illusion of duality dissolves, revealing the true nature of the Self. This peace is not dependent on external factors; it is the eternal, unshakable essence within us all." Amma

Supreme peace (paramamaya santhi) is a state that transcends all external conditions and arises from the dissolution of duality. As Amma says, "Supreme peace is realized when the illusion of duality dissolves, revealing the true nature of the Self." This peace is not contingent upon achievements, material wealth, or favorable circumstances;

rather, it is the eternal, unshakable essence within each individual. In this state, the individual recognizes their true nature as the Self, free from the illusions that divide and disturb the mind.

To attain such peace, one must develop a vyavrutha vishaya buddhi—an intellect turned inward, away from the distractions of external objects and experiences. This inward focus allows the mind to quiet itself and perceive directly the anandam (bliss) of the Self. When the intellect is unwavering (nischitha buddhi), it can experience this bliss without the interference of duality, as the division between subject and object dissolves. There is no longer an experiencer separate from the experience; instead, the individual abides in the non-dual realization of Brahman, where there is absolute certainty and clarity.

The worldly pleasures we experience—laukika anandhas—while real in their own way, are merely fleeting reflections of the ultimate bliss of Brahmananda. These transient joys are only fractions (amsa) of the full, limitless bliss that is inherent in Brahman, the ultimate reality. However, due to avidya (ignorance), we remain unaware of the source of all happiness, which lies within us. This ignorance manifests through desires, attachments to material goals, and identification with the body and mind. It creates the illusion that happiness can be found in the world of external objects, thus perpetuating the sense of separation and incompleteness.

The path to paramamaya santhi requires overcoming this avidya through self-inquiry, meditation, and detachment from external desires. When the mind is purified and freed from ignorance, it naturally turns inward to experience the infinite peace and bliss that is the essence of the Self. This peace, being inherent in our true nature, is not subject to fluctuations. It remains constant, regardless of external circumstances, because it is based on the realization of oneness with Brahman.

In this state, the individual recognizes that all external joys are simply reflections of the inner bliss of Brahman. By turning inward and quieting the mind, one transcends the limitations of worldly experiences and gains access to the infinite, unchanging bliss that lies at the core of existence. The individual no longer seeks happiness in the external world but rests in the peace and contentment that comes from self-realization.

Through this realization, the duality between the individual and the world dissolves. The individual no longer perceives themselves as separate from the rest of existence but recognizes the underlying unity of all beings and objects. This understanding brings about a state of paramamaya santhi, where the individual experiences the supreme peace of non-duality, free from the disturbances and conflicts that arise from the perception of separateness.

As the illusions created by avidya fall away, the individual experiences the true bliss of Brahmananda. This bliss is not a temporary state but the natural, eternal condition of the Self. It is untouched by the changes and challenges of the external world because it is rooted in the unchanging reality of Brahman.

In conclusion, the supreme peace and bliss of paramamaya santhi is the direct result of realizing the non-dual nature of the Self. By turning inward and purifying the mind, one can transcend the duality of subject and object, overcoming the illusions of separateness and ignorance. In this state, the individual experiences the infinite, unchanging peace that is the essence of their true nature—Brahmananda. This is the ultimate goal of spiritual practice: to realize the supreme peace that is not dependent on external factors but is the very foundation of existence itself.

CHAPTER-4

Deeper Knowledge and Dissolution of Ignorance

Mantra is Self

"The power of mantra is the signature of the Self, resonating with the divine. Through mantra japa, we connect with the essence of the Guru, Ishwara, and all that is sacred, for in truth, every face is the face of God." Amma

Mantras hold a special place in spiritual practice as they serve as bridges between the practitioner and the deeper reality of the Self (Atma). This power arises from the fact that mantras are not merely sounds or words; they carry the vibrational essence of the Self, connecting the individual to Ishwara (the divine), the Guru, and the ultimate truth. Through the repetition of mantra, one begins to tune into the sacred and realize the divine presence in all things, as every face becomes a reflection of God.

Mantra Japa (repetition of a mantra) is a profound practice in non-dualistic traditions like Advaita Vedanta, where the distinction between the practitioner, the act of reciting, and the divine being invoked gradually fades. The repetition of the mantra, particularly manasa japa (mental repetition), serves to quiet the mind and eliminate distractions. By repeating the mantra internally, the practitioner directs their focus inward, enabling the mind to dissolve into the sound vibrations. As the practitioner moves beyond surface-level sound, the deeper essence of the mantra is revealed, which is none other than pure consciousness, Atma Chaitanyam.

In this practice, the mantra is not an external tool but a direct expression of the Self. The recitation itself becomes a manifestation of Atma Vigjnanam (Self-knowledge), as the practitioner begins to realize that the mantra, the one reciting it, and the consciousness being awakened are all one and the same. This realization leads to a dissolution of the ego, as the practitioner understands that the distinctions between the subject (the reciter), the object (the mantra), and the act of reciting are illusions created by ignorance. Instead, the mantra becomes a gateway to the experience of non-duality, where all divisions cease to exist.

The eternal nature of mantras reflects the eternal and unchanging nature of the Self. In non-dual philosophy, the Self is timeless, infinite, and beyond the limitations of space and time. Mantras, being aligned with this non-dual truth, are also considered eternal. They arise from the same source as the Vedas, which are seen as spontaneous expressions of eternal wisdom. Just as the Self is not created or destroyed, the mantras too are seen as part of this cosmic, eternal expression of consciousness.

Through the continuous practice of manasa smruthi (mindful repetition), the practitioner begins to transcend the ordinary flow of thoughts, allowing the mantra to work at a deeper level. The repetition of the mantra helps to dissolve the ego and purify the mind, creating space for the direct experience of unity. The distinction between the one who is reciting and the object of recitation gradually dissolves. This brings the practitioner to a state where they are able to experience the oneness of existence, realizing that there is no separation between themselves, the mantra, and the divine essence being invoked.

In this state, the practitioner moves beyond the need for intellectual understanding or conceptual frameworks. The mantra becomes a living expression of truth, vibrating with the same energy that permeates the entire cosmos. The sound of the mantra and the consciousness it evokes are one and the same, both rooted in the eternal truth of the Self. As the practitioner deepens in their practice, they come to see the mantra not as something separate from themselves but as a direct reflection of their own inner nature.

As Amma's teaching suggests, this process leads to a realization that every aspect of life, every person, and every experience is a reflection of the divine. The mantra, in its power to connect the practitioner to the deeper reality of the Self, reveals that the entire universe is filled with the same divine essence. Every face becomes the face of God, and the practitioner comes to understand that the divine is not something distant or separate but is present in all things, including themselves.

This realization of oneness through mantra Japa aligns with the broader goal of Advaita Vedanta, which is the dissolution of the illusion of separateness and the direct experience of the non-dual Self. By consistently practicing mantra Japa, the seeker moves closer to this ultimate realization, where they no longer identify with the body-mind complex but see themselves as one with Brahman, the absolute reality.

In conclusion, the mantra is both a tool and an expression of the deeper truth within each individual. Through consistent practice, the practitioner connects with the divine essence that resides within them, gradually dissolving the sense of separation and realizing the oneness of all existence. As the practitioner becomes fully absorbed in the mantra, they move beyond the limitations of the mind and ego, experiencing the pure, unchanging consciousness that is the true nature of the Self.

Karma's Hold Released

"For the jnani, all actions, whether good or bad, are seen as part of the divine flow, leaving their inner peace undisturbed. The effects of past karma no longer bind them, as they realize the Self beyond the body and mind, free from the cycles of birth and death." Amma

For the jnani, all actions, whether good or bad, are part of the divine flow and no longer bind them to the cycles of birth and death. As Amma beautifully says, "The effects of past karma no longer bind them, as they realize the Self beyond the body and mind, free from the cycles of birth and death." In Advaita Vedanta, karma—both good and bad—only holds sway over those who identify with the body and mind, who are attached to the fruits of their actions. This attachment, based on ignorance (ajnana), keeps individuals entangled in cycles of pleasure and pain. However, the jnani (one who knows the Self) sees beyond this identification and remains undisturbed by the play of karma.

Karma is integral to the human experience, but for the jnani, it ceases to have a binding effect. The jnani understands that all actions—whether they bring pleasure or pain—are expressions of Brahman, the ultimate reality. As they no longer associate their identity with the body-mind complex, the jnani transcends dualities like joy and suffering. This detachment allows them to remain steady and peaceful in the face of life's inevitable ups and downs. Their inner peace is not shaken by external circumstances because they have realized that the true Self is beyond the transient world of actions and reactions.

Even prarabdha karma, the portion of one's past karma that has begun to bear fruit in the present life, does not affect the jnani. While the body and mind may still experience the results of past karma, such as illness or external challenges, the jnani remains free from attachment to these experiences. The prarabdha karma unfolds naturally, but the jnani views it from the perspective of jnana drushti (the vision of knowledge), recognizing it as part of the illusory nature of the world. Because they no longer identify with the ego, prarabdha karma does not accumulate further, and they are free from the cycle of future births and deaths.

The realization of the Self often comes through deep inquiry, solitude (ekantha), and the dissolution of the mind's distractions. In this stillness, the seeker uncovers the ultimate reality—ekamaya antham (the non-dual truth).

In solitude, the mind quiets down, allowing the individual to inquire into the nature of the Atma and its oneness with Brahman. This realization goes beyond all dualities and reveals the Self as the unchanging truth. The process of self-inquiry leads to an understanding that the body, mind, and world are temporary manifestations, while the Self remains eternal.

In Advaita Vedanta, the cycle of creation is governed by the universal Lord, Ishwara. Shrushti anupravesham refers to the involvement of the individual self (jiva) in the world of names and forms, where the waking and dream states arise from the causal state of deep sleep (sushupthi). Ishwara, as sarveshwaran (universal Lord), governs these states, allowing experiences to unfold based on the impressions carried from deep sleep. This cyclical nature of existence—moving through waking, dreaming, and deep sleep—is a reflection of the interconnectedness of all states of consciousness.

For the jnani, this entire cycle is seen as an appearance of Brahman, and through the knowledge of the Self (Atma Vidhya), the jnani recognizes that the Self is the only reality. The jnani no longer identifies with the transient states of waking, dreaming, or deep sleep but instead abides in the realization of the eternal Self, which transcends all states. This realization liberates the jnani from the illusion of separateness and the cycles of birth and death.

The concept of sarvajna Ishwara (the all-knowing Lord) reinforces the understanding that Ishwara is not separate from creation. The creator and the creation are one and the same. In this non-dual realization, the jnani sees all actions and experiences as expressions of the divine, and thus they no longer engage with the world through attachment or desire. For them, the distinction between the doer, the action, and the result dissolves, and what remains is the pure awareness of Brahman.

In conclusion, for the jnani, karma no longer has a hold. They see the unfolding of actions as part of the divine play, remaining unattached and unaffected by the results. Their realization of the Self allows them to transcend the cycles of birth, death, and rebirth, leading to ultimate freedom and inner peace. Through Atma Vidhya, they recognize that the true Self is beyond all dualities and beyond the illusions of the world, abiding in the unchanging, eternal reality of Brahman.

Atma-Jnani

"A Tatwa Jnani sees beyond the illusion of separateness, recognizing that all forms and distinctions are but expressions of the one universal Self. Just as gold remains unchanged regardless of the shape of the ornament, the Self is ever-present, beyond the layers of illusion." Amma

A Tatwa Jnani, or one who has realized the true nature of the Self, transcends the illusions of separateness and duality that cloud the understanding of ordinary individuals. As Amma beautifully expresses, "A Tatwa Jnani sees beyond the illusion of separateness, recognizing that all forms and distinctions are but expressions of the one universal Self." This realization is the hallmark of a jnani—someone who sees through the layers of illusion created by avidya (ignorance) and recognizes that all distinctions are merely superficial manifestations of the one universal Self, or Brahman.

In the state of realization, the Tatwa Jnani views the world through the lens of non-duality. Just as gold remains unchanged regardless of the form of the ornament, the Self (Atma) remains unaltered, regardless of the different layers or koshas (sheaths) that may cover it. These layers, such as the physical body (annamaya kosha) and the mind, are merely coverings, while the essence—the true Self—remains formless and eternal. The Jnani understands that the true Self is beyond the body and mind, and they see these layers as illusions that veil the real, unchanging nature of the Self.

At the moment of death, this knowledge brings profound liberation. For the Tatwa Jnani, death is not seen as an end or a transition into the unknown but as a natural continuation of the same non-dual reality they have already realized. Just as a gold ornament, when melted, returns to its original formless state, the dissolution of the body is simply the return of one of the forms to the formless Self. The Tatwa Jnani, having realized their oneness with Brahman, does not perceive death as a loss or as something to be feared. Instead, they remain established in the knowledge of their eternal nature, free from the dualities of birth and death.

The koshas, which represent different aspects of existence—physical, mental, and spiritual—are seen by the Tatwa Jnani as temporary coverings over the Atma. These layers are not separate from the Self, just as the different forms of ornaments are not separate from the gold they are made of. Once the Tatwa Jnani has realized this truth, they see through the illusion of separateness and duality that these layers create. The mind, body, and ego are no longer seen as defining aspects of identity but as temporary manifestations that arise and dissolve.

For the Tatwa Jnani, the distinction between life and death is an illusory one. The experience of birth, life, and death is a cycle that belongs to the body and mind, not to the Self. The Jnani, having transcended this cycle, lives in the constant awareness of the non-dual reality where there is no birth or death—only the eternal existence of Brahman. This profound realization brings about freedom from fear and the sense of separateness that drives most human experiences.

The Jnani's understanding of virat bhavam—their universal form—further reinforces this non-dual perspective. They see themselves as one with the entire cosmos, recognizing that all forms, whether human, animal, or inanimate, are simply expressions of the same underlying reality. This vision of oneness allows them to live without attachment or fear, fully embracing the understanding that the Self is all-pervasive and eternal.

At the moment of death, the Tatwa Jnani does not experience fear or anxiety, as they are no longer identified with the body or mind. Instead, they remain in the state of non-dual awareness, where the dissolution of the body is simply a return to the formless essence from which all forms arise. This realization of the Self as eternal and formless brings ultimate liberation, freeing the Jnani from the cycle of birth and death and the dualities that define worldly existence.

In this state of realization, the Tatwa Jnani fully embodies the understanding that the distinctions created by the koshas, the mind, and the world are mere illusions. Once these illusions are removed through self-knowledge, the underlying unity of all existence becomes clear. The Jnani lives in the awareness that everything in the cosmos is a manifestation of Brahman, the ultimate reality, and they see themselves as inseparable from this oneness.

Thus, for the Tatwa Jnani, death is not an event to be feared or resisted. It is simply the natural unfolding of the non-dual reality they have realized. Just as an ornament made of gold can take on different shapes without altering the gold itself, the Jnani understands that their true Self is beyond all forms and that the dissolution of the body is merely the melting away of one of those forms. In this state of understanding, the Jnani experiences ultimate liberation, free from the illusions of duality and separateness.

Body-Mind: Ego's Fuel

"Liberation is the realization that there is nothing separate from the Self, and thus no cause for fear. When one becomes Brahman, the illusions of duality—such as the eater and the eaten—dissolve, leaving only the infinite peace of oneness." Amma

Liberation, as Amma says, is the realization that nothing exists separate from the Self, and with that understanding, all causes for fear dissolve. This state of realization, where one becomes Brahman, removes the illusions of duality—such as the distinctions between the eater and the eaten—that define worldly existence. The ego and its attachments to the body and mind fuel this sense of separateness, but in the light of true knowledge, these illusions vanish, leaving only the infinite peace of oneness. The concern about fear in the process of liberation, therefore, stems from a fundamental misunderstanding of what it means to realize the Self.

Many fear that by attaining liberation and realizing their oneness with Brahman, their individual worldly existence will come to an end. This fear is often accompanied by the idea that they will become "food" for others or that their distinct identity will be consumed in the process. Such concerns arise from dualistic thinking, where distinctions between eater and eaten, subject and object, still hold sway. These distinctions, however, belong to the empirical world, the world of maya (illusion), where the ego perceives everything as separate and distinct. In the realm of maya, we identify with the body and mind, and this identification is what gives rise to fears about liberation.

However, the person of knowledge, or jnani, who has realized Brahman, transcends these dualistic distinctions. For the jnani, the concepts of eater and eaten, subject and object, exist only within the realm of relative experience, which is bound by ignorance. In the ultimate reality of

Brahman, these distinctions hold no significance. There is no separation between the eater and the eaten because there is no "other." The jnani understands that all forms and experiences in the world are temporary, illusory manifestations within the non-dual reality of Brahman.

The fear of losing individuality or becoming "food" for others is, therefore, based on ignorance. In the state of liberation, the person of knowledge recognizes that they are Brahman—the unchanging, all-pervading, and non-dual reality. In this realization, there is nothing separate from the Self, and thus nothing to fear. The jnani transcends the limitations of the body-mind complex and no longer identifies with the empirical experiences of pleasure and pain, consumption, or even physical existence. In the state of liberation, the distinctions that once gave rise to fear are understood to be illusory and false.

Worldly distinctions such as the enjoyment of desirable things, the notion of being an individual who consumes or is consumed, belong to the world of maya. These experiences are fleeting and temporary, tied to the false identification with the body and mind. Once the person of knowledge realizes the truth of Brahman, they understand that these experiences are merely projections of the mind, and they no longer identify with them. In the light of this realization, the jnani transcends the need for worldly pleasures and is no longer subject to the fears and anxieties that arise from attachment to them.

In liberation, there is no sense of separation or duality, and therefore no basis for fear. The person of knowledge becomes one with Brahman, realizing that their true nature is beyond the limitations of the physical body and mind. In this state of unity with Brahman, they experience the ultimate freedom and peace, free from the cycles of birth and death and the fear that accompanies attachment to the ego. Liberation is not the loss of individuality but the realization of the true Self, which is boundless, infinite, and eternal.

The idea of becoming "food" for others in liberation is based on the mistaken belief that the Self is something that can be consumed or lost. This fear arises from the dualistic perspective that separates the individual from the rest of existence. However, in the state of self-realization, the jnani understands that there is no "other" to fear. Brahman is the only reality, and it is beyond the dualities of eating and being eaten, pleasure and pain, or life and death. The jnani lives in a state of non-dual awareness, where the concepts of loss and gain no longer apply.

In this state of non-dual realization, the person of knowledge experiences liberation as a state of absolute fearlessness. There is no longer any sense of vulnerability or threat because the jnani knows that they are not the body-mind complex. They are the infinite, unchanging Brahman, and in this state, there is no external force that can cause harm or suffering. The jnani's experience of liberation is one of unshakable peace and freedom, where all fears about identity, individuality, and separation dissolve.

Thus, the liberation experienced by the jnani is the dissolution of all illusions, including the fear of losing individuality. In the light of true knowledge, the person of knowledge realizes that they are one with Brahman, and that there is nothing in existence that is separate from them. This realization brings with it an inner peace and freedom that cannot be shaken by external circumstances or worldly fears.

Reality Lies Beyond Projection

"The world is a projection of the Self, and through realizing the truth of our own nature, the illusion of creation dissolves, freeing us from the cycles of karma. For those seeking this understanding, meditation and devotion to the Guru serve as vital tools for deepening the inquiry into the ultimate reality." Amma

The mind, as Amma teaches, is a projection of the Self. This idea, rooted in Advaita Vedanta, suggests that the physical and material world we perceive is not separate from the Self, but rather an appearance, an illusion (maya). By realizing the true nature of our own existence, we dissolve the illusion of creation, which in turn liberates us from the cycles of karma. Both good (subha) and bad (asubha) actions lose their binding influence on a jnani, or one who has attained self-knowledge. This liberation—moksha—is the ultimate goal of spiritual inquiry, revealing that the Self alone is real and the world of names and forms is illusory.

The concept of projection aligns with the understanding that all creation is a manifestation of the Self. However, identifying with this projection rather than the true Self keeps individuals bound to the cycle of birth and death (samsara). Creation itself serves a purpose, but once one realizes the ultimate reality, the identification with creation must be transcended. In doing so, all perceptions of separation and duality dissolve, leaving the jnani free from karma and its consequences. The knowledge that reveals this truth is called Tatwajnan, or the knowledge of the ultimate reality. This knowledge discloses the non-dual nature of existence, where the Self is seen as the singular reality behind all appearances.

For seekers, however, the process of realizing this truth is not always immediate. Listening to the scriptures (shravanam) may plant the seeds of knowledge, but the truth may remain elusive. Therefore, practices like upasana (meditation) and mananam (reflection) become essential. Upasana allows seekers to focus their minds inward, quieting distractions and encouraging deep contemplation on the nature of the Self. This practice purifies the mind and fosters a deepening inquiry into the ultimate reality, helping the seeker develop clarity and concentration necessary for self-realization.

Mananam, or reflecting on the teachings heard during shravanam, further solidifies the intellectual understanding of the Self. This reflective process clarifies doubts and deepens one's conviction in the truth of non-duality. Through mananam, the teachings become ingrained in the seeker's consciousness, transforming intellectual knowledge into a lived experience. The combination of shravanam, upasana, and mananam provides a structured path for seekers to move from intellectual understanding to direct realization.

A crucial aspect of this journey is the role of the Guru. The Guru serves as both a guide and a living embodiment of the teachings, helping seekers navigate their spiritual paths. In Advaita Vedanta, approaching the Guru with humility, devotion, and sincerity—referred to as vidhivath upasannaya—is of utmost importance. This respectful approach allows the seeker to open themselves to the grace and wisdom of the Guru, which are essential for removing ignorance and realizing the Self. Devotion to the Guru strengthens the seeker's resolve and provides the necessary guidance for deepening their inquiry into the nature of existence.

The Guru's teachings, combined with the seeker's sincerity and effort, help to unveil the truth of non-duality. Through this process, the seeker begins to see the world not as a collection of separate entities but as expressions of the same divine presence. This understanding frees the individual from the illusions of separation and duality, leading to the realization that all is Brahman, the ultimate reality. The world, once perceived as external and separate, is now understood as a projection of the Self.

As the seeker deepens in their practice, the lines between the self and the world blur, and the oneness of existence becomes apparent. This realization brings a profound sense of liberation, as the attachments and desires that once governed the individual's life begin to fade. The seeker no longer identifies with the body, mind, or external circumstances but instead recognizes their true nature as the eternal Self, beyond all appearances and forms.

Ultimately, the realization of the Self as the singular reality leads to freedom from the cycles of karma. Since the jnani no longer identifies with the ego or body, they are unaffected by the results of past actions. The knowledge of non-duality reveals that there is no separate doer, and therefore, no karma to be accumulated. The jnani transcends the dualities of good and bad, pleasure and pain, and lives in the awareness of their oneness with Brahman.

In conclusion, realizing the truth of our own nature dissolves the illusion of creation and frees us from the cycles of karma. Meditation, reflection, and devotion to the Guru are vital tools for seekers on this path, helping to purify the mind and deepen the inquiry into the ultimate reality. By embracing these practices and approaching the Guru with sincerity, the seeker moves toward the direct experience of the Self, where all illusions dissolve, and liberation is attained.

Transcendent Liberation

"When the light of knowledge dispels ignorance, the illusion of worldly existence fades. True liberation comes not from escaping the world, but from realizing the eternal truth that transcends it." Amma

The Upanishadic statement "brahmavidāpnoti param" from the Taittiriya Upanishad (2-1-1), which means "the knower of Brahman reaches the highest," serves as the foundation for this understanding. The highest goal is not a physical or external achievement but the inner realization of Brahman—the eternal, infinite reality that transcends the material world.

Ignorance, or avidya, is the root cause of all suffering. It clouds our perception of reality and keeps us bound to the cycles of birth and death, caught in the web of desires and attachments. The light of knowledge (jnana) dispels this ignorance, enabling one to see beyond the superficial distinctions of the world. When one realizes the true nature of the Self, they understand that the Self is not limited by the body, mind, or external circumstances. It is infinite, unchanging, and beyond all dualities. This realization is what liberates an individual from the endless cycle of samsara (worldly existence), as ignorance is completely eradicated.

Amma's words remind us that true liberation does not require us to flee from the world or renounce it entirely. Instead, it involves recognizing the eternal truth that lies beyond the illusory nature of worldly experiences. The Upanishads teach that this knowledge helps one transcend the illusions and attachments that keep us bound to suffering. By seeing through the illusion of separateness and realizing the oneness of all existence, the individual attains a state of peace and freedom. Liberation is not about abandoning the world but about seeing the world through the lens of non-duality, where all forms and distinctions dissolve into the oneness of Brahman.

Fearlessness is a natural outcome of this realization. The Upanishads explain that fear arises from attachment to worldly desires and from identifying with the body and mind. As long as one remains attached to material existence, they remain vulnerable to fear. However, once the light of knowledge dispels ignorance, the individual transcends these attachments and enters a state of true fearlessness. They no longer fear death, loss, or suffering because they recognize that the Self is eternal and beyond harm. This fearlessness is a hallmark of the liberated soul, who rests in the awareness of their oneness with Brahman.

Furthermore, the Upanishads assert that the enlightened person is unaffected by actions. This is a profound shift from the usual human experience, where actions are performed with the expectation of results, whether good or bad. For the knower of Brahman, actions are no longer driven by personal desires or attachments. They perform actions selflessly, without attachment to the outcome, and are free from the bondage of karma. Virtue and vice, success and failure, pleasure and pain—these dualities no longer bind the jnani, as they have transcended the very framework that gives rise to such distinctions.

The jnani, or realized individual, also experiences a deep sense of equanimity. This state of balance is born out of their understanding that the Self is beyond the cycles of karma and the ups and downs of life. They are no longer disturbed by the fluctuations of external circumstances, whether good or bad. Their mind remains calm and undisturbed, rooted in the knowledge of the eternal truth. This state of equanimity brings a profound sense of inner peace, as the jnani no longer identifies with the transient and impermanent aspects of life.

Amma's teaching aligns perfectly with the wisdom of the Upanishads, emphasizing that the path to liberation is not about abandoning the world but about seeing through the illusion of separateness. True liberation is the realization that there is nothing outside of the Self—no external world to escape from, no dualities to overcome. In this realization, all illusions of the material world fade, leaving only the infinite peace and bliss of oneness with Brahman.

The journey toward this transcendent liberation is one of inner awakening. Through self-inquiry, meditation, and devotion, the seeker gradually removes the layers of ignorance that obscure the truth. The guidance of a Guru, like Amma, plays a vital role in this process, helping the seeker to navigate the complexities of the mind and ego and to focus on the ultimate goal of self-realization.

In conclusion, transcendent liberation is the ultimate goal of spiritual practice. It is the realization that the Self is not bound by the limitations of the material world and that the illusion of worldly existence dissolves in the light of true knowledge. Through this realization, fear, attachment, and suffering are eradicated, and the individual experiences the infinite peace and freedom of oneness with Brahman.

Timeless Presence

"Atma Jnanam is the eternal light that shines within. It is not something to be attained, but something to be realized. This knowledge is timeless, ever-present, and reveals the true nature of the Self as infinite and unchanging." Amma

The concept of Atma Jnanam, as Amma explains, is the eternal light that shines within, representing the timeless knowledge of the Self. This knowledge is not something that is attained externally but is realized as an ever-present truth that reveals the infinite, unchanging nature of the Self. In

Advaita Vedanta, this knowledge is inherent in Brahman, the ultimate reality, and is not subject to the limitations of time, space, or action. It is this timeless presence of jnanam, or knowledge, that pervades all of existence, making everything known while remaining unaffected by the dualities of the world.

Jnanam is an intrinsic attribute of Brahman and remains beyond the constraints of the physical senses. Human sense organs have limitations; they can only perceive objects within certain parameters, such as distance or light. Brahman, on the other hand, as pure consciousness, does not experience these limitations. Avyavahitham refers to the fact that Brahman's knowledge is inseparable from the objects it illumines. In other words, everything in existence is known through the consciousness of Brahman, which remains ever-present and boundless.

Brahman's omniscience, or Sarvajnatwam, allows it to possess complete knowledge of all changing objects in the universe, but without any attachment to action or the sense of "doership." This is the key difference between human knowledge, which is often tied to personal involvement or effort, and the knowledge of Brahman, which is passive and all-encompassing. Brahman knows all, but without the ego-driven need to act or participate. It simply illuminates all things with its consciousness, much like the sun illuminates objects without actively engaging with them.

In understanding the relationship between Brahman and the universe, we see that Brahman is not only the observer but the very foundation of all knowledge and existence. Without Brahman's consciousness, the world of objects, beings, and events would not exist or be perceived. This is why Brahman is referred to as Sarva Sreshtam, the supreme reality, and Sarvajnatha, the all-knowing. Its knowledge is not subject to the fluctuations of time, unlike human knowledge, which can grow or diminish. Brahman's knowledge is eternal, constant, and transcendent.

This timeless nature of Brahman's knowledge reveals the truth of non-duality. In the human experience, we perceive ourselves as separate individuals, distinct from the objects and beings around us. However, from the standpoint of Brahman, there is no such separation. The objects of the world and the consciousness that perceives them are not different from Brahman itself. All distinctions dissolve when one realizes the non-dual nature of existence, understanding that everything is interconnected through the light of Brahman's consciousness.

Amma's teaching aligns with this understanding, emphasizing that the true Self is not something to be acquired but something that is always present within. The realization of this truth transcends the illusion of separateness. Once ignorance is removed through self-knowledge, the individual understands that their true nature is identical to Brahman. This realization brings about liberation, freeing the individual from the cycles of birth, death, and the limitations of worldly existence.

In the realm of ignorance, or avidya, people are bound by dualities—pleasure and pain, success and failure, life and death. These dualities arise from the mistaken belief that the Self is separate from the world. However, when the light of knowledge dispels this ignorance, the individual sees the world as a projection of Brahman's consciousness. The dualities no longer have any power, and the individual rests in the peace and bliss of non-duality.

Brahman's knowledge is often described as self-luminous, meaning it does not require anything external to make it known. Just as the sun does not need another light to reveal itself, Brahman's consciousness shines forth naturally, illuminating all things without effort. The knowledge of

Brahman is ever-present, encompassing the universe and beyond. It is not limited by the passage of time or the changes in the world; it remains constant and infinite.

For the jnani, or the realized being, this understanding transforms their perception of the world. They no longer see themselves as separate from the objects they perceive. Instead, they recognize that everything is an expression of the same underlying consciousness—Brahman. This realization frees them from the attachments and desires that bind others to the material world, allowing them to live in a state of peace and liberation.

In conclusion, the timeless presence of Atma Jnanam, as Amma describes, is the realization that the Self is not distinct from the eternal, all-knowing consciousness of Brahman. This knowledge reveals the non-dual nature of reality, where all distinctions between subject and object, knower and known, dissolve. Brahman's knowledge is the light that illuminates all things, making the universe known while remaining ever-constant and unchanging. This is the essence of true liberation, where the individual transcends the illusion of separateness and realizes their oneness with the infinite, unchanging Self.

Discerning Intellect

"The infinite space that surrounds and pervades everything is like the Atma—vast, whole, and boundless. The Self is all-encompassing, untouched by divisions, ever-present within and beyond all that we perceive." Amma

Amma's quote, "The infinite space that surrounds and pervades everything is like the Atma—vast, whole, and boundless. The Self is all-encompassing, untouched by divisions, ever-present within and beyond all that we perceive," points to the nature of the Atma (Self) as infinite, indivisible, and beyond all limitations. This vastness and boundlessness of the Self are mirrored in the concept of space, which pervades everything yet remains untouched by the objects within it. The Atma, similarly, remains ever-present and whole, even as it seems to be encased within the individual body and mind.

In Advaita Vedanta, the intellect (buddhi) is closely tied to the process of realizing this boundless nature of the Self. The buddhi is considered the instrument of discernment, capable of separating the real from the unreal, the eternal from the transient. While the intellect is often associated with reasoning and decision-making in worldly matters, it also plays a vital role in spiritual practice. Through the purified intellect, one can penetrate the layers of ignorance that obscure the true nature of the Self and begin to see the underlying unity between the individual self (jiva) and Brahman.

The intellect acts as a bridge between the individual self and Brahman. It is often compared to the subtle space within the heart, where one reflects on their deeper nature. Just as infinite space contains and pervades all things without being affected by them, the Atma is the substratum of all experiences, remaining unaffected by the changes in the body, mind, or external world. This vastness of the Atma can be realized when the intellect, refined by self-inquiry and meditation, is turned inward.

In spiritual practice, the process of turning inward is essential for discerning the nature of the Self. The intellect, when clouded by ignorance (avidya), perceives the world through the lens of duality—distinguishing between the self and others, the body and the world. However, when the intellect becomes purified through practices like shravana (listening to teachings), manana (contemplation), and nididhyasana (meditation), it begins to perceive the deeper truth of non-duality. It starts recognizing that the individual self is not separate from the all-encompassing Brahman.

This inward journey requires the intellect to rise above the distractions of the mind and senses, which constantly pull it toward external objects and desires. By focusing on the subtle space of the heart, where the Self resides, the intellect can transcend the divisions of the external world. This inward focus helps the practitioner to gradually shift from identifying with the body and mind to identifying with the infinite and boundless Self. The practice of discerning between the transient and the eternal is key to this realization.

As the intellect becomes more refined, it begins to dissolve the divisions that were once perceived as real. The distinctions between the body and the mind, the self and others, begin to fade, revealing the truth of oneness. Just as space is not divided by the objects within it, the Atma is not fragmented by the individual forms it inhabits. It remains whole and indivisible, pervading everything yet untouched by the limitations of form.

Amma's teaching highlights that the Self is all-encompassing and ever-present, both within and beyond what we perceive. The process of realizing this truth is an inward journey, guided by the intellect but culminating in the direct experience of non-duality. The intellect, when purified and focused, becomes the vehicle through which the individual realizes their true nature as Brahman. This realization dispels the illusion of separateness and allows the individual to rest in the boundless peace of the Self.

In the ultimate state of realization, the intellect itself is transcended, as the distinctions between knower and known, subject and object, dissolve. The individual no longer experiences themselves as a separate entity but recognizes their unity with the entire cosmos. This state of oneness, where the individual self merges with the universal Self, brings about liberation (moksha). In this state, the individual is free from the cycles of birth and death, and all forms of duality disappear.

The discernment cultivated by the intellect is essential in the early stages of spiritual practice, but once the truth of non-duality is realized, the intellect's role shifts. It no longer functions as a tool for distinguishing between things but becomes the means by which the individual perceives the unity of all existence. In this sense, the intellect serves as a mirror, reflecting the infinite and boundless nature of the Self.

Ultimately, the intellect reveals the truth that the Atma is not confined by the body, mind, or even the universe itself. The Atma is the underlying reality that pervades everything, just as space pervades all objects yet remains untouched by them. This realization brings about the dissolution of ignorance and the experience of supreme peace and freedom.

In conclusion, the intellect, when properly directed, is a powerful tool for discerning the true nature of the Self. By turning inward and focusing on the infinite space within the heart, the individual can move closer to realizing the unity between the self and Brahman. This realization dispels the illusions of separateness, allowing the individual to experience the boundless, ever-present nature of the Self, untouched by divisions and limitations. As Amma's quote suggests, the infinite space that surrounds and pervades everything is like the Atma, and recognizing this truth leads to the ultimate realization of oneness.

True Insights

"True understanding comes through the light of discernment, revealing the essence of Ishwara within. Through Atma Jnana, we realize that the path to liberation is not outside but within the heart, where the Self and the Divine are one." Amma

Amma›s profound quote, "True understanding comes through the light of discernment, revealing the essence of Ishwara within. Through Atma Jnana, we realize that the path to liberation is not outside but within the heart, where the Self and the Divine are one," underscores the essence of true knowledge and the journey of self-realization. The path of Brahma Jnana, or knowledge of Brahman, is an inward journey that reveals the oneness between the Self and the Divine, ultimately leading to liberation. This journey is deeply intertwined with discerning intellect, self-inquiry, and direct experience beyond superficial understanding.

Brahma Jnana revolves around understanding Brahman, the ultimate reality, through attributes such as truth (Satyam), knowledge (Jnanam), and infinity (Anantam). Brahman is vast, cosmic, and beyond ordinary comprehension, and understanding these key attributes is central to realizing its true nature. Satyam refers to Brahman's unchanging essence, Jnanam emphasizes that Brahman is pure consciousness, and Anantam highlights that Brahman is infinite and boundless. However, simply grasping Brahman conceptually is insufficient for liberation; one must realize that Brahman is their own Self. This deeper, personal understanding dissolves ignorance and the false perception of duality.

When seekers mistakenly view Brahman as something separate from themselves, they are trapped in duality—the belief that the Self and the universe are distinct. Liberation comes when one understands the non-dual nature of Brahman and the Self. Aparoksha Jnanam, or direct knowledge, is the ultimate realization of non-duality, where the distinction between knower and known vanishes. The Sarvatma Bhavam, the vision of oneness, emerges when the seeker realizes that the same underlying essence exists in all beings, dissolving all apparent differences. This knowledge is not just intellectual but an experiential understanding that liberates one from samsara—the cycle of birth and death.

To experience Brahman as the Supreme Reality, one must go beyond indirect knowledge, which remains conceptual. The Vigjnanam, or highest knowledge, comes through direct experience, where the seeker realizes their oneness with Brahman. Brahman is not an object to be understood through the intellect but is the very foundation of all existence. The Upanishads describe Brahman as Bhuma—the infinite, where no otherness exists. In this realization, there is only unity, and one perceives everything as the Self, leading to ultimate freedom and peace.

A key aspect of Brahma Jnana is the distinction between names and forms (Nama-Rupa) and the essential reality behind them. While the world is filled with diversity and differences in appearance, the realized individual sees these as mere illusions, understanding that all distinctions are superimposed on the unchanging Brahman. Just as a pot may have different shapes but remains clay at its core, all forms and beings are expressions of the same Brahman. This recognition of unity in diversity is at the heart of non-duality.

Amma emphasizes that liberation is not something to be sought outside but realized within. The journey inward, through meditation and contemplation, reveals the true nature of the Self, which is infinite, unchanging, and identical with Brahman. This inward focus allows the seeker to purify the mind, dispel ignorance, and directly experience the truth of non-duality. Only when the seeker turns away from the distractions of the external world and focuses inward can they realize the eternal oneness that underlies all of existence.

Furthermore, the purification of the mind is essential in this journey. As Amma notes, ignorance and doubts cloud the understanding of the Self. The mind, filled with desires and attachments, obstructs the light of knowledge. Through self-inquiry, meditation, and devotion to the Guru, the mind becomes purified, enabling the seeker to experience the direct, unmediated knowledge of Brahman. The process of shravana (listening), manana (reflection), and nididhyasana (meditation) helps dissolve ignorance, leading to the direct experience of the Self.

In understanding the non-dual nature of Brahman, the distinctions of subject and object, knower and known, dissolve. The seeker realizes that Brahman is the substratum of all experience, not just an external object to be known. This is the ultimate realization of non-duality, where the individual merges with the universal Self, and all experiences of duality fall away. In this state, one transcends the limitations of the body, mind, and world, experiencing the boundless freedom of Brahman.

The journey toward this realization is deeply connected to discrimination (viveka) and detachment (vairagya). Discrimination allows the seeker to distinguish between the real (Brahman) and the unreal (the world of appearances). Detachment helps in loosening the grip of worldly attachments, enabling the mind to focus inward. With these tools, the seeker can move beyond the limitations of names and forms, recognizing their essential oneness with Brahman.

Amma's teaching also highlights the role of the Guru in this journey. The Guru is the embodiment of the knowledge of Brahman and serves as a guide for the seeker, helping them navigate the path of self-realization. Through devotion and surrender to the Guru, the seeker can overcome the obstacles of ignorance and ego, receiving the grace necessary for the ultimate realization of oneness with Brahman. The Guru's teachings help the seeker understand that the Self and Brahman are not separate but are one and the same.

In this state of realization, the individual no longer sees themselves as a separate entity. The Tatwa Jnani (knower of truth) recognizes that all distinctions—between self and other, body and mind—are illusory projections of the mind. The Atma (Self) is infinite, formless, and ever-present, beyond the limitations of time and space. This understanding brings about the dissolution of all fears, attachments, and desires, leading to liberation.

Finally, the realization of non-duality brings with it a profound sense of peace and freedom. The individual who has realized their oneness with Brahman is no longer bound by the cycles of karma, nor are they affected by the dualities of pleasure and pain, success and failure. They live in a state of equanimity, recognizing that all actions are part of the divine flow. In this state of liberation, the individual abides in the eternal, unchanging bliss of the Self, free from all limitations and suffering.

In conclusion, Brahma Jnana, as Amma points out, is not about acquiring external knowledge but realizing the truth of the Self within. Through the purification of the mind, the guidance of the Guru, and the practice of self-inquiry, the seeker attains the direct knowledge of Brahman. This knowledge reveals the oneness of all existence, dissolving the illusions of duality and leading to liberation.

Love is Presence

"The oneness of the Self is pure love. When we realize that all are expressions of the same divine essence, love flows naturally, without boundaries, embracing all beings as one." Amma

Amma's profound teaching that "the oneness of the Self is pure love" echoes the essence of the Upanishads, particularly the teachings of Tat Tvam Asi ("Thou art That") from the Chandogya Upanishad, which reveals the inherent unity between the individual soul (Atman) and the ultimate reality (Brahman). This oneness reflects the understanding that everything in existence is an expression of the same divine essence, and when we internalize this, love naturally flows. This love is not confined to personal attachments or relationships but is boundless, extending to all beings as expressions of the same Self. The realization that we are part of this wholeness transforms our perception of the world, allowing love to arise effortlessly as the purest form of existence.

In the Brihadaranyaka Upanishad (I.iv.10), it is said, "Sarvam Khalvidam Brahma" ("All this is Brahman"), emphasizing that all beings and the entire universe are manifestations of the one, undivided reality. Amma's teaching complements this understanding perfectly. When we recognize that everything we encounter—people, nature, experiences—are all expressions of the same divine essence, we dissolve the barriers that divide us. This boundless love, which flows from the recognition of unity, is not shaped by preferences or biases. It is unconditional and universal, embracing all without distinction. This state of love is the natural outcome of perceiving the oneness of all life.

This recognition of unity and love also profoundly shifts our understanding of relationships. The Isha Upanishad (verse 6) tells us, "He who sees all beings in his own Self, and his own Self in all beings, loses all fear." When we begin to see others as not separate individuals but as reflections of the same Self within us, we transcend the limitations of ego and separateness. This oneness fosters compassion, empathy, and a deeper connection to all life, nurturing peace and harmony. It encourages us to see the world not through the lens of division, but as an interconnected, living whole.

Rather than viewing life as a series of isolated events or individuals as disconnected entities, this Vedantic perspective, aligned with Amma's teaching, presents life as a unified whole. The Katha Upanishad (II.2.13) reminds us: "As pure water poured into pure water becomes the same, so becomes the Self of the knower of Brahman." The oneness of life is not an abstract concept but a lived reality that can be experienced in every moment. When we realize that all forms and experiences are but different expressions of the same underlying reality, we transcend duality and experience our natural state of existence—Beingness.

The Taittiriya Upanishad (II.7) teaches that "Brahman is Satyam, Jnanam, and Anantam" (truth, knowledge, and infinity). When we recognize the oneness of the Self as pure love, as Amma describes, we come to a profound realization that everything—whether relationships, actions, or experiences—reflects the same divine essence. This understanding dissolves the boundaries that separate us from others and the world, leading to a life of love, unity, and inner peace. It is a recognition that there is nowhere to go, for we are already one with all that exists, and love is the presence that holds everything together. This is the highest teaching of the Upanishads, brought to life through Amma's words.

CHAPTER-5

Dissolution of Ego and the Unchanging Self

Innate Nature

"True liberation is beyond form, where the Self is free from all superimposed identities. For the realized one, there is no lack in bliss or freedom, as both are ever-present in the fullness of knowledge." Amma

This quote encapsulates the essence of aroopa mukthi—superimposed forms or liberation from the bondage of form and identity. This form of liberation is essential for those who are still entangled in the illusions of the material world, where forms create a sense of separation and limitation. However, for a Tatwa Jnani—a realized being who has transcended the duality of form and formlessness—there is no such attachment or need for liberation. They have already realized their true nature as the infinite Self, which is beyond all forms.

The Tatwa Jnani lives in the awareness of paripurnam, or complete fullness. This fullness is not something they seek to attain but is their natural state of being. The forms and appearances that bind others are irrelevant to the Jnani, as they no longer see distinctions between form and formlessness. For them, the experience of liberation is not about moving away from form but about abiding in the realization that all forms are expressions of the same non-dual reality. The Tatwa Jnani does not reject forms but sees them as part of the ever-present, unchanging Self.

For the realized being, the concept of aroopa mukthi—liberation from form—is irrelevant because they have already transcended the limitations of form through the direct experience of the Self. There is no longer a need to liberate oneself from anything, as the Tatwa Jnani lives in the constant awareness of their true nature as Brahman, the ultimate reality. This awareness frees them from all concepts of duality and separation, allowing them to remain in a state of complete and undisturbed liberation.

While others may strive to transcend form to experience liberation, the Tatwa Jnani is already established in the realization that there is no real distinction between form and formlessness. In the state of paripurnam—complete knowledge—the Tatwa Jnani recognizes that all forms are merely expressions of the same underlying reality. There is no need to escape or reject form, as form itself is not an obstacle to liberation. Instead, it is the false identification with form that creates the illusion of bondage.

Ultimately, the Tatwa Jnani's experience of liberation is one of wholeness and completeness. There is no sense of lack or incompleteness, as the Tatwa Jnani is fully established in the knowledge of the Self. The dualities of form and formlessness, bondage and liberation, no longer hold any meaning for the realized one, as they have transcended all distinctions and experience the infinite bliss of non-duality.

Thus, for the Tatwa Jnani, aroopa mukthi is not an external goal but a natural state of being. They are free from all superimposed identities and attachments to form, living in the constant awareness of the eternal Self. This realization brings with it the ultimate freedom and bliss, as the Tatwa Jnani abides in the infinite and unchanging truth of Brahman.

Self-Knowledge Unveils Unity

"True understanding arises from the direct perception of oneness, where knowledge transcends names and forms. In realizing the Self as Brahman, we see that ignorance has no real existence, and what remains is the eternal truth beyond concepts and perceptions." Amma

Amma's quote perfectly aligns with the core teaching of Advaita Vedanta—the non-dual nature of reality. The realization of the Self as Brahman represents the dissolution of avidya (ignorance), which falsely presents the world of forms and distinctions as real. When one perceives this unity, there is a profound recognition that the dualities of speaker and listener, subject and object, are mere illusions.

The Self, being infinite and unchanging, remains untouched by any experience or conceptual framework. This is illustrated in the state of sushupthi (deep sleep), where no duality is experienced. In this state, the mind is absent, and there is no awareness of separateness, yet existence continues uninterrupted. The buddhi (intellect) cannot comprehend or negate the reality of the Self, for it operates within the realm of duality, while the Self is beyond such distinctions. Therefore, all experiences and perceptions that seem to be separate from the Self are ultimately anirvachaniyam (indescribable or unreal).

The shift from ignorance to knowledge, known as sankramanam, is not a physical or mental movement. It is a subtle shift in understanding where one comes to see the truth of non-duality. The dissolution of ignorance reveals that the Self is always present and unchanging, and jnanam (knowledge) merely removes the veil of ignorance. This does not imply a new experience but the realization of what has always been—paramanandam (supreme bliss), which is inherent in the Self. Since the Self is beyond duality, it is established in abhayam (fearlessness), for in non-duality, there is no second entity to cause fear.

Thus, through Atma Jnana (Self-knowledge), the individual dissolves the false identifications with the body, mind, and ego, and recognizes the one, indivisible reality that pervades all existence. This realization brings about the end of duality and the full understanding that there is nothing other than the Self, which is Brahman. All that remains is the timeless, eternal truth, beyond the limits of perception and conceptualization.

Awakening to Consciousness

"Consciousness, the ultimate reality, remains pure and untouched by ignorance or enlightenment. True wisdom comes from realizing that Consciousness itself is eternal and unchanging, beyond the fleeting states of the mind." Amma

The nature of nescience (avidya), as described in Advaita Vedanta, is both beginningless and incomprehensible. It is not something tangible but exists in relation to pure Consciousness, relying on it for its apparent existence. This avidya is the root cause of the internal organ, or antahkarana (mind), which undergoes transformation based on its inherent qualities—sattva (purity) or tamas (ignorance). When the internal organ is influenced by sattva, it manifests as clear knowledge, while tamas gives rise to error and delusion. However, these transformations do not affect Consciousness itself.

The antahkarana is like a mirror that reflects Consciousness, but the reflection may appear either pure or distorted, depending on the condition of the mind. Consciousness, being the eternal observer, remains unchanged regardless of the state of the internal organ. Just as light may appear colored when passed through a colored lens, Consciousness may appear as enlightened or deluded based on the mind's state. But in truth, Consciousness itself is beyond both states, remaining unchanging, pure, and untouched by mental modifications.

Avidya exists solely because of a lack of understanding of the true nature of Consciousness. It leads to the mistaken belief that Consciousness is subject to the transformations of the mind and senses. However, this nescience is not a real quality of Consciousness but an illusion created by ignorance. The internal organ, influenced by sattva or tamas, manifests knowledge or error, but these are merely attributes of the mind. They have no bearing on Consciousness, which is ever-pure and self-luminous.

The reflection of Consciousness upon the mind results in various experiences—of knowledge, ignorance, pleasure, and pain. Yet, these experiences do not alter the true nature of Consciousness, just as the sun remains unaffected by the reflections it casts on water.

To realize true enlightenment, one must perceive the Self as independent of mental transformations, understanding that the fluctuations of knowledge and ignorance belong to the mind alone. The Self is beyond duality, always self-luminous and eternal. This realization is the dissolution of avidya, allowing the seeker to experience the true, unchanging nature of Consciousness.

The final step toward enlightenment involves recognizing that Consciousness is ever-free from ignorance and error. Once this realization dawns, all delusion dissolves, and the individual sees that the Self is neither bound by nor dependent on mental states. The individual comes to rest in the eternal, pure light of Consciousness, recognizing it as the one true reality, beyond all mental constructs.

In this state of realization, as Amma teaches, the light of Consciousness shines clearly, revealing the essence of our being as pure and infinite. The seeker no longer identifies with the mind's transformations but remains rooted in the eternal presence of the Self, experiencing the boundless peace and bliss of true liberation.

The Bliss of Being

"The realization that 'I am love' dissolves the separation between the individual and the universal. In this oneness, we recognize that the Self and Ishwara are the same—boundless, all-knowing, and ever-present within all." Amma

Amma's profound statement, "I am Love," captures the essence of Advaita Vedanta, the philosophy of non-duality. It emphasizes the ultimate realization that the individual self (jiva) and the universal Self (Ishwara) are not separate entities but one and the same. This understanding reveals the oneness of all existence and dissolves the illusion of separateness, leading to the recognition of the Self as identical with Ishwara.

The recognition that "I am love" leads to the dissolution of fear and separation. The jnani understands that Ishwara and the Self are one, and this realization brings about a profound sense of fearlessness (abhayam). There is no "other" to fear because there is no distinction between the individual and the universal. The jnani resides in a state of inner peace, free from the limitations imposed by duality.

This understanding also brings about moksha (liberation), where the individual is freed from the cycle of birth and death (samsara). The karmic cycle—which binds individuals to the consequences of their actions—loses its hold on the jnani. With the dissolution of the ego and the recognition of oneness, the jnani is no longer bound by karma, as they are no longer acting from the standpoint of separateness.

The bliss of the Self (Ananda) is not something external that the individual must seek; it is the innate nature of the Self. In realizing this, the jnani experiences Sahaja Ananda—a natural, spontaneous bliss that arises from the understanding of non-duality. This state of bliss is unconditional, as it is not dependent on external circumstances or experiences.

Amma's teaching encourages seekers to look beyond the limitations of the ego and the body-mind complex. By turning inward and contemplating the true nature of the Self, one can transcend the illusions of the waking state and experience the infinite bliss that is the true nature of existence. This self-knowledge leads to the recognition that the Self and Ishwara are not two, but one.

In conclusion, Amma's statement, "I am Love," is a call to realize the non-dual nature of the Self and Ishwara. By recognizing this oneness, one transcends the illusions of duality, dissolving the false separation between the individual and the universal. In this realization, the seeker experiences the infinite, boundless bliss that is the essence of both the Self and Ishwara, leading to liberation and the ultimate truth beyond all concepts and perceptions.

Atma the Reality

"The Atma sees no difference, only oneness, while the ego creates the illusion of separation. When we negate this sense of separation, we discover true love—love that flows from the understanding that we are all one." Amma

The Atma, or true Self, is the essence of non-differentiation, perceiving no separation between itself and the universe. This realization of oneness is the cornerstone of Advaita Vedanta, where the Self is understood as indivisible from the world and the source of all existence. As stated in the Brihadaranyaka Upanishad : "He who sees all beings in his own Self, and his own Self in all beings, loses all fear." In this state of awareness, there is no distinction between the individual and the universe. In contrast, the ego introduces a sense of separation, creating distinctions between the self and others, between the subject and the object. This illusion of duality is the root of suffering and ignorance.

The concept of Sarvaananyatha—the absence of any differentiation or "otherness"—is central to this understanding. The Chandogya Upanishad (6.1.4) expresses this through the example of clay: "All modification is only a name based upon words; the clay alone is real." Similarly, the Atma, like gold in an ornament, is the substance behind all forms. The various appearances in the world—just as gold takes on many forms as ornaments—are not separate from their underlying reality. Brahman, the ultimate truth, is the essential substance, while the world of forms and names is temporary and dependent on it. Mundaka Upanishad (2.1.10) elaborates, saying, "Brahman is the only truth; the world is an illusion. The soul is nothing but Brahman." When one truly grasps this, the illusion of separation dissolves, and the reality of oneness becomes clear.

When we transcend the ego and its illusory projections, we discover true love—a love that arises from the recognition of oneness. As the Isha Upanishad (verse 6) states, "He who sees all beings in the very Self, and the Self in all beings, feels no hatred by virtue of that (realisation)." This love is not limited or conditional, as it does not see "the other" as separate. Instead, it flows from the understanding that all beings are expressions of the same underlying reality. This realization brings compassion and universal love, for the distinctions between "Self" and "other" dissolve in the light of Atma Jnana (Self-knowledge).

The world and its myriad forms, which appear distinct and separate, are ultimately unreal when compared to the underlying truth of Brahman. The Just as gold remains gold regardless of the shape it takes as an ornament, the world, with all its forms and distinctions, remains one with Brahman. To realize this truth is to transcend the illusion of separateness and to abide in the knowledge that everything is one. Therefore, Upanishad teaches that in the ultimate state of reality, there is "neither inside nor outside, neither diversity nor duality." It is the pure non-dual state where the Self alone remains, and everything else is recognized as a mere play of illusion.

When we negate the sense of separation, we realize that what we had taken to be distinct entities were, in fact, all part of the same Brahma, the eternal and unchanging reality. The sense of duality fades, and what remains is the oneness of existence—the knowledge that all forms and names are temporary, but the essence, the Atma, is eternal.

In conclusion, Amma's teaching encourages us to move beyond the ego's illusions of division and to see the world through the eyes of the Atma, which recognizes only unity. In doing so, we discover true love, the love that comes from the understanding of oneness, and we realize that Brahma is the ultimate reality, beyond all distinctions and forms. This understanding brings about a profound inner peace and the dissolution of all illusions, revealing the Atma as the eternal and boundless reality behind all appearances.

Ishwara Viewpoint

"Knowledge dispels ignorance, revealing the truth of our existence, yet it does not grant the power to change the world—only Ishwara holds that capacity. Even after realizing the oneness of the Self, we remain instruments in the hands of the Divine, with all actions flowing through Ishwara's will." Amma

The essence of non-duality (Advaita) is found in the teaching that jiva (the individual self) and Ishwara (God) are not two distinct entities, but share the same underlying reality—Brahman. The perception of separateness, which creates duality, is due to avidya (ignorance). Through Atma jnana (Self-knowledge), this illusion of separateness is dissolved, and the individual realizes their unity with Ishwara. This realization leads to fearlessness, as all sense of "otherness" fades, and there is nothing external left to fear.

However, while knowledge can remove the illusion of duality and bring one to the realization of oneness, it does not grant the individual the power to change the world or alter reality itself. Only Ishwara, the supreme reality, holds the capacity to govern the universe. Even after one attains Atma jnana, they remain an instrument of the divine, acting according to Ishwara's will. In this sense, the realized being surrenders their personal will, understanding that all actions are simply the expressions of the divine will manifesting through them.

Therefore, the removal of fear and the experience of liberation do not come from an attempt to control or change the external world. Instead, they arise from the inner realization that the individual self is one with Ishwara, that the apparent differences are illusory, and that all actions are part of the divine play. This understanding leads to profound peace and allows the individual to move through life with equanimity, free from the illusions that once bound them

Ultimate Unchanging Reality

"The real and unreal are not separate; they arise from the same source. When we see beyond the illusion of duality, we recognize that all is rooted in the same divine essence." Amma

Sat (the ultimate reality) and Mithya (the apparent reality) are understood not as two distinct entities but as two aspects of the same foundational truth—Brahman. This view is encapsulated in the phrase "Sathyam abhavath yadidham kincha," meaning that everything in the world exists only because of Brahman, the unchanging reality. All that we perceive, from the forms and names that make up the world (nama and rupa), is a manifestation of this singular, divine essence.

Mithya, or the apparent reality, refers to the transient, changing world of experiences that we encounter daily. While these experiences seem real, they are ultimately dependent on Brahman. This does not mean that Mithya is false, but rather that it is a temporary expression of the eternal truth, Sat. Mithya, with all its changing forms, exists as a surface level of reality, while Brahman—unchanging and eternal—forms the true foundation of all existence.

According to Amma's teachings and Advaita Vedanta, the journey of self-realization involves recognizing this non-duality. The seeker is guided to see beyond the illusion of separateness, where the world of diversity appears to be distinct from the Self. However, through deeper understanding, one realizes that all creation is a reflection of the same underlying reality, Brahman. This realization dissolves the false perceptions of duality and reveals the oneness of existence.

When one comes to fully understand their true nature as Brahman, they move beyond the distractions and entanglements of the material world. The focus shifts from the external appearances of creation to the inner self, which is an expression of the same Brahman that pervades all things. This realization is the key to moksha (liberation), where the individual no longer identifies with the body-mind complex but instead with the infinite and eternal Brahman.

The teachings of Advaita emphasize that this non-duality is not something to be acquired, but something that is innately present and simply needs to be realized. Once this realization occurs, the individual transcends the illusion of separateness, recognizing that all forms and names in the world are merely temporary manifestations of the one Brahman. There is nothing truly separate, nothing independent of the divine essence.

In this state of realization, one sees that Sat and Mithya are not opposing forces but complementary aspects of the same reality. While Mithya represents the changing, visible world, it is not apart from Brahman—the eternal truth that underlies all. This profound understanding of the oneness of reality leads to peace, liberation, and the dissolution of all duality.

Immutable Self

"When duality is dissolved, the illusion of separateness fades, and what remains is the absolute bliss of oneness. In this state, we experience the pure joy of the Self, eternal and unchanging." Amma

The root cause of fear, suffering, and the perception of duality in our lives is avidya (ignorance). It is avidya that creates the illusion of separateness, making us believe that we are distinct from others, the world, and even the divine. This false perception gives rise to vulnerability, impermanence, and the fear of loss or harm. In contrast, the state of nonduality (Advaita), which is the realization that there is no second entity or "other," is free from fear. Once this realization occurs, fear dissolves because there is no longer anything external to fear.

For an ajnani (one who is ignorant), the world of nama rupa (name and form) appears to be the ultimate reality. This perception of multiplicity is akin to someone with a vision defect seeing two moons in the sky. Just as the extra moon is an illusion caused by physical impairment, the perception of duality and separation is the result of ignorance. The ajnani remains trapped in this world of forms, experiencing suffering, attachment, and fear due to the belief in separation from the true Self.

However, for the Vidhwan (one who has realized their swaswarupam—their true nature), the false identification with the body, mind, and world dissolves through the realization of Advaita bhavam (the nondual understanding). This profound realization negates the samsaric identification of being a samsari (a bound individual subject to suffering). The Vidhwan transcends the illusions of duality and sees the underlying oneness of all existence—Atma (the Self). In this state of nondual awareness, they recognize that external circumstances, such as disease or death, have no real impact on their true nature.

Through this realization, the Vidhwan achieves abhayam (fearlessness). Since fear is rooted in the perception of "otherness," when the false sense of separateness is dissolved, fear can no longer exist. Alongside fearlessness comes anandham (bliss) and shanthi (peace), as the Vidhwan experiences the joy of their true nature, which is free from all forms of suffering. This joy is not fleeting, like the pleasures of the material world, but an enduring bliss that comes from recognizing one's oneness with Brahman, the infinite and eternal reality.

In this state of nonduality, the individual no longer sees themselves as a separate entity moving through a world of others. They understand that they are not distinct from the world or from Brahman, the supreme reality. This understanding dissolves all notions of duality, and the Vidhwan rests in the pure, blissful awareness of their own true nature, untouched by the fluctuations and challenges of the external world.

Thus, the Vidhwan experiences liberation from suffering, fear, and bondage through the realization of the Atma as the one unchanging reality. In this state, there is nothing external to fear, and the individual abides in the eternal peace of oneness with the divine. Amma's teaching guides us to recognize this truth within ourselves, encouraging us to move beyond duality and experience the immutable bliss of the Self.

The Right Knowledge

"The highest attainment is realizing the Self. Through the knowledge of who we truly are, all doubts dissolve, and we come to rest in the infinite peace and bliss of our own divine nature." Amma

The realization of the Self is considered the highest and most transformative attainment in Advaita Vedanta. This knowledge, often referred to as Atma Jnana (Self-knowledge), marks the end of ignorance (avidya), which is the root cause of suffering and worldly bondage. When one understands their true nature, they see beyond the illusions of the material world and external attachments. This understanding dissolves all misconceptions, bringing profound inner peace and liberation from the cycle of birth and death.

The Upanishads highlight the necessity of this knowledge, asserting that "the knower of the ultimate reality reaches the highest." This statement underlines the supreme value of realizing the Self—for it is only through this knowledge that one can be free from the limitations imposed by the body, mind, and external influences. Ignorance creates the illusion of separateness and attachment to worldly experiences, causing an individual to remain bound to suffering. By knowing the Self, these false identifications are eradicated, revealing the infinite and unchanging reality that lies at the core of existence.

Just as the acquisition of any practical skill requires effort and understanding of its usefulness, the pursuit of Self-knowledge also begins with the recognition of its importance. When the seeker understands the transformative power of this knowledge, they are motivated to engage in the spiritual practices that lead to realization. The journey toward Self-realization involves the progressive steps of shravanam (listening), mananam (reflection), and nididhyasana (meditation). These steps provide the seeker with a structured approach to internalize and directly experience the truth of their divine nature.

Through shravanam, the individual listens to the teachings of the Upanishads and other sacred texts. These teachings plant the seeds of inquiry and begin to shift the seeker's perception from the outer world to the inner reality. Mananam, or reflection, allows the individual to contemplate the teachings deeply, clarifying doubts and intellectually understanding the nature of the Self. This reflective process helps remove the misconceptions that arise from habitual thinking patterns, clearing the way for deeper insights.

However, mananam alone is not sufficient for complete realization. The final step, nididhyasana, or meditation, leads the seeker into direct experience. Through meditation, the seeker transcends intellectual knowledge and enters the realm of aparoksha anubhuti (direct realization), where they experience the Self without the interference of the mind and ego. This experience of the Self brings a permanent end to doubts, suffering, and the limitations of worldly existence.

Ultimately, the pursuit of Self-knowledge is the path to moksha (liberation). It frees the individual from the cycle of samsara (worldly existence) and allows them to abide in their true nature, which is beyond time, space, and causality. In this state of oneness with Brahman, there is no longer a sense of separation, only the realization of the indivisible, absolute truth that underlies all creation. The knower of the Self lives in this liberated state, free from the limitations of the mind and body, resting in the boundless ananda (bliss) of their divine essence.

Self Shines Unaffected

"Existence, consciousness, and bliss may seem to imply duality, but the true Self transcends all opposites. The role of the Guru and scriptures is to remove the veil of ignorance, allowing the direct experience of the eternal oneness that is our true nature." Amma

In Advaita Vedanta, the Self (Atma) is often described through the attributes of sat (existence), chit (consciousness), and anandam (bliss). While these qualities convey the nature of the Atma, they can also create a perception of duality. For example, we might interpret "existence" as contrasting with "non-existence" or "bliss" with "suffering." These dualistic notions arise from the mind's tendency to categorize experiences in opposites, limiting our understanding to relative, conditioned thinking.

However, the Atma transcends all such oppositions. It is not bound by dualities like existence versus non-existence or consciousness versus unconsciousness. The Atma stands beyond these distinctions, as it is the non-dual reality where all such differences dissolve. It cannot be grasped through comparisons or intellectual definitions, as it is the ultimate, unchanging essence behind all experiences. The Atma does not exist in relation to anything else—it is the ground of all being, where dualities vanish, and only oneness remains.

The Atma is not something that can be grasped as an object of knowledge, nor can it be perceived by the senses or comprehended intellectually. Unlike other objects that we can observe, understand, and define, the Atma is the subject of all knowledge. It is the awareness that allows all experiences to be perceived, but it cannot itself be perceived as an object. The scriptures and the Guru act as guides on the path, helping to clear away the ignorance (avidya) that clouds our understanding of the Self.

The Guru and scriptures do not "reveal" the Atma in the way we reveal an external object. Their role is to direct the seeker's attention inward, to point out the Self that is already present but obscured by ignorance. Through teachings, self-inquiry, and meditation, the seeker is led to realize the truth that was always there: that the Atma is the eternal, changeless reality underlying all appearances. The Atma is already self-luminous, meaning it reveals itself without needing anything external to illumine it. The problem is not with the Atma itself but with the seeker's identification with the body, mind, and ego. These limited identifications create the illusion of separateness and veil the true nature of the Self. The teachings serve to remove this veil of ignorance, allowing the Atma to be known not as an object of experience but as the subject—the pure awareness that underlies all experiences.

As Amma suggests, liberation lies not in achieving something new or external, but in recognizing the Atma's eternal presence. The Guru and scriptures play a crucial role in guiding seekers, but ultimately, the realization of the Atma is a direct, personal experience—a moment when all false identifications fall away, and the true nature of the Self is known. This is aparoksha jnanam, direct knowledge of the Atma as one's own essential nature.

In this state of direct realization, the dualities of existence/non-existence and bliss/suffering no longer apply. The seeker, now a jnani (knower of the Self), understands that the Atma is the eternal, unchanging reality. This knowledge brings about liberation from the cycles of fear, suffering, and ignorance, allowing the individual to rest in the infinite peace and bliss that is their true essence, ever-present and unaffected by the world of change.

CHAPTER-6

Realization and Freedom

The Illusion of Doership

"The realization of non-dual consciousness reveals that the Self and Brahman are one, free from all illusions of separateness. True knowledge dissolves the false 'I' and 'mine,' allowing the light of the eternal Self to shine, untouched by ignorance." Amma

Advaita Vigjnanam, or the knowledge of non-duality, brings about the profound realization of Paramatma bhava—the recognition that the jiva (individual self) is not separate from Brahman (the ultimate reality). When this realization occurs, the Brahmajnani (one who knows Brahman) no longer sees themselves as an individual entity possessing knowledge about Brahman, but as Brahman itself. This state of being transcends the limitations of individuality, as the Brahmajnani understands their true nature as the infinite, formless, and undivided reality of Brahman.

The Brahmajnani is free from the shackles of ajnanam (ignorance), which had previously created the illusion of identification with the koshas (the five sheaths that cover the Self: physical body, energy, mind, intellect, and bliss sheath). These layers, perceived through ignorance, foster the false belief in a separate self, bound by the notions of "I" and "mine." This identification with the koshas leads to the dualistic perception of separation between the individual and the rest of creation, perpetuating a cycle of attachment and suffering.

The purpose of vidhya (knowledge) is to dispel avidya (ignorance) and its consequences. Vidhya acts as the antidote to ignorance, gradually removing the false identification with the body and mind. Once the Brahmajnani comprehends that their true essence is beyond the confines of the koshas, they understand that the Atma (Self) is not a distinct entity but one with Brahman—the infinite, unchanging reality.

As vidhya removes the darkness of ignorance, the light of self-knowledge begins to shine. In this light, all distinctions and dualities that were once considered real are revealed as illusions, projections of the limited mind. Once avidya is dissolved, the individual no longer perceives themselves as a separate being but as the eternal, undivided Brahman. The realization of this oneness leads to complete liberation from the cycles of samsara (birth and death).

In this state of non-dual realization, the individual recognizes that there is no longer a "doer" acting independently, as all actions are seen as part of the divine play orchestrated by Ishwara (the supreme divine). The false ego, which had previously claimed ownership of actions and experiences, dissolves completely. What remains is the pure Atma, shining in its natural state, free from the bondage of individual identity and ignorance.

Through this realization, the Brahmajnani experiences a deep sense of ananda (bliss) and purnam (completeness). This state of eternal bliss and fulfillment is not dependent on external circumstances or achievements, but is the natural, ever-present essence of the Self. The individual, now liberated from the limitations of ignorance, abides in the realization of oneness with Brahman, experiencing the ultimate freedom and peace that come from true self-knowledge.

Thus, vidhya leads the seeker beyond the illusions of duality and separateness, bringing them into the light of the eternal Self, where liberation and bliss are the natural state of being

Ego the Illusion

"The Atma is the infinite, the entirety of existence, while the ego is the source of limitation and separateness. When we dissolve the ego, we realize the boundless nature of the Self, which is ever whole and free." Amma

The Atma, or the Self, is the infinite essence that underlies all of creation. Unlike the ego, which imposes limitations and separateness, the Atma is boundless and limitless, encompassing the entirety of existence. The ego is the illusion (maya) that creates a sense of division between the individual and the rest of creation, leading to the belief in duality. The Atma, however, remains untouched by these limitations. It is the true, unchanging reality that transcends all forms of separation imposed by the ego.

Atma's nature as infinite means it is beyond the confines of space and time. It cannot be categorized or restricted by any intellectual constructs. The vastness of creation, with all its forms, is merely an expression of this limitless essence. However, the finite mind struggles to comprehend the infinite because it is conditioned by dualistic thinking and limited by its attachment to the body and ego. The ego, being the source of this limitation, perceives itself as a separate entity within the universe, causing fear, desire, and suffering.

In contrast, the Atma, like space, is ever-present and not confined to any particular form or location. Space exists within everything, just as the Atma pervades all beings and objects. It is the substratum of existence, the unchanging reality upon which the transient world of names and forms appears. The ego, by falsely identifying with the body and mind, creates the illusion of being an individual entity, distinct from the Atma. This false identification is the root of all suffering and separation.

Dissolving the ego is the key to realizing the true nature of the Self. The ego gives rise to the sense of "I" and "mine," creating attachments to the body, mind, and external objects. These attachments bind the individual to the cycle of birth and death, perpetuating the illusion of separateness. When the ego is dissolved through self-inquiry, meditation, and the grace of the Guru, the individual realizes that they are not the limited body or mind but the infinite Atma. This realization brings freedom from the limitations of the ego and reveals the boundless nature of the Self.

In this state of self-realization, the individual experiences the Atma as whole, complete, and ever-free. There is no longer any sense of lack or incompleteness, as the individual recognizes their oneness with the infinite. The ego's limitations dissolve, and with them, the false perception of duality. What remains is the experience of non-duality (Advaita), where the Self is seen as the one reality that pervades all of creation. This state of realization brings about a profound sense of peace and bliss, as the individual is no longer subject to the fluctuations of the mind and external circumstances.

This understanding of the Atma as infinite and beyond all boundaries leads to the realization that the ego is nothing more than an illusion. It is a false construct that obscures the true nature of the Self. By recognizing the ego's illusory nature and dissolving its hold, one can experience the Atma in its fullness, free from the limitations of separateness and division. In this state, the individual no longer identifies with the small self (the ego) but with the universal Self that is present in all things.

Thus, Amma's teaching reminds us that the dissolution of the ego is the path to the realization of the infinite, ever-whole Atma. When the ego's illusion is dispelled, the individual recognizes their true nature as one with the entirety of existence, beyond all limitations and boundaries. This is the ultimate freedom—the realization of the Self as boundless, eternal, and free.

Self-Knowledge

"Realizing the true nature of Paramatma dissolves all doubts and fears, revealing the formless and infinite essence within. The wise are free from ignorance and rest in the truth, while those bound by ignorance remain caught in illusion and separation." Amma

Attaining the realization of Paramatma Tatwa—the understanding of the Supreme Self—requires dispelling both ajnana (ignorance) and samsaya (doubt) about the formless and attributeless nature of Paramatma. Ignorance gives rise to the illusion that we are separate from the supreme reality, causing us to identify with the body, mind, and ego. This false identification results in suffering, fear, and attachment to the impermanent experiences of the material world.

When ignorance is removed, one realizes the true nature of Paramatma, which is beyond all forms and attributes. Paramatma is the ultimate, indivisible reality that pervades everything. This realization naturally leads to abhayam (fearlessness) because the individual transcends the changes and fluctuations of the world and the false sense of self. In this state of realization, all sense of separation dissolves, and there is no longer any fear of loss, harm, or death, as the Self is understood to be eternal, formless, and unchanging.

The difference between a Vidhwan (wise person) and an Avidhwan (ignorant person) lies in their understanding of Paramatma Tatwa. The Vidhwan has overcome ignorance and doubt, fully realizing that their true nature is one with Paramatma. They see through the veil of avidya (ignorance) and recognize that all distinctions are false projections created by the mind. As a result, the Vidhwan lives in a state of fearlessness, inner peace, and freedom, unaffected by the transient nature of worldly experiences.

For the Avidhwan, however, ignorance continues to cloud their perception of reality. This ignorance creates a false sense of identity and separation, leading to doubts about the nature of the Self and the supreme reality. The Avidhwan remains caught in the cycle of fear, attachment, and suffering, unable to see beyond the illusion of duality. This keeps them trapped in the endless pursuit of temporary pleasures and avoidance of pain, without realizing the true nature of their being.

In essence, the realization of Paramatma Tatwa is what separates the wise from the ignorant. The Vidhwan, having dispelled ignorance, rests in the truth of non-duality, experiencing the bliss and peace of being one with the formless and attributeless Paramatma. This state of realization brings about a deep sense of unity with all of existence, where the individual recognizes their oneness with the entire cosmos.

Meanwhile, the Avidhwan continues to be entangled in maya (illusion), perceiving the world through the distorted lens of ignorance. This ignorance perpetuates the cycle of birth and death, keeping them bound to the limitations of the body, mind, and ego. The Avidhwan is unaware that the supreme reality they seek lies within them, as their own true nature.

Therefore, the journey toward self-knowledge involves recognizing that the Self and Paramatma are not separate. It is through the dissolution of ignorance and the realization of this oneness that one attains true liberation, freeing themselves from the limitations of the ego and the illusion of separateness.

Wholeness

"The true fulfillment lies in knowing the infinite (Anantham) nature of the Self. When we realize the wholeness of the Atma, we experience a boundless peace, where there is no lack—only completeness and divine unity." Amma

The term Anantham, meaning "that which has no end," signifies the infinite and boundless nature of Brahman. It is a central concept in Advaita Vedanta, establishing that Brahman is beyond all limitations and restrictions. The recognition of Anantham negates the idea of nasa (destruction), asserting the permanence and eternal nature of Brahman. Similarly, the negation of parichinnathwam (limitedness) reinforces the all-encompassing quality of Brahman, pointing to the fact that there are no boundaries or divisions within the ultimate reality.

The Upanishads declare that Atma (the Self) is indeed Brahman. This profound statement reveals the identity of the individual self with the ultimate, non-dual reality. By recognizing the true nature of the Self, one realizes their essential oneness with Brahman. The use of the term Atma in place of Brahman signifies that there is no real distinction between the individual self and the infinite, except in terms of perception due to ignorance (avidya). In truth, the Self and Brahman are inherently connected, and this realization dissolves all sense of separation.

The true fulfillment that Amma speaks of lies not in intellectual understanding or theoretical knowledge about Brahman but in the direct realization of Brahman as one's own essential nature. While paroksha jnanam (indirect knowledge) may come from studying scriptures or listening to teachings, it is only through aparoksha jnanam (direct, experiential knowledge) that one fully recognizes their unity with Brahman. This internal contemplation and self-inquiry lead to the discovery that the Anandam (bliss) one seeks is not outside but is the very essence of one's being.

The Purvapakshi (objector) raises questions about how an individual, who appears to be parichinnam (limited), can be identical to Brahman, which is aparichinna (limitless). This objection is rooted in the difficulty of understanding how the finite self, conditioned by the body and mind, can be equated with the infinite, unconditioned reality of Brahman. The Purvapakshi also questions the notion of jnana kathruthwam (being the knower) and its identity with Brahman, suggesting that the role of the knower involves action and is thus subject to nasam (destruction), making it impermanent and dependent on external factors.

In addressing these objections, the Upanishads clarify that the limitations experienced by the individual self are the result of ignorance and not the true nature of the Self. Through knowledge (jnana), these limitations are negated, and one comes to recognize their eternal, infinite nature. The kathruthwam (doership) associated with the ego and the body-mind complex is seen as a temporary phenomenon, but the underlying consciousness (Atma) is unaffected by such limitations. It is not subject to change or destruction and remains ever-pure and formless.

Ultimately, understanding Anantham involves negating all notions of limitation and recognizing that Brahman is eternal and infinite. The Upanishads continuously emphasize the identity of the individual self with Brahman, guiding seekers toward the realization that their true nature is beyond form and limitation. By recognizing this, one attains true fulfillment, a state of wholeness where the illusion of separation dissolves, and the individual abides in the infinite bliss of their own essential nature.

In this realization, the Purvapakshi's concerns about limitations and the interpretation of Brahman as a doer are resolved. The individual recognizes that Brahman is not an actor bound by the results of actions but is the infinite substratum of all existence, free from all dualities. This leads to the ultimate experience of completeness and divine unity, where there is no lack, only the boundless peace that Amma describes.

Reality Beyond the Jiva

"Externally, the layers of the jiva and Ishwara may seem separate, but within, they are one. The essence of both is the same divine reality, waiting to be realized through inner reflection." Amma

Brahman, the ultimate reality, is often described as Sat-Chit-Ananda (existence, consciousness, and bliss). Yet, Brahman transcends the limitations imposed by the Pancha Kosas (the five sheaths) that veil the true nature of the Atma (Self). While the Anandamaya Kosha (the sheath of bliss) might seem to embody Brahman's blissful aspect, Brahman is not confined to this or any of the sheaths. The Pancha Kosas—Annamaya (physical body), Pranamaya (life force), Manomaya (mind), Vijnanamaya (intellect), and Anandamaya—are simply layers or coverings that obscure the true essence of the Self.

Through Pancha Kosa Viveka, a process of discernment, one can differentiate between the koshas and recognize that these layers are mere coverings, not the essence of the Self. Each kosha represents a different level of experience and existence, but they are not the ultimate reality. The Atma—the unchanging substratum—is like gold that remains unchanged despite being molded into various forms. The realization of Brahman requires transcending these koshas and understanding that they are not the Self but transient layers that must be transcended to grasp the ultimate truth of Brahman.

The significance of recognizing Brahman beyond the koshas lies in the realization that as long as one identifies with these sheaths, one remains trapped by Avidya (ignorance) and subject to suffering. The koshas create a sense of separation and individuality, which perpetuates the illusion of duality. Without the knowledge that Brahman is the all-pervading Atma, individuals experience life as fragmented, disconnected from the underlying reality. They remain bound by concepts, dualities, and false identifications, leading to confusion and dissatisfaction.

By moving beyond identification with the koshas, one transcends the limitations of the body, mind, and intellect. The koshas are seen for what they are: tools for navigating the relative world, but not the true Self. Through self-inquiry and the guidance of the Guru, one can dissolve the attachments to these layers, leading to the realization of Brahman, which is the unchanging reality underlying all experiences.

The vikalpas (conceptual distinctions) created by the mind and intellect further cloud the perception of Brahman. These mental constructs arise from the limitations of human understanding, confining one to a world of distinctions and categories. Yet, Brahman is beyond all conceptualization and intellectual definitions. It is directly realized as the Sarva Adharamaya Atma—the all-pervading foundation of existence. This realization brings fulfillment, moksha (liberation), and a profound sense of unity with all creation.

In this state of non-duality (Advaita), the individual experiences Purnam (completeness). There is no longer a sense of separation between the jiva (individual self) and Ishwara (God). The external differences between the two are seen as illusions created by the koshas. Beneath these layers, both the jiva and Ishwara share the same divine essence, which is Brahman. This understanding dissolves the false perception of separateness, allowing one to rest in the truth of oneness.

The transcendence of the koshas and the dissolution of conceptual boundaries leads to the recognition of the Atma as the infinite, unchanging truth that pervades all existence. This realization frees the individual from the limitations of ignorance, bringing about lasting peace and the experience of divine unity.

Thus, as Amma beautifully expresses, the essence of both jiva and Ishwara is the same divine reality. Through inner reflection and the practice of Pancha Kosa Viveka, one can realize the oneness within, dissolving all layers of separation and arriving at the ultimate truth of Brahman, which is eternal, boundless, and ever-present.

Existence is Essence

"The Atma is the embodiment of wholeness, and this wholeness is pure love. When we experience the unity of the Self, we realize that love is the very fabric of existence, connecting all beings as one." Amma

Atma (Self) is the ultimate reality that underlies all creation. This reality is the source and substance of the universe, permeating everything without exception. When Amma says, "the Atma is the embodiment of wholeness," she highlights the nature of the Self as inherently complete, lacking nothing. This wholeness is synonymous with pure love, emphasizing that the experience of non-duality is not just intellectual but an expression of deep, unconditional love that transcends all distinctions.

The Isness of the Atma reflects that it is beyond all limitations of form, time, or place. It is the essence of all beings, meaning that every form of life and existence is a manifestation of this one, indivisible reality. From the smallest atom to the vast galaxies, everything is an expression of the same underlying Brahman. This wholeness binds all beings together, making love the fundamental force that connects everything, as Amma eloquently expresses. The recognition of this oneness dispels the illusion of separateness, leading to the realization that all divisions—whether personal, social, or cosmic—are mere surface appearances.

By realizing the unity of the Self, the knowledge of the Self becomes not just an intellectual pursuit but a lived experience. This knowledge, or Jnana, is the direct perception that the knower, the known, and the act of knowing are one and the same. In ordinary experience, we distinguish between the subject (the knower) and the object (the known), but in the state of self-realization, this division disappears. The individual perceives that there is no "other" to know—there is only the Self, pure consciousness, knowing itself.

When we fully realize this truth, we experience a profound sense of unity. The idea of an individual self separate from the universe or others becomes obsolete. The supreme Self—Brahman—and the individual self—Jiva—are understood to be one. This realization of non-duality dissolves the illusion of separateness and reveals the true nature of reality as an interconnected whole.

Through this understanding, one comes to perceive that love is not something that flows between separate individuals; rather, it is the fundamental fabric of existence. This love is not personal or conditional but is the natural expression of oneness. In this state, pure love flows effortlessly because the individual recognizes that there is no division between themselves and others. Everything is part of the same oneness.

The experience of wholeness leads to a profound transformation in how one relates to the world. Instead of seeing life through the lens of ego-driven desires and separations, the realized person sees all beings as expressions of the same divine reality. This leads to a deep compassion for all life, for there is no longer an "other" to compete with or fear. All are seen as extensions of the same Self.

This realization also brings freedom from suffering, for suffering arises from the perception of lack, incompleteness, and separation. When one realizes that the Atma is whole and complete, these sources of suffering fall away. There is nothing to gain or lose, as everything is already a part of the infinite wholeness of Brahman. The experience of love in this state is not tied to external circumstances or conditions—it is the natural state of being.

In conclusion, Amma's teaching reminds us that the Atma is the embodiment of wholeness and love. The realization of the unity of the Self dissolves the illusion of separateness and reveals that love is the very fabric of existence. This realization leads to an experience of boundless peace and the recognition that all beings are interconnected in the one divine reality. Through inner reflection and the knowledge of the Self, we come to understand the essence of our existence, where love and oneness are the ultimate truths.

Main Tenets of Self Knowledge

"In the knowledge of Self, we realize that forgiveness, compassion, service, and equality are the true expressions of divine love. When we embody these qualities, we reflect the essence of Ishwara, who is present in all." Amma

The essence of Brahma Vidya, the knowledge of Brahman, reveals that the Self is not separate from Brahman, the infinite and formless reality that underlies everything. This knowledge leads to a profound realization that the Self is fearless, unbound by the limitations of the physical world. In knowing this, one finds liberation from the endless cycle of samsara (birth and death). As stated in the Vedic texts, "The knower of Brahman attains the highest." This emphasizes that understanding the nature of Brahman leads to the ultimate purpose of existence—moksha (liberation).

Brahma Vidya centers around three key aspects: Prayojanam (the goal), Phalam (the result), and Sambandham (the connection between the seeker and the truth). The goal is to attain Paramatma (the Supreme Self), and the result is a profound realization of oneness with Brahman through the teachings of the Upanishads and spiritual disciplines. Brahman is described as greater than the greatest, and those who know Brahman come to understand the limitless vastness of this ultimate reality.

In the realm of karma, goals are achieved through action and effort, much like reaching a destination by traveling. However, in the realm of knowledge (jnana), simply knowing is itself the goal. There is no separate process of acquiring something outside of oneself. The moment one realizes the truth, the goal is instantly achieved. In Brahma Vidya, knowing and attainment are not distinct from one another.

A common question arises: How can someone "attain" Brahman if Brahman is everywhere and without limits? This apparent paradox is resolved by understanding that the concept of "attainment" applies to limited objects or places, but Brahman, being infinite, does not need to be reached or acquired. The knower of Brahman "attains" it by recognizing that they are already one with Brahman. This realization is not about acquiring something new but about seeing the eternal truth of one's own nature.

This leads to the understanding that in the realm of knowledge, there is no action or achievement, only the direct experience of truth. Much like a spiritual vision or darshan, the act of seeing is itself the realization. Just as the jiva (individual self) is the same as the Supreme Self or Paramatma, so too does one realize that the Self is already one with Brahman. This can be compared to the story of ten villagers searching for a tenth person, only to realize the tenth person was among them all along. The realization comes not through logic or reasoning but through direct experience.

Our failure to recognize this truth stems from ignorance (avidya), which creates a false identification with the body, mind, and ego. Once these illusions are removed, the truth of Brahman becomes self-evident, much like counting the villagers to reveal the tenth person. This realization of our true nature is direct and undeniable—it does not depend on comparisons or measurements but on recognizing the infinite nature of the Self.

Ignorance, which clouds our understanding, is the only barrier between us and the realization of Brahman. Brahma Vidya does not aim to teach us something new, but rather to reveal what has always been true—that the Self is one with the infinite Brahman. This knowledge dispels the darkness of ignorance, allowing the light of self-knowledge to shine, bringing about the full realization of oneness.

With this understanding complete, one moves toward the essence of Brahma Jnana—the path of liberation through understanding, discernment, and the dissolution of the false sense of separation.

Ishwara

"There is no real difference between Jiva and Ishwara. Both are expressions of the same divine essence—one infinite reality appearing as many." Amma

In Advaita Vedanta, Ishwara (God) is understood as Brahman conditioned by ignorance or illusion (avidya/maya). While Brahman in its pure form is beyond all distinctions and dualities, in relation to the world, Ishwara becomes the source and foundation of creation. Ishwara is both the material cause (the substance of the world) and the efficient cause (the intelligence behind creation), thus manifesting as the creator and sustainer of the universe. This conditioned form of Brahman is referred to as saguna Brahman, possessing attributes such as omnipotence, omniscience, and the ability to create, while remaining a reflection of the unconditioned, infinite Brahman beyond all forms.

So, Ishwara (the supreme being) and jiva (the individual soul) are ultimately the same in essence, both manifestations of the one Brahman. However, the distinction between them lies primarily in their relationship with avidya (ignorance) and maya (illusion). Ishwara is swathanthra—independent and beyond the influence of avidya, while the jiva is parathantra—dependent and subject to the limitations of ignorance. This fundamental ignorance clouds the jiva's perception of reality, causing it to identify with the body, mind, and ego, which leads to a sense of separation from the divine.

Ishwara, as Brahman conditioned by maya, oversees and controls the manifest world, but remains unaffected by it. Maya is under Ishwara's control, and though maya creates the appearance of multiplicity and duality, it does not bind Ishwara. In contrast, the jiva, under the influence of avidya, is entangled in the illusion of separateness and duality, mistakenly believing itself to be a limited being separate from Brahman.

While Ishwara is described as swayam purnam (complete within himself) and apthakaman (fulfilled), meaning he has no unfulfilled desires or needs, the jiva experiences kamana (desires) due to the influence of avidya. The jiva seeks fulfillment through external experiences and is driven by the pursuit of worldly desires and actions. On the other hand, Ishwara's will or kamana arises from a place of total fullness and completeness. Ishwara acts not out of need or deficiency but out of his inherent purnam (wholeness), while the jiva, in its ignorance, acts out of a perceived sense of lack and incompleteness.

The jiva, influenced by the delusions of the mind, believes that the pursuit of external objects will bring lasting happiness and fulfillment. However, these desires only bind the jiva further in the cycle of samsara (birth and death), leading to more suffering and attachment. Ishwara, in contrast, is free from all attachments and desires, as he is already in a state of Ananda (bliss) and completeness.

Through the process of jnana (knowledge) and bhakti (devotion), the jiva can transcend the limitations imposed by avidya and realize its true nature as non-different from Ishwara. This realization dissolves the illusion of duality and brings about moksha (liberation), where the jiva understands that it is none other than Brahman, the infinite and eternal reality. The Upanishadic saying Tat Tvam Asi (You are That) signifies this profound realization that the jiva and Ishwara are one.

In this state of realization, the jiva recognizes that the very desires and actions it once sought were illusions born of ignorance. With this knowledge, the jiva no longer seeks external validation or fulfillment, as it now abides in the awareness of its oneness with Ishwara, experiencing the boundless peace and bliss of Brahman.

Thus, while jiva and Ishwara may appear different due to their association with maya and avidya, their essence is the same divine reality—one infinite existence manifesting as many. The distinction dissolves once the jiva realizes its true nature, leading to the ultimate state of unity and wholeness with Ishwara.

Beyond Doubts: The Realization of Atman

"The true result of Atma Vidhya is the dissolution of ignorance, doubt, and misperception, clearing the path to self-realization. When these obstacles are removed, the light of the Self naturally shines, revealing the truth of our divine nature." Amma

The journey toward Atma Vidhya (knowledge of the Self) is transformative, as it leads to the dissolution of ignorance, doubt, and misapprehension. These three obstacles—Ajnanam (ignorance about one's true nature), Samsayam (doubt regarding the knowledge of the Self), and Viparyayam (misperception or incorrect identification with the body, mind, and ego)—veil the realization of one's inherent divinity. These barriers obstruct the direct experience of the Atma, which is infinite, ever-present, and formless.

Ignorance is the root of all misconceptions about the Self. It causes individuals to believe that their identity is limited to their physical and mental form, leading to the false assumption that they are separate from the ultimate reality, Brahman. Atma Vidhya works by eliminating this foundational ignorance, enabling one to see through the illusion of separateness. Once ignorance is dispelled, the true nature of the Self becomes evident—it is not a limited entity but the infinite, unchanging Atma.

Doubt, or Samsayam, arises when there is uncertainty about the nature of the Self. Even if one has heard the teachings of the Upanishads or spiritual texts, doubt can linger in the mind, preventing firm conviction in the truth. Atma Vidhya removes this doubt through direct experience, where the knowledge of the Self becomes unshakable. The jnani (knower of the Self) no longer wavers between belief and disbelief but rests in the certainty of their true nature as Brahman.

Misapprehension, or Viparyayam, refers to the incorrect identification with the body, mind, and ego. This false identification is what keeps individuals bound to the world of duality, where they experience pleasure and pain, birth and death, as real. Through the process of self-inquiry, guided by the teachings of Atma Vidhya, this misidentification is corrected.

When these obstacles—ignorance, doubt, and misapprehension—are removed, the Self naturally shines forth. Atma Vidhya does not add anything new to the individual but removes what is false, allowing the inherent truth of the Self to be fully realized. The Atma, which is ever-luminous and self-revealing, does not need external light to be known; it simply needs the veils of ignorance and false identification to be lifted. Once this happens, the individual recognizes their oneness with Brahman.

The result of Atma Vidhya is a state of clarity, peace, and freedom. One realizes that they are not the limited individual they once thought they were but the eternal, unchanging Brahman. This realization brings about a profound sense of wholeness and completeness, as the individual no longer seeks external validation or fulfillment. They are free from the limitations imposed by the body, mind, and ego, and experience the bliss of the Self.

In this state of realization, there is no longer a sense of separateness or duality. The individual understands that all distinctions—between self and other, subject and object—are mere illusions created by ignorance. The non-dual nature of existence becomes clear, and the individual abides in the truth of oneness with all creation. This experience is not an intellectual understanding but a direct realization of the Atma, which is infinite, formless, and ever-present.

The journey of Atma Vidhya leads to the ultimate freedom from the cycle of samsara (birth and death). By dissolving ignorance, doubt, and misapprehension, the individual is no longer bound by the limitations of the material world. They attain moksha, or liberation, which is characterized by the direct experience of eternal bliss and inner peace, free from the fluctuations of the external world.

In conclusion, the fruit of Atma Vidhya lies in the complete elimination of ignorance, doubt, and misperception, leading to the realization of the Self as Brahman. This knowledge brings about a profound transformation, where the individual no longer identifies with the body, mind, and ego but with the infinite, unchanging Atma. This realization leads to liberation, where one experiences the boundless peace and bliss of oneness, free from the limitations of duality.

Natural Contentment

"The wise are not swayed by fleeting happiness; they dwell in the natural state of inner peace and contentment. In this state, they are free, resting in the eternal bliss of the Self." Amma

In Advaita Vedanta, the vidhwan (wise one) is described as living in a state of sahaja anandham, or natural bliss, which is independent of external circumstances. This realization of Ananda Swarupam—the embodiment of bliss—is the cornerstone of the vidhwan's life. Unlike the sopadhika anandham (conditional happiness) that arises from external sources, sahaja anandham is eternal and unconditioned. It stems from the deep realization that happiness is not something to be attained from the world but is the very essence of the Self.

The wise one's actions are rooted in this understanding. Their activities are not motivated by a need to find happiness in the external world. Instead, they engage with the world from a place of wholeness, knowing that their true nature is Ananda, or bliss. They no longer seek fulfillment through desires or external achievements, as they understand that true satisfaction can only come from recognizing their oneness with Brahman—the unchanging, infinite reality.

This distinction between sopadhika anandham (temporary happiness dependent on external conditions) and sahaja anandham (inherent happiness) is key in Advaita Vedanta. The avidya (ignorance) of the ordinary individual leads them to pursue happiness through external objects and experiences, believing that these will provide lasting satisfaction. However, the vidhwan has transcended this limited perspective, understanding that external pleasures are fleeting and inherently unsatisfactory.

The vidhwan, having realized sahaja anandham, is no longer affected by the fluctuations of the waking state, where happiness is pursued through desires and attachments. In this state of realization, there is no need to chase after fleeting joys, as the vidhwan rests in the unchanging bliss of their true self. This is the ultimate contentment, a state of inner peace that is beyond the grasp of the ego and the desires of the mind.

Moreover, the wise one sees the impermanence of the waking world and its objects, recognizing that all forms are transient and subject to change. The pursuit of happiness through external means is seen as futile, as these sources of joy inevitably fade. Instead, the vidhwan abides in the awareness of their oneness with Brahman, where there is no differentiation between subject and object, between the seeker and the sought.

This realization brings about a profound freedom—freedom from the cycle of desire and dissatisfaction, from the dualities of pleasure and pain, and from the sense of lack that drives individuals to seek happiness outside themselves. The vidhwan knows that they are already whole, already complete, and that nothing in the external world can add to or diminish this inherent fullness.

In sahaja anandham, there is no striving, no effort to maintain or grasp at happiness, as it is the natural state of the Self. This blissful awareness is not a result of any particular action or achievement; it is simply the recognition of one's true nature as the eternal Atma. The wise one lives in this state effortlessly, embodying the peace and contentment that comes from knowing the Self.

In this state, the vidhwan is unmoved by external circumstances—whether praised or blamed, whether experiencing success or failure, the wise one remains in the unshakable bliss of the Self. This equanimity arises from their direct realization of non-duality—the understanding that all distinctions and separations are illusory, and that the only reality is Brahman, the infinite, formless, and blissful substratum of all existence.

Thus, the vidhwan transcends the limitations of the waking world, no longer seeking fulfillment through desires or external conditions. Their contentment comes from within, from the deep and abiding realization that they are already whole and free. This state of sahaja anandham is the culmination of the spiritual journey, where the vidhwan rests in the eternal bliss of the Self, untouched by the fleeting joys and sorrows of the material world.

In conclusion, natural contentment is the hallmark of the wise one who has realized their true nature as the embodiment of bliss. By transcending the fluctuations of external circumstances and desires, the vidhwan lives in a state of sahaja anandham, free from the limitations of the waking world and the cycle of seeking and dissatisfaction. This is the ultimate realization of the Self, where one rests in the infinite peace and wholeness of Brahman, the eternal and unchanging reality.

CHAPTER-7

Abiding in the Light of Self-Knowledge

Highest Bliss

"True bliss arises from within, independent of worldly objects and experiences. The joy we find in the world is just a fleeting reflection of the infinite bliss that resides in the Self." Amma

In Advaita Vedanta, Vyavrutha Vishaya Buddhigamya Anandam refers to the bliss that is realized when the intellect, or buddhi, turns inward, away from the distractions of external objects and experiences. This inward gaze leads to the direct experience of Atma Swarupa Anandam, the inherent bliss of the Self. This bliss is distinct from Laukika Anandam—the limited, temporary happiness derived from worldly pleasures and objects, which is merely a reflection of the deeper, infinite bliss that is the nature of the Paramatma (the Supreme Self).

Laukika Anandam arises from external experiences and is fleeting, a shadow of the Sahajamaya Anandam (natural bliss) that resides within every being. In contrast, Sahajamaya Anandam is the natural and ever-present state of the Atma, which can only be realized when the mind turns away from external dependencies and focuses on its true nature. This bliss is unchanging, complete, and self-sufficient, unaffected by the fluctuations of external events.

The reason most beings experience only Laukika Anandam is due to the presence of Avidya (ignorance). Avidya creates a veil that obscures the inherent bliss of the Self, leading to the perception of duality. In this state of ignorance, individuals are trapped by kama (desires) and karma (actions), constantly seeking happiness in external things while remaining unaware of the bliss that naturally resides within them. Even the highest beings are subject to this ignorance as long as they identify with the body-mind complex and remain under the influence of duality.

Avidya perpetuates the illusion of separation between the subject (the individual self) and the object (the external world). As long as this illusion persists, the individual remains bound by desires and the cycle of karma, unable to experience the Atma Swarupa Anandam that is their true nature. The key to breaking free from this cycle is through Vidya—the knowledge that dispels ignorance.

Vidya brings about the realization that all dualities are illusions, and that the self and the world are not separate entities. When Avidya is destroyed, the veil that obscures the bliss of the Self is lifted, and one can experience Sahajamaya Anandam—the natural, effortless bliss that arises from recognizing the unity of all existence.

The realization of this bliss is immediate and direct, not something that is achieved through effort or concentration while still holding onto ignorance. Sahajamaya Anandam is not a temporary state of happiness that arises from fulfilling desires; rather, it is the eternal, unchanging joy that is inherent in the Atma itself. This bliss is indivisible and complete, unaffected by the ups and downs of the external world.

The wise one, having realized Atma Swarupa Anandam, abides in this state of natural contentment and bliss. They no longer seek happiness from external objects or experiences because they have discovered the Ananda (bliss) that is their true nature. In this state, there is no separation between the individual and the universal, between the knower and the known. All dualities dissolve, and what remains is the one eternal reality—the Self, which is infinite and all-pervading.

As Amma beautifully expresses, the joy found in the world is but a fleeting reflection of the infinite bliss that resides in the Self. By turning inward and removing the veil of Avidya, one can experience the Sahajamaya Anandam—the natural, ever-present bliss that is the true nature of the Self, transcending all dualities and limitations. This is the ultimate state of realization, where one abides in the light of Self-knowledge, free from ignorance, desires, and the illusions of the external world.

Freedom is Peace

"Complete bliss arises in the heart that is free from desires, untouched by the pull of worldly cravings. True fulfillment comes when one understands the deeper meaning of life, purifies their actions, and renounces all desires." Amma

In Advaita Vedanta, Ananda Purnatha refers to the state of complete and unbroken bliss experienced by a Tatwa Jnani—one who has realized the non-dual nature of the Self. This profound bliss arises from the absence of desires, a condition known as akamahatham. Desires are the primary source of mental disturbances and dissatisfaction, keeping the mind agitated and longing for external gratification. For the akamahatham, however, the mind is calm, steady, and free from the distractions of worldly temptations or internal cravings. This leads to a continuous, undisturbed state of paramananda prapthi—the attainment of ultimate bliss.

The Tatwa Jnani transcends the cycle of desires and attachments. Since desires are the root cause of restlessness and incompleteness, their absence allows the Tatwa Jnani to experience Ananda Purnatha as their natural state. In this state, bliss is not dependent on external factors but arises from the realization of the true nature of the Self. Paramanandam, or ultimate bliss, is the culmination of spiritual realization, a state where the individual has gone beyond all cravings and attachments.

To reach this state of paramanandam, three essential sadhanas (spiritual practices) are necessary:

Understanding the true meaning of the scriptures (Shrothreeyasya):

A deep understanding of spiritual teachings and scriptures is vital for dispelling ignorance and guiding the seeker toward the ultimate truth. This knowledge forms the foundation of the path to Self-realization, offering clarity and insight into the nature of existence and the Self.

Eliminating sinful actions (Avrajanam):
Purity of action is crucial in creating the right environment for spiritual progress. Negative karma, accumulated through harmful or selfish actions, serves as an obstacle on the path to enlightenment. By purifying one's actions and adhering to dharma (righteousness), the mind becomes clearer, calmer, and more focused on higher truths.

Freedom from desires (Akamahathwam):
Desires are the source of mental agitation and incompleteness. The Tatwa Jnani, having transcended desires, experiences contentment and peace, as their mind no longer seeks fulfillment in external objects or experiences. This freedom from desires is the key to experiencing unbroken bliss, allowing the individual to rest in the inherent joy of their true nature.

As Amma emphasizes, true peace and bliss arise when the heart is free from desires and the mind is untouched by worldly cravings. This state of Ananda Purnatha—complete and unbroken bliss—is possible only for one who has purified their actions, understood the deeper meaning of life, and renounced all desires. Such an individual is not swayed by external temptations or material goals, as they have realized that true fulfillment comes from within, not from the transient pleasures of the world.

The path to paramananda is not a passive one. It involves active engagement with spiritual teachings, ethical living, and self-discipline. By following these three essential practices—scriptural understanding, purity of action, and freedom from desires—the seeker moves closer to the state of paramanandam, where the mind, free from disturbances, rests in the eternal bliss of the Self.

For the Tatwa Jnani, life is no longer a quest for external satisfaction, as they have realized their oneness with the infinite. Their bliss is not subject to the fluctuations of external circumstances, as it arises from the recognition of their true nature as Ananda Swarupam—the embodiment of bliss. This realization leads to a life of freedom, contentment, and inner peace, where all desires have been transcended, and only the bliss of the Self remains.

Introspection Leads to Self

"As the layers of body and mind are peeled away, the illusion of separateness dissolves, and the true Self is revealed—pure, infinite, and untouched by the changing world." Amma

In Advaita Vedanta, the primary reason for the identification of the Self with the body and mind is avidya (ignorance). An ajnani (ignorant person) mistakenly identifies their true nature based on the external attributes of the pancha kosas (five sheaths), which obscure the realization of the Atma (Self). The practice of Pancha Kosa Viveka is prescribed to distinguish the true Self from these layers or coverings that create the illusion of separateness. This introspective practice aims to help the seeker gradually strip away the layers of identification with the non-Self and realize the pure, infinite nature of the Atma.

The pancha kosas consist of the Annamaya kosha (physical body), Pranamaya kosha (vital energy), Manomaya kosha (mind), Vijnanamaya kosha (intellect), and Anandamaya kosha (bliss sheath). While these koshas are necessary for experiencing life, they do not represent the true essence of the individual. They are transient, changing, and subject to decay, whereas the Atma is eternal, formless, and unaffected by the world's fluctuations. By employing viveka (discrimination) to recognize that these sheaths are not the Self, the seeker can move beyond the illusions they create.

A helpful metaphor used to illustrate this process is observing the moon through the branches of a tree. Just as the branches may obstruct a clear view of the moon, the layers of body and mind cloud the perception of the Atma. However, with careful focus and discernment, one can look beyond these obstructions to see the true light of the Self. Another metaphor is the bird and the nest, where Puushan (the nourishing aspect of the divine) is likened to a bird living in a nest. While the bird resides within the nest, it is not the nest itself—similarly, the Self resides within the body but remains distinct from it.

The Self is often referred to as the foundation or adhishtanam of all experience, the underlying reality that supports the body, mind, and intellect. Despite being veiled by the koshas, the Atma remains unchanged and serves as the source of all perception and consciousness. This is why the Self is described as the "middle part" or central essence, symbolizing its role as the core of one's being that is beyond the physical and mental layers.

The removal of the koshas reveals the Atma as Sat-Chit-Ananda (existence, consciousness, and bliss), qualities that reflect the boundless, formless nature of the Self. When these layers are recognized as temporary and separate from the true Self, the illusion of separateness dissolves, and the individual experiences their oneness with the infinite. This realization marks the end of avidya (ignorance) and the beginning of true knowledge (vidya).

Amma's teaching highlights that introspection is the key to this self-discovery. By turning inward and peeling away the layers of attachment to the body and mind, the seeker transcends the false identifications that create suffering and separation. This introspective journey is not about rejecting the world but about understanding the deeper reality that underlies it, the Atma, which is untouched by the changes of the physical or mental realms.

In the state of Atma Jnana (knowledge of the Self), the individual rests in the experience of ananda (bliss), where there is no longer any distinction between the observer and the observed. The Self is realized as the unchanging witness to all experiences, beyond the constraints of time, space, and causality. This recognition of the true Self brings about moksha (liberation), freeing the individual from the cycle of birth and death and allowing them to live in the eternal peace of non-duality.

Thus, the practice of introspection and Pancha Kosa Viveka guides the seeker toward the realization that the Self is the pure, infinite essence that remains after all illusions are dissolved. It is in this realization that true freedom, contentment, and love are found, as Amma so beautifully expresses.

Sublating Differences into Wholeness

"The physical body, vital energy, and senses create our experience of the waking world, yet the true essence lies beyond them. In deep sleep, all distinctions dissolve, reminding us that everything arises from and returns to the infinite Self." — Amma

The individual's waking experience is shaped by three key components: the annam (physical body), the pranan (vital energy), and the indriyas (senses). These elements allow us to interact with the external world, leading to our perception of reality in the jagrath (waking state). The waking state is characterized by constant engagement with the material world through sensory input, action, and thought. However, while these interactions seem real and all-encompassing, they are not the ultimate expression of truth.

In Advaita Vedanta, the true essence of both the individual and the universe is not found in these waking experiences or in the realm of creation itself. Instead, the essence lies in the sushupthi (deep sleep state), which is often considered the most profound and foundational state of consciousness. In deep sleep, all distinctions of body, mind, ego, and external reality dissolve. This state represents a profound oneness—a state where duality disappears, and the individual rests in the unmanifest, formless state of pure existence.

Amma's teaching points to the transformative experience of sushupthi as a reminder that beyond all waking and dream states lies the true infinite Self. During the waking state, we experience duality and multiplicity, but in deep sleep, there is no sense of separation or individuality. It is a return to the source, the unmanifest state where the self remains as pure consciousness, untouched by the changing world of forms and experiences.

In this cyclical process of creation, experience, and dissolution, sushupthi represents the origin and the destination. The waking state, with its multiplicity of experiences, thoughts, and actions, is merely a temporary manifestation that arises from this deeper state of unity and stillness. After the experiences of waking and dreaming, we return to deep sleep, where the distinctions and differences experienced in waking life are sublated into the wholeness of pure being.

Amma's quote highlights the impermanence of the waking state and encourages seekers to recognize that everything—

including the physical body, senses, and thoughts—arises from the unmanifest and will eventually return to it. This teaching serves as a reminder that the waking world is fleeting and transient, while the Self is the eternal, unchanging substratum.

The three states of consciousness—waking (jagrath), dream (swapna), and deep sleep (sushupthi)—are often compared to the three levels of reality in Advaita Vedanta: the apparent reality, the transactional reality, and the absolute reality. While the waking state corresponds to the apparent reality, where distinctions and dualities exist, the state of deep sleep corresponds to the absolute reality, where all separations are dissolved into oneness.

Through self-inquiry and introspection, the seeker is encouraged to recognize that the Self (Atma) is ever-present in all three states of consciousness. However, it is only in the state of deep sleep—free from the distractions of the mind, body, and senses—that the pure nature of the Self is most fully experienced. By contemplating the nature of sushupthi, one is reminded of the essential unity that underlies all states of being.

Ultimately, Amma's teaching directs us to seek the unchanging essence that lies beyond the fleeting experiences of life. By understanding that the waking world and its experiences are temporary and transitory, we are reminded of the importance of spiritual practice and introspection to realize the infinite Self. The process of sublating differences into wholeness through deep reflection leads to the recognition of the true nature of the Self, beyond the illusions of duality and separateness.

This understanding fosters a deeper peace and contentment, as one learns to identify not with the ever-changing experiences of the waking world but with the eternal Self that is present in all states of consciousness. In realizing this non-dual truth, one transcends the limited perception of individuality and rests in the boundless wholeness that is the essence of existence.

Thus, the teaching of sublating differences into wholeness serves as a powerful reminder that the true essence of life and existence lies beyond the layers of experience and is rooted in the infinite Self, where all distinctions dissolve into the unity of pure consciousness.

Essence of Oneness

"The Self is non-dual, the source and substance of all. In realizing this oneness, we understand that everything we see and experience is the same divine essence, without separation or division." Amma

The concept of "ekatwaath Brahmanaha" emphasizes the non-dual nature of Brahman, asserting that Brahman is indivisible and without parts or divisions. This understanding is essential in Advaita Vedanta, where Brahman is described as niramsam (without parts) and niravayawam (without divisions), meaning that Brahman is whole, complete, and without fragmentation. As a result, the notion of Brahman "entering" the jiva (individual soul) in any specific or limited form is metaphorical rather than literal. The Atma (Self) is not distinct from Brahman; thus, the idea of Brahman entering into the jiva would imply a dualistic distinction, which contradicts the very nature of Brahman.

When the Upanishads say, "Tadh shrushtva tadheva anupravishath" ("Having created, it then entered"), this is to be understood symbolically. It conveys the idea that Brahman is the substratum of creation and is ever-present in every aspect of creation, including the jiva. The phrase signifies that Brahman manifests as the jiva rather than entering it as something separate. The jiva, therefore, is an expression of Brahman's existence, inseparably connected to it. This reflects the non-dual understanding that Brahman and the jiva are one, with no true separation between the creator and the created.

In Advaita Vedanta, the focus is not on the act of creation but on the realization of Brahman, the ultimate, unchanging truth behind all appearances. The phrase "Brahma anugamascha" underscores the importance of understanding and knowing Brahman. It reminds seekers that self-realization involves transcending the external layers of existence, such as the annamaya kosha (the physical body), pranamaya kosha (life force), manomaya kosha (mind), and vijnanamaya kosha (intellect), until one perceives the anandamaya kosha (the bliss sheath), where the infinite nature of Brahman, Anantha, is revealed.

The metaphor of Brahman "entering" creation can also be understood as a description of the seeker's journey to self-realization. It suggests that the process of realization is not an external event but an internal recognition that Brahman has always been present as the essence of the jiva. Through introspection and self-inquiry, guided by the buddhi (intellect), the seeker realizes that the perceiver and the perceived, the creator and the created, are the same undivided reality—Brahman.

The idea of "entering" thus serves as a metaphor for the seeker's inner journey. The realization that the knower, the known, and the act of knowing are all aspects of the same Self leads to liberation. The "antharkarna guha" (the cave of the heart), symbolizing the innermost space where the Atma resides, is understood to be one with Brahman. When this truth becomes clear, the seeker recognizes that the Self is not separate from the supreme reality, leading to the dissolution of the illusion of duality.

The essence of this teaching is that the ultimate reality is non-dual. The oneness of existence is realized when the veil of ignorance is lifted. As Amma highlights, all experiences and forms we encounter are manifestations of the same divine essence, and there is no fundamental separation or division. The recognition of this non-dual truth is the culmination of the spiritual path, where the seeker comes to rest in the knowledge that the Self and Brahman are one.

This realization leads to moksha (liberation), where the seeker understands that the knower, the object of knowledge, and the act of knowing are all expressions of the same reality—Brahman. It is in this unity that the true nature of existence is revealed, and the individual recognizes their eternal connection to the divine.

Fearlessness

"Fearlessness arises when we realize the inner Self. The wise, by abiding in their true nature, are untouched by fear, resting in the infinite strength and peace of the Self." Amma

The Vidhwan (wise person), through the journey of self-realization, reaches the state of abhayam (fearlessness). This transformation occurs by recognizing and abiding in their true nature, known as swarupam. The ego (aham) and attachments to external objects, ideas, and relationships (mama) create an illusion of separateness, which gives rise to fear. Fear stems from the belief that the self is isolated and vulnerable in a dualistic world.

Fear arises due to the perception of duality, the belief that the individual self is separate from the world and other beings. In this perception of separateness, the possibility of harm, loss, or suffering becomes real, thus creating fear. However, when the Vidhwan realizes their true nature as one with the infinite Paramatma (Supreme Self), this illusion of separation dissolves. The realization of swarupa prathishta (abidance in one's true nature) allows the Vidhwan to understand that everything is a manifestation of the same divine essence. Therefore, there is nothing external to fear because all existence is unified.

In this state, the Vidhwan no longer identifies with the limited body and mind, nor with the ego that creates a sense of individuality and isolation. The self is now experienced as infinite, whole, and complete, free from the divisions that give rise to fear. This understanding is central to Advaita Vedanta, where the realization of non-duality (Advaita) leads to the dissolution of the false sense of individuality. Since Brahman (the ultimate reality) is inherently free from fear and duality, and the Vidhwan has come to recognize their oneness with Brahman, fear cannot exist in this state of unity.

The natural outcome of swarupa prathishta is abhayam, the complete freedom from fear. By realizing that the Self is not separate from anything in the universe, the Vidhwan transcends the notion of an "other" that could cause harm or pose a threat. The profound realization of non-duality brings a deep and abiding peace, rooted in the knowledge that the Self is eternal, unchanging, and all-encompassing.

This state of fearlessness is not simply an emotional or psychological state, but a spiritual realization that transforms how one perceives and interacts with the world. The Vidhwan sees the entire cosmos as an extension of their own being and experiences the bliss of oneness. In this state of unity, there is no longer any basis for fear, as the individual self merges into the all-encompassing Brahman.

The dissolution of fear brings with it the experience of infinite strength and peace, qualities that are inherent in the realization of the Self. The Vidhwan abides in this inner strength, knowing that they are no longer subject to the dualities of life—such as success and failure, gain and loss—that typically generate fear. Instead, they rest in the unshakable peace of their true nature, which is beyond all change and fluctuation.

In conclusion, the realization of the non-dual nature of the Self dissolves the false distinctions that give rise to fear. The Vidhwan, by recognizing their oneness with Brahman, experiences abhayam—the profound fearlessness that comes from understanding that there is no separation between the self and the rest of existence. This fearlessness is the natural outcome of self-realization, leading to a life rooted in eternal peace and strength, free from the illusions of duality.

Unconditional Happiness

"Happiness that depends on external objects is fleeting and temporary. True joy comes from within, where the eternal bliss of the Self resides, untouched by worldly changes." Amma

The happiness that we typically experience in the waking state is known as sopadhika anandham, meaning it is conditional and arises from our attachment to external objects or vishayas. For instance, when we acquire something we desire, we feel happiness, but this happiness is temporary and dependent on the presence of that object or situation. It vanishes when the object is removed or when our attachment fades, making this happiness artificial and fleeting.

Even the happiness experienced in deep sleep, although more peaceful and profound, is still considered sopadhika anandham. In this state, we are free from external objects and worldly concerns, but the happiness we experience is still an anubhava vedhyam—an experiential happiness.

When we wake up, we often reflect on the peacefulness of our sleep, but this reflection still places happiness in the realm of experience, making it dependent on a particular state.

Sahaja anandham, on the other hand, refers to the natural and innate happiness that is beyond the duality of experiencer and experienced. Unlike sopadhika anandham, which is dependent on external objects or internal states, sahaja anandham is the intrinsic nature of the Self (Atma). This happiness is ever-present and does not arise from any specific situation or condition. It is the pure bliss that is unconditional, not an emotion or feeling that we can grasp or experience in the way we usually understand happiness.

In contrast to the fleeting happiness of waking life and deep sleep, sahaja anandham is the pure, unchanging bliss that is part of our true nature. This happiness is not something we acquire or lose; it is always there, regardless of external circumstances or mental states. Sahaja anandham is the natural state of being, a happiness that is devoid of attachment and duality, untouched by the ups and downs of life.

To reach this state of unconditional happiness, one must move beyond identifying with the body and mind, which are sources of conditional happiness. As long as we rely on external objects or temporary experiences to bring us happiness, we will continue to experience fluctuations in our joy. However, when we recognize that happiness is our true nature, we realize that it is always present within us.

The attachment to external objects and the identification with the mind create a sense of incompleteness, leading us to believe that we need something outside of ourselves to be happy. This attachment keeps us in a cycle of desire and disappointment, constantly chasing after temporary sources of joy. But the Self, which is eternal and unchanging, is the source of sahaja anandham—the bliss that is not dependent on any external factors.

In Advaita Vedanta, the understanding of sahaja anandham is central to self-realization. By recognizing that true happiness comes from within, we can transcend the limitations of the waking and dream states, where happiness is often tied to external conditions. The wise person, or vidhwan, understands that happiness is not something to be sought externally, but is the innate state of the Self.

In conclusion, true joy arises from realizing the Self and experiencing the unconditional happiness that is ever-present, untouched by worldly changes. While the happiness of the waking and deep sleep states is fleeting and dependent, sahaja anandham is the blissful state that is always whole and complete, requiring no external validation or fulfillment.

Maya

"Maya creates the veil of superimposition and false identification, but through the grace of Ishwara and the wisdom imparted by the Guru, this veil is lifted. The knowledge of the Self reveals the eternal truth beyond illusion." Amma

In Advaita Vedanta, Adhyasam, or superimposition, refers to the mistaken attribution of qualities that do not belong to the Self. It is the confusion between the conscious, living reality (the Self or Atma) and the non-living, inert aspects of existence (such as the body, mind, and senses). This confusion arises from Maya, the force of illusion that causes us to identify the unreal as real and to attribute qualities of the impermanent world to the eternal Self.

Maya creates a veil of illusion, leading us to superimpose the qualities of the body, mind, and ego onto the Atma. As a result, we believe that the limitations of the body—such as aging, suffering, and death—belong to the Self. However, the true Self is beyond all qualities and limitations; it is changeless, eternal, and free from the cycle of birth and death.

This false identification leads to the bondage of samsara, where individuals perceive themselves as limited beings subject to fear, desire, and suffering. Through the grace of Ishwara (the Supreme Lord) and the wisdom imparted by the Guru, the seeker is guided to recognize the illusory nature of Maya and the superimpositions that obscure the true nature of the Self.

The process of lifting the veil of Maya involves discriminative wisdom (Viveka), where one learns to separate the real from the unreal. This practice is referred to as Pancha Kosa Viveka, the discernment between the five sheaths (koshas) of the body and mind that cover the Self. The seeker must realize that the physical body, vital energy, mind, intellect, and even the sheath of bliss are all temporary coverings of the Atma, which itself is eternal and unchanging.

By understanding that these temporary attributes do not belong to the Self, one begins to see through the illusion created by Maya. The qualities of the body—such as pleasure and pain, success and failure—are part of the temporary world of name and form, and do not define the true nature of the Atma. The mind's identifications with these qualities create the sense of ego and separation, leading to suffering.

However, with the wisdom of the Guru and scriptural teachings, the superimposition of these attributes on the Self is gradually dissolved. The seeker realizes that the Self is the pure consciousness that witnesses all experiences but is not affected by them. The Self is like the space within a pot—even though the pot may change in size or shape, the space remains unchanged and unaffected.

The removal of ignorance (avidya) through self-knowledge (Atma Vidya) leads to the direct experience of the Self as Sat-Chit-Ananda (existence, consciousness, bliss). This knowledge reveals that all dualities—such as joy and sorrow, pleasure and pain—are mere projections of the mind, and that the truth of the Self is beyond duality, rooted in eternal bliss.

Ultimately, when the veil of Maya is lifted, the individual realizes that the Self is Brahman, the infinite reality. There is no longer a sense of separation between the individual (jiva) and the universal (Ishwara). The superimposed differences between creator and creation, knower and known, dissolve, revealing the oneness of all existence.

In conclusion, the knowledge of the Self reveals the eternal truth beyond the illusion created by Maya. Through the guidance of the Guru and the grace of Ishwara, the seeker can transcend the false identification with the temporary and experience the boundless freedom of the true Self

Indwelling Bliss

"Searching for happiness outside is born of ignorance, for true joy is found within. The wise turn inward, discovering the boundless peace that has always been their true nature." Amma

In Advaita Vedanta, the Supreme Self (Paramatma) is the singular source of true and everlasting happiness. This Ekarupamaya Paramatma is the undivided essence of all beings, and Anandham (bliss) is its intrinsic nature. Every individual self (jiva) shares this inherent bliss, but due to avidya (ignorance), this truth remains obscured. Individuals mistakenly search for happiness in the external world, attaching themselves to fleeting pleasures and material gains, unaware that the true bliss they seek resides within.

Avidya, or ignorance, veils the Paramatma within and causes the jiva to identify with the body and mind, perceiving itself as a limited, separate entity. This leads to the belief that happiness can be found in external objects, relationships, and experiences. The cycle of desire and attachment that follows creates dukham (suffering), as the individual becomes entangled in the impermanence of worldly joys, which are inevitably accompanied by loss, disappointment, and dissatisfaction.

In contrast, the Vidhwan (the wise person) has realized the true nature of the Self. Through self-knowledge (Atma Vidya), they have overcome avidya and see through the illusion of duality and separateness. The Vidhwan experiences the sahaja anandham—the boundless bliss that arises naturally from within, independent of external conditions. This bliss is the Atma's very essence, eternal and unchanging. The Avidhwan (ignorant person), on the other hand, remains bound by maya and dualistic thinking, continuing to search for joy in the impermanent world, only to experience suffering as a result.

The difference between a Vidhwan and an Avidhwan is not in the external circumstances they face, but in their inner realization. The Vidhwan has understood that they are not the limited body and mind, but the infinite Paramatma, beyond all worldly limitations. This realization brings about abhayam (fearlessness) and anandham (bliss), as they no longer see themselves as separate from the source of all joy. The Avidhwan, by contrast, remains trapped in the illusion of separateness, perceiving life as a series of gains and losses, and thus continues to suffer from the fluctuations of pleasure and pain.

The path of wisdom (jnana marga) leads to the dissolution of avidya and the direct realization of one's true nature as Paramatma. This realization is not merely an intellectual understanding, but a direct experience of the Self as Sat-Chit-Ananda—existence, consciousness, and bliss. When avidya is removed, the individual no longer seeks happiness outside but abides in the eternal bliss that has always been their true essence.

Ishwara (the Divine) and the Guru play a crucial role in guiding the seeker towards this inner realization. Through the grace of Ishwara and the teachings of the Guru, the veil of ignorance is gradually lifted. The seeker is encouraged to turn inward, away from the distractions of the external world, and to engage in practices like self-inquiry and meditation, which reveal the oneness of the jiva and Paramatma.

Ultimately, the realization that the source of true joy lies within leads to liberation (moksha). The individual no longer identifies with the transient ego but recognizes their oneness with the infinite, unchanging reality of Brahman. This state of eternal bliss and wholeness is the final goal of Atma Vidya, where all desires are transcended, and the individual rests in the unconditional happiness of the Self.

In summary, the wise realize that true joy comes from within, untouched by the impermanence of the world. By dissolving ignorance and recognizing the eternal nature of the Self, they experience the boundless peace and bliss that is their true nature.

Self-Recognition

"The True Self is direct and immediate, always present and waiting to be realized. It is not distant or hidden but shines within each of us, accessible in every moment when we turn inward with awareness." Amma

In Advaita Vedanta, the realization of the True Self is described as direct and immediate. Unlike other forms of knowledge that require external validation, the knowledge of the Self, or Atma Vidya, is self-evident. It does not need proof because it is innate and always present within. The True Self is not something that needs to be discovered or brought into existence but something that is already shining within us, waiting to be recognized.

The intellect (buddhi), often considered the seat of individual knowledge, plays a pivotal role in the process of realization. The intellect is like a mirror that can either reflect the light of the Self clearly or distort it when clouded by ignorance. In its purified state, the intellect enables the direct perception of the True Self, revealing the universal consciousness that is Brahman. However, when the intellect is influenced by desires, attachments, and ignorance, it creates a sense of separateness, leading to misidentification with the body and mind.

Direct knowledge (aparoksha jnana) is the immediate and doubtless realization of one's true nature. It is not something that is learned or acquired over time but is the unfolding of the truth that has always been present. In contrast, indirect knowledge (paroksha jnana) refers to intellectual understanding, where the individual may know the teachings of non-duality but has not yet had the direct experience of the Self. True realization occurs when the individual moves beyond concepts and experiences the Self directly.

This direct knowledge is like the immediate awareness we have of our own existence. We never question whether we exist because our existence is self-evident. Similarly, the True Self is always known, even if we are not fully conscious of it. It is the awareness behind all experiences, always present and waiting to be recognized once the veil of ignorance is lifted.

The mind and the intellect are often seen as obstacles to realizing the Self, but they can also be instruments of realization when properly directed. When the intellect is sharpened and turned inward through practices like self-inquiry and meditation, it begins to reflect the light of the Self more clearly. This process of introspection allows one to see beyond the temporary identifications with the body, emotions, and thoughts, leading to the recognition of the unchanging reality that is the Self.

One of the fundamental teachings of Vedanta is that the Self is ever-present. It is not hidden or distant but is immediate and directly accessible to those who turn their attention inward. The Guru and the scriptures serve as guides in this process, pointing the seeker towards the inner reality and helping them remove the layers of ignorance that obscure the truth.

The True Self is described as Sat-Chit-Ananda—Beingness and Knowingness equals Bliss. These are not attributes of the Self but are its very essence. The Self is Existence itself, the Consciousness that illuminates all experiences, and the Bliss that is untouched by worldly suffering. The realization of the Self leads to a profound sense of peace and fulfillment as the seeker understands that nothing external can provide the lasting happiness that is already present within.

In this state of Self-realization, all doubts and uncertainties dissolve. The seeker no longer identifies with the limitations of the body-mind complex but rests in the infinite nature of the Self. This realization is immediate and final, as it reveals the eternal truth that has always been present, but was previously obscured by ignorance.

Ultimately, Self-knowledge is about turning inward and recognizing that the true essence of our being is not something we need to acquire but something we need to realize. The light of the Self is always shining within us, and through awareness, introspection, and the guidance of the Guru, we can come to see that we are already whole, complete, and one with the infinite reality.

In conclusion, direct knowledge of the Self leads to the dissolution of ignorance and the recognition of one's true nature. The intellect, when purified, serves as the instrument through which the Self is realized. This realization is immediate, ever-present, and leads to the infinite peace and bliss that resides within all of us.

Sat

"Ishwara is the living essence that pervades everything, even inanimate objects. Though they may seem different, all are united in oneness, filled with the same divine presence." — Amma

In Advaita Vedanta, Sat refers to pure existence, reality, or being, representing the unchanging and eternal nature of the Absolute (Brahman). The Absolute is described as pure Being, beyond time, space, and all dualities. It is the foundational reality that underlies all existence, remaining constant and unaffected by the transient world of forms and names. In this view, Brahman is Sat, the ultimate truth and reality, and all else is considered an illusory manifestation (maya) in relation to this pure, eternal Being.

Brahman is the substratum of all that exists, the eternal, unchanging reality, and is unsublated in the three periods of time (past, present, and future) and the three states (waking, dream, and deep sleep) is Sat. Unlike the unconscious or inanimate objects we encounter in the material world, Brahman is described as chetana, or consciousness. It is not merely the cause of the universe but also the living essence that animates all existence, including both sentient beings and inanimate objects.

In Bhagavad Gita 2:16, it is said, "The unreal has no being; the real never ceases to be. The truth about both has been seen by the seers of the essence." This verse emphasizes that Sat (the real, the existent) is eternal and unchanging, while the asat (the unreal, non-existence) has no true substance. Brahman, as Sat, cannot arise from Asath, or non-existence. This makes Brahman fundamentally different from things like seeds or mud, which may serve as causes for specific objects but are themselves subject to change, decay, and destruction. Brahman, however, is self-sufficient and eternal.

The essence of Brahman is described through qualities such as kamayatha (will) and Sarvajnam (omniscience). These qualities differentiate Brahman from the individual jiva (soul), which is bound by ignorance and limited by the physical body and mind. While seeds or mud may have the potential to create specific forms like plants or pots, they do not possess will or knowledge. In contrast, Brahman is described as possessing Sathya Jnana Lakshanaha—meaning it is endowed with the qualities of truth and knowledge.

Ishwara, the personal aspect of Brahman, is seen as the creator, sustainer, and destroyer of the universe. Ishwara is the embodiment of Sat, the living essence that animates all of creation. Through maya (the cosmic illusion), Ishwara manifests the universe, making it appear as though there is diversity and separation. However, in truth, everything is a manifestation of the same Brahman, the non-dual reality. This divine presence pervades even the inanimate objects, which, though appearing lifeless, are still filled with the essence of Brahman.

The jiva (individual soul) often perceives itself as separate from Ishwara and the world, due to the veil of avidya (ignorance). This ignorance leads to the false identification with the body and mind, creating the illusion of duality. However, the knowledge of Sat—the realization that Brahman is the ultimate reality—dissolves this illusion. The Vidhwan (wise person) sees beyond the superficial differences and recognizes the oneness of all existence. Whether animate or inanimate, all are expressions of Brahman.

Even though inanimate objects like seeds, mud, or stones seem distinct and lacking in consciousness, they are still pervaded by Ishwara, who is the source and essence of all. The difference lies in the manifestation of consciousness—while the jiva expresses this consciousness in a more apparent way, inanimate objects reflect it in a subtler form. However, the underlying reality remains the same. In this sense, everything in the universe, whether living or non-living, is united in the oneness of Brahman.

As Amma explains, the perception of difference is merely an illusion created by the mind. When we realize the truth of oneness, we understand that the same divine essence fills everything. The wise person, who has transcended ignorance, sees the unity in diversity and experiences the eternal presence of Brahman in all.

This understanding leads to a state of fearlessness and inner peace, as the illusion of separateness dissolves. The individual no longer identifies with the limited self or the body but rests in the awareness of being one with the infinite reality. This is the goal of self-realization, where one sees everything as an expression of the same divine essence and abides in the bliss of oneness.

In conclusion, the Sat or ultimate reality is not bound by the limitations of time, space, or objects. It is the living essence that pervades all of creation, both animate and inanimate. Through the grace of Ishwara and the wisdom of the Guru, the veil of maya is lifted, and the truth of non-duality is revealed, leading to the realization that everything is a manifestation of the same divine presence—Brahman.

Cognition Beyond Duality

"The Self is infinite, beyond all boundaries of duality and ego. When the ego dissolves, we realize that there is no separation—only the oneness of pure consciousness, ever free and ever whole." — Amma

This quote emphasizes the infinite nature of Brahman, where the perception of separateness, or seeing things as distinct from oneself, dissolves. In our ordinary experience, we tend to perceive objects as separate from ourselves, creating a subject-object duality. However, when one realizes the Infinite Self, this perception of duality vanishes. The Self, or Atma, cannot be experienced as an object outside of oneself because it is the all-encompassing Brahman. In the realm of the infinite, there is no "other" to perceive, no division between knower and known.

This is the essence of Advaita Vedanta, which teaches that Brahman is the ultimate reality, and it is non-dual—meaning there is no separation, no multiplicity, only oneness. The phrase "anything else" highlights this central idea: in the experience of the Self, there is no other entity or object to perceive or know. The infinite nature of the Self means that it transcends all categories of knower and known, subject and object. This is called Turiya, which is beyond waking, dreaming, and deep sleep. In this state, all duality disappears, and only the pure awareness of the Self remains.

When the ego, which creates a sense of separateness, dissolves, we experience the Self as infinite and unbounded. The ego (Ahamkara) is the cause of dualistic thinking, dividing the world into "I" and "other," creating the illusion of separation. It gives rise to the identification with the body, mind, and individuality. However, when this false identification is dropped, what remains is the pure consciousness of the Self—eternal, infinite, and whole. Amma's statement, "When the ego dissolves, we realize that there is no separation," points directly to this truth of non-duality, where the individual self merges with the universal Brahman.

The experience of oneness is not a conceptual or intellectual understanding, but a direct realization that everything is a manifestation of the same underlying reality. The Self is the source of all knowledge, but it cannot be known in the usual sense because it is not an object of knowledge. This is the core teaching of the Upanishads: the Self is the eternal subject that illumines all things, yet it itself is beyond being known as an object. In the words of the Kena Upanishad: "It is not that which is seen but the seer of all things."

In the state of Self-realization, one transcends the limitations of the body-mind complex and understands that the Self is eternal, untouched by time, space, or causality. This understanding leads to fearlessness, as there is nothing external or separate that can cause fear. The Self, being whole and complete, is the source of Ananda (bliss), which is experienced as one's true nature once the veil of ignorance is lifted.

The realization of the Self dissolves the limitations of time and space, as these are constructs that exist only within the realm of duality. In the non-dual state, there is no past, present, or future, no here or there—everything is now and here, in the eternal presence of the Self. The Self is not confined by the body or the mind; it is limitless, all-pervading, and indivisible.

As Amma suggests, true happiness and peace come from the direct realization of the Self. The illusion of separation is the root of all suffering, and the dissolution of this illusion leads to the experience of freedom and bliss. The wise ones, who have realized this truth, live in a state of continuous joy, unaffected by the fluctuations of the material world. They understand that all distinctions—between the individual and the universal, the material and the spiritual—are ultimately illusory.

In conclusion, Amma's teachings point to the truth: the Self is infinite, beyond all distinctions of duality. When we realize this, the illusion of separateness dissolves, and we abide in the eternal oneness of pure consciousness, untouched by the changes of the world. The Self, ever free and ever whole, is the ultimate reality that we all share.

No Becoming, Only Being

"The scriptures repeatedly affirm that the Self and Brahman are one, guiding us to realize our divine essence. Through this knowledge, we transcend ignorance and awaken to the infinite truth that has always been within."
— Amma

The teachings of the Upanishads and other sacred texts repeatedly emphasize the non-dual nature of the Self (Atman) and Brahman, the ultimate reality. The profound realization that "I am Brahman" is the essence of all spiritual teachings in Advaita Vedanta. This knowledge is not just theoretical but is a direct, transformative experience that dissolves the ignorance (avidya) that keeps us trapped in the cycle of birth and death.

In having this knowledge, one sees through the illusion of duality, realizing that the distinctions between self and world, subject and object, are false constructs of the mind. This realization leads to a state of absolute knowing, where the truth is never contradicted by any future experience because it reflects the unchanging reality of Brahman.

The Brhadaranyaka Upanishad encapsulates this transformation by describing the person who knows the Self as becoming "self-controlled, calm." The realization of one's true nature as Brahman brings about an inner peace that arises from the cessation of desire. Since the realized being understands that there is nothing external to acquire or pursue, they no longer engage in actions driven by craving or fear. Their being is whole and complete.

Renunciation plays a central role in the path to liberation. The Svetāśvatara Upanishad points to those who have transcended the conventional stages of life.) and turned entirely toward the quest for liberation. By renouncing attachments, they focus solely on Self-realization. This renunciation is not merely a rejection of the physical world but a deep inward shift where one disengages from the illusion of separateness and desires.

The Kaivalya Upanishad further reinforces this idea, stating that immortality, or liberation, is not attained through karma, wealth, or progeny, but through renunciation. This message underscores that worldly accomplishments, no matter how great, do not bring lasting fulfillment or freedom. It is only by relinquishing the ego's desires and attachments and turning inward toward the Self that one finds moksha, or liberation.

The Smriti texts align with these Upanishadic teachings, stating that once an individual attains Self-knowledge, they should embrace a life of inactivity in the sense of renouncing worldly ambitions and the pursuit of external results. This is not a passive or purposeless inactivity, but rather a cessation of ego-driven action. A person who realizes their identity as Brahman no longer seeks to achieve anything through action because they recognize that they are already complete.

Sannyasa, or the path of renunciation, is encouraged for those who have reached this realization. The Smriti explains that after attaining knowledge, one should move toward a life of contemplation and renunciation, away from the distractions of the material world. Sannyasa is not about physical isolation but about renouncing attachment to the fruits of action. This lifestyle is most conducive to realizing the eternal truth of Brahman, allowing one to fully immerse in the contemplation of the Self.

The Upanishads consistently teach that ignorance (avidya) is the root cause of all suffering and bondage. Ignorance is what makes one identify with the body, mind, and ego, mistaking these transient forms for the true Self. The knowledge that the Self and Brahman are one cuts through this ignorance, much like the rising sun dispels the darkness of night.

When one attains this knowledge, doubt and misapprehension fall away. There is no longer any confusion about who one truly is. The realization of the Self is not merely intellectual; it is a deep, lived experience where one understands that all sense of separateness was a product of the mind. With the dissolution of ignorance, the individual no longer sees themselves as a finite being struggling within the world, but as the infinite Brahman, which transcends all dualities and limitations.

The realization that "I am Brahman" leads to the direct experience of non-duality, where the illusion of separateness is completely dissolved. One who abides in this truth understands that the Self is eternal, formless, and free from all distinctions of time, space, and causality. This is the highest knowledge, as described in the Chandogya Upanishad: "In that state, one does not see anything else, hear anything else, or know anything else."

In this state of Self-realization, there is no becoming, only being. The individual no longer seeks to achieve or attain anything, because they have realized that they are already complete and whole. The pursuit of external validation or fulfillment ceases, and the realized one rests in the absolute peace of their own true nature. As Amma's quote suggests, the teachings of the Upanishads and Smriti point to the ultimate realization that the Self and Brahman are one. This knowledge is the key to transcending the illusion of separateness, dissolving ignorance, and attaining liberation. Through renunciation, contemplation, and the dissolution of desires, one can awaken to the infinite truth that has always been within, leading to a state of unconditional peace and freedom.

Natural State

"In Advaita, there is no separation between the experiencer and the experience of bliss—both are one and the same. True joy arises when we realize that ananda is our inherent nature, free from the desires and illusions of the external world." Amma

In the philosophy of Advaita Vedanta, the essence of non-duality is the realization that there is no separation between the anandhi (the one who experiences bliss) and ananda (bliss itself). This is because bliss is not something external that one can acquire through the relationship between a subject and object, such as a person and an external source of happiness. Instead, Advaita teaches that ananda is the inherent, natural state of the Self (Atma).

For a Tatwa Jnani—one who has attained the wisdom of the true nature of reality—there is no longer any ajnana (ignorance), samsayam (doubts), or the pursuit of external objects for fulfillment. The Tatwa Jnani recognizes their swaswarupa (true nature) as swabhavika ananda (innate bliss). This recognition marks the realization that true happiness does not arise from external sources or sensory experiences but is an intrinsic part of their very being.

In the ordinary experience of life, individuals often engage in a vishaya-vishayi bhavam—a dualistic relationship where they perceive external objects of desire and seek happiness by acquiring or interacting with these objects. However, in Advaita, this dualistic approach is transcended. The Tatwa Jnani no longer seeks joy through external objects or experiences, knowing that their true nature is already blissful. There is a profound understanding that ananda is not something to be achieved but is always present within the Self.

When one abides in this Self-realization, there is no distinction between the experiencer and the experience of bliss. The Tatwa Jnani no longer perceives themselves as separate from the source of joy. They do not depend on external circumstances to experience happiness because they have discovered that the bliss they once sought outside was always present within.

In this state of non-dual awareness, the Tatwa Jnani dwells in sahaja ananda, or the natural, effortless bliss that is inherent to the Self. This bliss is not subject to fluctuations or conditions, as it does not arise from interactions with the external world. It is an unbroken, continuous state of joy that exists independent of changing circumstances. The Tatwa Jnani understands that ananda is the very fabric of their existence and remains unshaken by the illusions of separation and duality.

Because of this realization, the Tatwa Jnani is no longer influenced by desires for worldly experiences, as they are fully content in the knowledge that they are one with Brahman, the infinite source of all existence and bliss. In this understanding, they live in a state of unconditional joy, free from the limitations of the body and mind. Ananda is their true nature, and it shines forth without any external cause.

Thus, the realization of Advaita leads to the dissolution of all sense of separation, where the individual and the experience of bliss merge into one. The Tatwa Jnani abides in the natural state of sahaja ananda, the ever-present bliss that is the essence of the Self. This state is the ultimate realization that ananda is not a transient feeling but the eternal truth of one's being.

Conviction in Self

"When ignorance and doubt are removed, one is firmly established in the true Self, realizing that bliss is inseparable from their own nature. Just as heat is not separate from fire, the joy we seek is always within us, part of our very being." Amma

In the realization of Tatwa Jnani, the negation of ajnana (ignorance) and the removal of all doubts about one's swaswarupa (true nature) result in swarupa prathishtan, the firm abidance in one's true Self. This is the conviction that one no longer needs to seek happiness externally or through the dualistic lens of subject and object. The Tatwa Jnani has realized that Atma Swarupam—the true nature of the Self—is inherently ananda (bliss), which is not distinct from their being.

Just as heat cannot be separated from fire, ananda is inseparable from the Self. The Tatwa Jnani understands that bliss is not an external experience to be pursued but the natural state of their existence. This profound realization leads to kruthakruthyan, a state where the Jnani feels that they have accomplished all that needed to be done. There is no further desire or goal because they are already complete in their recognition of ananda as their essence.

Moving deeper, this understanding leads to the concept of the Paramananda Purusha, the ultimate blissful being who pervades both the Adhithyan (cosmic) realm and the jiva (individual being). This Paramananda Purusha is the same in essence, regardless of the form or the realm in which it is perceived. Much like space that exists inside pots of different shapes and sizes, anandam (bliss) remains unchanged and undivided across all manifestations. The pots may vary in form, but the space within them is the same; similarly, the bliss of Paramatma (the supreme Self) pervades all forms without distinction.

By negating the notions of uthkarsha (increase) and apakarsha (decrease), the non-dual nature of Paramatma is emphasized. Whether experienced in the cosmic or individual realm, the essence of bliss does not change—it remains whole, undivided, and eternal. There is no differentiation in the magnitude of bliss, and it is not subject to growth or reduction. Paramatma's nature as anandam is ever-present, and all beings are expressions of this same ananda.

The Tatwa Jnani experiences no division in essence, understanding that the bliss they experience is the same bliss that permeates the universe. This realization erases any sense of separateness between the individual and the cosmic realms, affirming the unity of Paramatma in all. The Paramananda Purusha, whether cosmic or individual, remains eternally blissful, unchanging, and complete, reinforcing that the ultimate truth of existence is one of eternal bliss and oneness.

Thus, the Tatwa Jnani abides in the conviction that ananda is their own nature, never apart from their being, and their fulfillment lies in this eternal Self-recognition. The joy that all beings seek externally is already present within, as the essence of the Self. This understanding leads to the dissolution of all desires, attachments, and dualistic perceptions, leaving only the unbroken, eternal bliss of the Self.

Intrinsic Nature

"The Divine, after creating the universe, entered into all that exists. This means that the creator and creation are not separate—the same divine presence pervades everything, both within and beyond." — Amma

The Sruti (sacred scripture) verse "Tadh shrushtva tadheva anupravishath" meaning "Having created, it then entered," presents the profound idea that Brahman (the ultimate reality) not only creates the universe but also pervades and animates it. This raises the question: can Brahman, being non-dual and infinite, truly "enter" into the individual soul (jiva) as if they were separate entities?

The clay and pot analogy helps clarify this concept. When a pot is formed, the clay itself takes the shape of the pot; the pot is simply a manifestation of the clay. There is no additional or separate "entry" of the clay into the pot because the pot is nothing but clay in a different form. Likewise, Brahman, the ultimate substratum of all existence, does not need to "enter" the jiva as something separate. The jiva is merely an expression or form of Brahman, just as the pot is of the clay.

In this light, Brahman is both the material and efficient cause of the universe. Brahman is not external to creation but is its very essence, much like clay is to the pot. This concept challenges the conventional idea that Brahman, or Ishwara (God), enters creation in a physical sense. Since Brahman is all-pervading, non-dual, and eternal, there is no need for any separate process of entry—Brahman is the underlying reality in all beings and forms.

Thus, the jiva (individual soul) is not separate from Brahman; it is an expression of Brahman itself. The distinction between creator and creation, between Brahman and jiva, is notional and based on ignorance (avidya). Once this ignorance is removed through knowledge (jnana), the individual recognizes that their true nature is Brahman, just as the pot is nothing but clay.

Ishwara and creation are not distinct realities but two aspects of the same oneness. The divine presence permeates everything, within and beyond, because Brahman is the essence of all. This understanding dissolves the illusion of separation between the jiva and Brahman, leading to the realization that there is no external process of creation or entry—there is only Brahman, appearing in different forms and names.

In the Advaita Vedanta tradition, this teaching forms the basis for the realization of non-duality. The ultimate truth is that the individual soul (jiva) is Brahman, and all distinctions between creator, creation, and individual are mere illusions arising from ignorance. The Tat Twam Asi ("That Thou Art") principle emphasizes this, guiding the seeker to realize their intrinsic oneness with the infinite, formless Brahman.

When the veil of ignorance (avidya) is lifted through self-knowledge (Atma Vidya), the individual no longer perceives themselves as separate from the divine or the universe. They recognize that their essential nature is the same as Brahman, the source of all creation. This is the ultimate realization in Advaita Vedanta—that the jiva, creation, and Ishwara are one, undivided, and inseparable.

Thus, Amma's teaching of the divine presence pervading everything echoes the fundamental truth of non-duality. The divine essence resides not only within every being but also pervades the entire universe, showing that all forms, whether perceived as individual or collective, are simply manifestations of the one Brahman. This recognition leads to liberation, where the seeker understands that the Self and the Divine are one and the same, eternally whole and indivisible.

Role of Self-Knowledge

"True knowledge is not attained through external means but through direct experience of the Self. Listening, reflecting, and meditating on the truth lead to the dissolution of ignorance, allowing the light of wisdom to shine from within." Amma

The realization of Self-knowledge in Advaita Vedanta is not merely an intellectual exercise but an inward journey of direct experience. The elimination of ajnanam (ignorance) and the attainment of jnana (knowledge) require more than the study of scriptures or the guidance of teachers. While these are essential starting points, they serve primarily to direct the seeker toward a deeper realization—swaanubhava (direct experience of the Self).

Amma's teaching emphasizes that true knowledge cannot be fully acquired through external sources alone, much like hearing about the path to the Himalayas is not the same as actually embarking on the journey and experiencing the mountains firsthand. The process of knowing the Self must be inwardly realized, as intellectual understanding, while helpful, does not lead to the direct awareness of one's true nature.

In Advaita, the path to Self-knowledge begins with shravana (listening). This involves hearing the teachings of the scriptures and the Guru, which plant the seeds of understanding. However, these seeds must be nurtured. Listening alone does not eliminate the avidya (ignorance) that obscures the direct experience of the Self. It provides the seeker with the conceptual framework and inspiration for further contemplation.

Following shravana, the seeker must engage in manana (reflection), a deeper form of contemplation that helps to internalize the teachings. Manana helps the seeker clear doubts and conflicts that arise from intellectual reasoning. Through continuous reflection, the seeker moves from a theoretical understanding to a more profound, personal realization of the teachings. Yet, even at this stage, the truth remains conceptual until the seeker directly experiences it.

The final and most transformative step is nidhidhyasana (meditation), where the seeker deeply immerses in the contemplation of the Self. Here, the mind moves beyond dualistic thinking, breaking free from its habitual identification with the body, mind, and ego. This meditative absorption leads to the dissolution of ego-consciousness and the direct experience of the Self as Atma—the unchanging, eternal consciousness that is Brahman.

As Amma highlights, the dissolution of ignorance happens not through intellectual knowledge but through the inward illumination that arises during nidhidhyasana. The seeker experiences swaswarupa (one's true nature) as boundless, infinite, and non-dual. The light of wisdom that shines from within replaces all misconceptions of separateness, division, or attachment.

By transcending ego-identification, the seeker realizes that their true nature is free from the limitations of the external world and the body. In this state of realization, the understanding of non-duality (Advaita) becomes clear—there is no division between the individual self and Brahman, no separation between the experiencer and the experience.

This inner journey of shravana, manana, and nidhidhyasana unfolds progressively. The teachings from external sources serve as the guide, but the actual Self-realization happens through inward experience. Only by immersing in these stages can the seeker transcend maya (illusion) and experience the oneness of existence.

In conclusion, as Amma's quote beautifully captures, Self-knowledge is not merely about accumulating information or intellectual understanding but about direct experience. It is through listening, reflecting, and meditating that the seeker moves from the realm of conceptual understanding to the direct realization of the Self, revealing the eternal truth that has always been within.

Satyam Jñānam Anantam Brahma

"The Self is the embodiment of truth, knowledge, and infinity. When we realize this, we understand that the Divine is not separate from us but is the very essence of who we are." — Amma

The phrase «Satyam Jñānam Anantam Brahma," from the Taittiriya Upanishad (2-1-1), translates to "Truth, Knowledge, and Infinity is Brahman" and serves as a clear definition of Brahman, the ultimate reality in Advaita Vedanta. These three words—Satyam (Truth), Jñānam (Knowledge), and Anantam (Infinity)—are not merely descriptive terms but encapsulate the very essence of Brahman, pointing to its eternal, unchanging nature. Through this understanding, one can realize that Brahman is not an abstract concept but the fundamental reality that pervades all existence, including one's own Self.

The word Satyam emphasizes that Brahman is the unchanging truth that remains constant, unlike the transient, temporary nature of the material world. In the Chandogya Upanishad, for instance, it is explained that forms like a clay pot are subject to change, but the clay itself remains unchanged. The pot, though it seems real, is only a temporary manifestation, dependent on language and perception. This analogy helps clarify that Brahman is like the clay—real, unchanging, and the substratum of all forms.

Jñānam (knowledge) in this context refers to Brahman as pure consciousness or awareness. It is not intellectual knowledge but the underlying consciousness that makes all experiences and knowledge possible. This awareness is not bound by the limitations of time, space, or objects; it is the eternal, self-revealing light of consciousness that illuminates everything. Brahman is not a separate knower or an object of knowledge but the very source of knowing itself.

Anantam (infinity) signifies that Brahman is limitless and all-encompassing. It transcends all boundaries and distinctions, such as time, space, and causality. Brahman is not confined by any particular form or attribute; it is the infinite reality that pervades everything. Just as space is present within and beyond every object, Brahman is within all beings and yet beyond all distinctions.

Together, Satyam, Jñānam, and Anantam form a complete definition of Brahman. These qualities demonstrate that Brahman is the ultimate, non-dual reality that transcends the relative world of names and forms. It is the eternal truth that does not change, the pure consciousness that is the basis of all knowledge, and the infinite reality that is beyond all limitations.

Amma's quote aligns beautifully with this Upanishadic teaching. By recognizing the Self as the embodiment of Truth, Knowledge, and Infinity, one realizes that the Divine is not something external or separate from oneself. The Self is not bound by the illusions of the material world or by the ego. It is, in essence, Brahman—pure, eternal, and infinite.

This realization dissolves the false perception of duality—the belief that we are separate from the Divine or from each other. As the Chandogya Upanishad asserts, just as the pot is nothing but clay in essence, so too is the jiva (individual soul) nothing but Brahman in essence. The names and forms we perceive are fleeting and impermanent, but Brahman remains constant, the foundation of all existence.

In Advaita, liberation (moksha) is achieved when one directly experiences this truth—when the ego-driven distinctions between the self and the world dissolve, and the oneness of Brahman is realized. This realization leads to ananda (bliss) because it is the recognition of one's true, infinite nature. There is no more fear, attachment, or suffering, as all these arise from the false identification with the body, mind, and ego.

By understanding Brahman as Satyam Jñānam Anantam, we move beyond the illusions of separateness and duality. The Self is not merely a part of the Divine—it is the Divine, the very essence of all that exists. This realization, as Amma highlights, brings a profound transformation, allowing us to experience the infinite truth that has always been within us.

Through this understanding, we come to know that Brahman is the ultimate reality, and we ourselves are inseparable from it. This knowledge is not something we acquire from outside but is a direct realization of our own true nature. When this truth is fully grasped, the seeker transcends the cycle of ignorance and illusion and abides in the bliss of oneness with Brahman.

Seeing Through the Mirage

"The world we perceive is like a mirage, an illusion created by ignorance, while the true reality is the eternal Self. When the veil of ignorance is lifted, we see beyond the illusion and recognize the oneness that lies beneath all forms." Amma

In Advaita Vedanta, the core teaching is that everything other than the Atma (Self) is regarded as avidya (ignorance). This ignorance distorts our perception of reality, making the world appear as real and separate from us. However, the enlightened, or jnanis, understand this world to be like a mirage, much like a person with cataracts sees two moons. The second moon is not real but an illusion created by faulty vision. Similarly, the world of names and forms is not the ultimate reality but a projection caused by ignorance.

For those who have attained vidhya (knowledge), this illusion is seen through, and they perceive the underlying non-dual reality of Brahman. They understand that the diversity of the world is a product of the mind's projections, not a reflection of the true, unchanging Self. While the ajnani (one still in ignorance) may be trapped in this illusory perception, moments of deeper awareness occasionally allow them to transcend these limitations.

Deep concentration can offer a glimpse beyond the illusion. When the mind becomes fully absorbed in a task, such as a hunter sharpening an arrow, the awareness of the external world and even the body itself fades into the background. The hunter, engrossed in his activity, temporarily loses the perception of the world around him, akin to a meditative state. This suspension of the external world hints at the underlying reality, where the distractions of sensory objects are no longer present.

Similarly, deep sleep serves as a state where the distinctions of the waking world dissolve. Both the ajnani and the jnani experience non-perception of the world in this state. During deep sleep, the mind ceases to engage with thoughts, desires, or sensory input, and there is a natural return to peace. While the ajnani might see this as a fleeting, unconscious experience, the jnani recognizes this deep, undisturbed state as a reflection of the Atma, where there is no duality, only the non-dual Self.

Amma's quote encapsulates this insight, reminding us that the external world is an illusion born of ignorance. When the veil of avidya is lifted, the reality of oneness is revealed. The separateness that seems so real in the waking state dissolves, and the individual realizes that they are not separate from the Divine or from the world—they are the very essence of it.

In moments of non-perception, whether through deep concentration or deep sleep, we receive hints of this deeper reality. These states temporarily free us from the identification with the body, mind, and world. For the jnani, this transcendence is not an occasional experience but a continuous realization. The world no longer binds or distracts them, as they rest in the constant awareness of the Atma as the only true reality.

Thus, for the enlightened, the Self is always present, shining through the veil of illusion. The distractions of the waking world are seen for what they are—temporary, fleeting manifestations of the one true reality. The jnani abides in the understanding that the world is a projection of the mind, born of ignorance, and that the Self is the eternal, unchanging truth that remains when the illusion fades.

This knowledge allows the jnani to live in a state of fearlessness and inner peace, knowing that the essence of all beings and forms is the same, undivided Self. The perception of separateness no longer holds any sway, and they experience the bliss of non-duality, where the distinctions of the world have dissolved into the oneness of Brahman.

The Silence of the True Self

"In deep sleep, we return to a natural state of pure consciousness, untouched by the illusions of the waking world. This is a glimpse of our true Self, where there is no duality, only the peace of existence beyond ignorance."
Amma

In Advaita Vedanta, the state of deep sleep offers a profound insight into the nature of the Atma (Self). During deep sleep, one experiences a state of pure, undisturbed consciousness, where the ego, mind, and senses are completely at rest. The ajnani (ignorant individual) may not realize it, but this state of deep sleep provides a glimpse of the Self, free from the dualities and illusions of the waking and dream states. In this state, there is no awareness of the body, mind, or external objects, and thus no experience of duality.

This absence of duality in deep sleep is crucial in understanding the swarupam (true nature) of the Atma. The mind and senses, which create the distinctions of subject and object in the waking state, are silent. In this profound stillness, there is no identification with the body, thoughts, or emotions, and thus no attachments or desires. What remains is a state of pure being—an undivided consciousness that is not disturbed by the perceptions or movements of the external world.

However, for the ajnani, deep sleep is an unconscious return to the Self. It is not a fully conscious realization of the Atma. For the jnani (the enlightened one), deep sleep is recognized as a reflection of the ever-present Atma. The jnani knows that this pure state of being, experienced temporarily during deep sleep, is the same consciousness that pervades all states—waking, dream, and deep sleep. In contrast to the unconscious experience of deep sleep, the jnani abides in this state of non-duality consciously, even while awake.

In the context of deep sleep, agrahanam refers to the inability to consciously grasp one's existence. Even though there is no active perception or cognition during this state, the individual's existence cannot be denied. The Atma remains, unperceived but ever-present. This highlights the unchanging nature of the Self, which exists beyond the fluctuations of the mind and the distractions of external objects.

Sushupthi (deep sleep) is considered by many as a state that reveals the paramaardham (highest truth). In both the waking and dream states, the mind creates dualities—perceiving the world as separate from the self, experiencing desires, fears, and attachments. But in deep sleep, all these dualities dissolve, and what remains is a state of oneness, free from the ego and external perception. This state brings the individual closer to experiencing their true nature, though unconsciously.

The Atma serves as the substratum of all states of consciousness—waking, dream, and deep sleep. It is the ever-present reality that underlies all experiences. In deep sleep, while the mind and senses are inactive, the Atma remains untouched by duality. The stillness and silence of deep sleep reflect the unchanging essence of the Self, free from the movements of the mind and the illusions of the external world.

In this unconscious state, the individual is in direct contact with their essential swarupam. Although this experience is not fully realized, it reveals the Atma's nature as the ever-present foundation of all states of consciousness. The key difference between deep sleep and moksha (liberation) is that in liberation, the individual consciously abides in this state of pure, undivided being at all times, whereas in deep sleep, the experience is unconscious.

Amma's quote beautifully encapsulates this understanding. Deep sleep offers a temporary return to the Self, free from the illusions of the waking world. While in this state, the individual experiences the peace of existence beyond duality, revealing a glimpse of their true nature. This profound stillness, untouched by desires and fears, is a reminder of the Atma, the eternal Self that is always present, even when hidden by the fluctuations of the mind.

For the jnani, this state of peace and stillness is not limited to deep sleep but is realized as the constant, unchanging nature of the Self. By recognizing the Atma as the only reality, the jnani transcends the dualities of the waking and dream states, abiding in the eternal bliss of pure consciousness, where no illusions of the mind can disturb the silence of the true Self.

The Unchanging Self in Deep Sleep

"Deep sleep is not a void, but a state where we are closest to our true essence, free from the distractions of duality and ignorance. It is a reminder that our pure being exists in all states of consciousness, untouched by the world's illusions." Amma

In Advaita Vedanta, the state of deep sleep offers a profound glimpse into the true nature of the Atma (Self). Unlike the waking or dream states, where the ego and mind create dualities and distinctions, deep sleep represents a state of pure, undisturbed being, free from the influence of the senses and mind. This state of avasthuthwam (absence of things) reflects the recognition that even when all perceptions of the external world and individual identity cease, the core Self remains ever-present. Far from being a void, deep sleep is a state where the ego, desires, and dualities dissolve, leaving the individual momentarily in touch with their essential nature—Atma, which is always present but often obscured by the distractions of the waking and dream states.

In deep sleep, the ego and individual identity dissolve, offering a temporary reprieve from the ignorance (avidya) that creates the dualities experienced in the waking state. During this state, one experiences non-duality, as the distinction between subject and object disappears. It is not a state of unconsciousness, but rather a pure form of existence where the Self is untouched by external distractions. This state reflects the swarupa (true nature) of the Self, where ignorance and the illusions of the external world no longer cloud one's awareness.

A common objection arises: Is the non-perception of duality a valid experience? In deep sleep, one experiences the non-perception of duality, where there is no distinction between subject and object. This experience is real and reveals the underlying nature of the Self. It demonstrates that duality is an illusion created by the mind in the waking and dream states and that the absence of duality is the true state of existence.

Some argue that the non-perception of duality in deep sleep is like being distracted. However, this comparison is flawed. In deep sleep, there is a complete cessation of dualistic experiences, including distractions. This state is not a temporary avoidance of external awareness but a profound absorption in the Self, where duality no longer exists. The non-perception of duality in deep sleep is a direct reflection of the Atma's true nature.

The perception of duality in the waking and dream states is a result of ignorance. These states are temporary manifestations of ignorance, and the duality perceived within them is illusory. When ignorance is dispelled through self-realization, duality ceases to exist, as demonstrated by the experience of non-duality in deep sleep.

Some suggest that non-perception of duality in sleep is due to ignorance, but this is not the case. The non-perception of duality in deep sleep reflects the natural state of the Self. In deep sleep, there is no experience of duality because the mind and senses are at rest, allowing the Atma to shine without interference. This state is distinct from the waking and dream states, which are characterized by fleeting and illusory perceptions caused by ignorance.

Non-Dual Truth Revealed

"In deep sleep, the Self rests in its natural state, free from the burdens of ego and attachment. However, while it offers a glimpse of peace, it is not the ultimate realization, as it is still influenced by the underlying ignorance that veils true knowledge." Amma

In the state of deep sleep (sushupthi), the Atma (Self) rests in its natural state, untouched by the distractions of the body, mind, or the external world. In this state, the ego (aham) and the sense of ownership (mama), which characterize the waking state, completely dissolve. The Atma is freed from these layers of identity, experiencing a kind of peace that is absent in the waking and dream states, where dualities dominate.

In deep sleep, the absence of the ego allows the Atma to shine more clearly, without being clouded by the constant sense of "I" and "mine" that we cling to while awake. The mind, body, and external senses are at rest, providing a temporary suspension of the ego.

In this sense, deep sleep is a state of agrahanam, or non-perception, where all perceptions of duality disappear. The external world and even the internal sense of self are not perceived. This temporary dissolution of duality offers a reflection of the underlying oneness (ekathwam) that is the true nature of the Atma. While the experience of non-duality in deep sleep hints at the truth of the Self, it is incomplete, as it is not accompanied by the conscious realization that defines true Self-knowledge (Atma Jnana).

The Atma is nirvikara—unchanging, without modifications—whether one is in the waking state (jagrath), the dream state (swapna), or deep sleep (sushupthi). The Atma remains constant and unaffected by the changes that happen to the body and mind. In deep sleep, the absence of ego and perception allows the Atma to exist in its pure form. Still, this pure form is not consciously experienced by the individual due to the absence of instruments of knowledge (e.g. body-mind complex). This is why deep sleep is considered an indirect reflection of the Self, rather than the full, conscious realization of it.

The ultimate goal of moksha (liberation) is not to remain in a state of unconscious peace, as in deep sleep, but to consciously realize the Atma in all states of existence. This realization brings a permanent understanding that the Atma is ever-present, unchanging, and unaffected by the illusions and dualities of the waking world. In this state, the individual is freed from the cycle of birth and death, liberated from the fluctuations of ego-driven experiences, and rests in the permanent state of being that is the true nature of the Self.

Thus, while deep sleep offers a glimpse of the peace and oneness inherent in the Atma, it is not the final state of realization. True liberation occurs when one consciously abides in the knowledge of the Self, recognizing the Atma as ever-present, unchanging, and beyond the reach of ignorance.

Stillness Reveals True Self

"To discover the true nature of the Self, we must look beyond the mind and body. In the stillness of the heart, we find the divine essence that is unchanging, pure, and infinite." — Amma

In order to discover the true nature of the Self, as Amma says, we must look beyond the mind and body. The mind is filled with constant thoughts, distractions, and the illusion of duality. The body, too, is impermanent, subject to change and decay. But within the stillness of the heart lies the essence of who we are—the divine Self, which is unchanging, pure, and infinite. This realization, according to Advaita Vedanta, is the key to understanding Brahman, the ultimate reality.

Brahman is often misunderstood as an abstract, distant concept. However, the deeper understanding reveals that Brahman is not separate from us. It is the very essence of our being, the source of all existence. The Upanishads tell us, "The knower of Brahman attains the highest," pointing to the fact that Brahman can be known directly. It arises when we move beyond the limitations of the mind and body, entering the stillness where the true Self is revealed.

In that stillness, we realize that Brahman is not an external entity to be sought but is, in fact, our own deepest essence. This realization transforms our understanding of life. No longer do we identify solely with the temporary, changing aspects of existence—the body, the mind, and the external world. Instead, we come to know ourselves as the unchanging reality that pervades all things. This understanding brings a profound sense of peace and fulfillment.

Brahman, described as Satyam (truth), Jnanam (knowledge), and Anantam (infinity), is the substratum of all that exists. It is not something to be gained but something to be realized as our own true nature. The journey to understanding Brahman is a journey inward, where we come to recognize that the individual self, or Atma, is one with Brahman. This oneness is not just a philosophical concept—it is a lived experience of unity with all that is.

When we realize Brahman, we transcend the superficial distinctions of the material world. The ego, which creates the sense of separation and individual identity, dissolves in the light of this realization. What remains is the awareness of oneness with the universal Self, the recognition that the same divine presence exists in all beings. This realization leads to the highest state of spiritual awakening—moksha, or liberation.

As Amma beautifully expresses, true self-realization is not about adding something new to ourselves. It is about removing the layers of ignorance, doubts, and false identifications that obscure our true nature. When these layers are stripped away, what remains is the pure, infinite Self—Brahman, the ultimate reality. In this realization, we find a peace that is unshakable and a joy that is eternal.

Thus, the stillness of the heart becomes the gateway to the ultimate truth. It is in this stillness that the noise of the world fades, and the light of the Self shines forth, revealing the divine essence that has always been present. The realization of Brahman brings about a transformation in how we see ourselves and the world around us. It is the key to true freedom and lasting happiness.

The Infinite Nature of Reality

"The Self is beyond all limitations—untouched by the illusions of time, space, or individuality. In realizing its non-dual nature, we uncover the infinite existence that has always been and always will be." — Amma

The Self, as Amma says, is beyond all limitations. It is not bound by time, space, or individuality, but is infinite and eternal. In realizing the non-dual nature of the Self, we uncover the truth that the essence of reality has always been infinite, untouched by the fleeting illusions of the external world. This realization leads us to understand that the Self is the ultimate reality—Brahman—undivided and whole.

If the Self could be understood like an ordinary object, teachings and scriptures about the Self would be unnecessary. The very purpose of spiritual instruction is to guide individuals toward something they have not yet directly experienced. Brahman is not limited by characteristics such as being a "knower" because that would imply a restricted role. Brahman, as described in the Upanishads, is pure existence, truth, and knowledge—qualities that transcend any action or role.

The term "satya" refers to this unchanging reality—something that exists eternally, without contradiction. "Jñāna" (knowledge) emphasizes that Brahman is self-revealing awareness, and "ananta" (infinity) points to Brahman's limitless nature. These terms—truth, knowledge, and infinity—are meant to negate any opposing qualities and affirm Brahman's ultimate, limitless reality. Brahman, being the source and essence of all creation, pervades the universe while also being the innermost Self of every individual.

Just as the sun's light is inseparable from the sun, Brahman's consciousness is inseparable from its essence. This consciousness illuminates all states of mind, whether they are active or dormant, but it itself remains untouched by change. Those who confuse the changing states of mind with changes in the Self fail to recognize the true nature of Brahman's unchanging consciousness.

Brahman is omniscient—knowing all that exists—but this knowledge is not dependent on sensory perception or mental processes. Unlike human knowledge, which relies on the senses, Brahman's knowledge is inherent and independent. It is not a form of action, but an eternal state of being. Brahman knows all, not through a process of observation or interaction, but because everything is a manifestation of Brahman. There is no "other" for Brahman to know because all is one.

This omniscience of Brahman is described in the Upanishads: "The knower's function of knowing can never be lost, because It is immortal; but there is not that second thing separated from It, which It can know" (Brihadaranyaka. IV. i. 30). Brahman's knowledge is not a dynamic process but a state of being. Words like "truth" and "knowledge" are used to describe Brahman, but they only point to aspects of its nature. Brahman, in its essence, is beyond all descriptions and definitions. These terms help differentiate Brahman from the changing, impermanent world, but they do not fully encapsulate Brahman's infinite and unbounded reality.

In realizing this, we understand that the Self, or Brahman, is the ultimate reality—eternal, infinite, and unchanging. When the veil of ignorance is lifted, we see that there is no duality between the knower and the known, between the individual and the infinite. All is one, rooted in the same divine essence, and this realization reveals the limitless nature of existence that has always been within us.

Fear Arises from Duality

"Fear arises not from Ishwara but from the illusion of duality and attachment to the limited self. Through spiritual practice and the grace of Ishwara, we purify the mind and dissolve ignorance, realizing the oneness that frees us from all fear." Amma

Fear arises not from Ishwara, but from the illusion of duality and the attachment to the limited self (jiva). Amma's teaching reveals that it is the perception of separateness from Ishwara and the world that creates vulnerability and fear. When the jiva sees itself as distinct and subject to external forces, insecurity and fear of loss, death, and suffering naturally follow. However, when one realizes that the jiva and Ishwara are not separate but are expressions of the same non-dual reality, the root of fear dissolves.

Through spiritual practice (sadhana) and the purification of the mind (chitta sudhi), one can transcend this illusion of duality. Practices like meditation, self-inquiry, and devotion help calm the mind and reduce egoic attachments. The purification of the mind is essential to eliminate ignorance (avidya), which is the fundamental cause of fear. Ishwara plays a vital role as the bestower of grace, aiding in this purification process. With Ishwara's grace, the mind gains clarity, enabling one to see the truth of the Self and Ishwara as one.

This understanding of non-duality (Advaita) leads to the recognition that there is no "other" to fear. The oneness with Ishwara brings about abhaya (fearlessness) and inner peace. Thus, Ishwara is not the cause of fear but the means to freedom from it. By dedicating oneself to spiritual practice and receiving the grace of Ishwara, one dissolves ignorance and attains fearlessness.

To attain the knowledge of Advaita, one must go through the processes of shravanam (listening to Vedantic teachings) and mananam (reflecting on those teachings). Shravanam involves hearing the teachings of scriptures that explain the nature of the Self, such as the mahavakyas like "Tat Twam Asi" ("You are That"), which reveal the oneness of the individual soul with Brahman. Under the guidance of a realized teacher, this process helps the aspirant intellectually grasp the non-dual nature of reality.

Mananam, or contemplation, follows shravanam and is essential for removing any doubts or misunderstandings. It allows the seeker to internalize the teachings, moving beyond the superficial world of forms to grasp the underlying oneness of all existence. Through shravanam and mananam, the aspirant gains clear knowledge of their true nature as Atma, which is one with Brahman. This knowledge eliminates avidya, revealing samsara as an illusion created by the mind.

While spiritual practices such as meditation, devotion, and ethical living may not directly lead to liberation without tatwa bodham, they play an important role in preparing the mind. These practices develop one's yogyatha (eligibility) by purifying the mind, reducing desires, and creating mental clarity needed for the reception of jnana (knowledge).

Meditation (dhyana) helps calm the mind and develop focus. Devotion (bhakti) fosters surrender and reduces the ego. Selfless service (karma yoga) transcends personal desires, and ethical living (dharma) aligns one's actions with higher values, purifying the mind. Together, these practices pave the way for the seeker to gain the knowledge that leads to liberation and the realization of non-duality.

Liberation in Timeless Awareness

"The scriptures reveal that the enlightened soul rests in the direct knowledge of the Self, free from ignorance, while the unenlightened remains bound by illusion. True liberation comes when the light of wisdom dispels the darkness of ignorance, making the distinction clear." — Amma

The distinction between enlightened and unenlightened souls is clearly established through various scriptural references, especially from the Upanishads. These texts highlight differences in their states of consciousness, attitudes toward worldly actions, and obligations.

The Brihadaranyaka Upanishad states, "Where everything becomes his Self" (Br. II. iv. 14), describing the state of the enlightened soul. For such individuals, the empirical world of duality, which includes actions, auxiliaries, and fruits (results of actions), is no longer relevant. The enlightened soul has realized the non-dual nature of reality, where everything is recognized as one with the Self. In this state, there is detachment from worldly pursuits and no identification with the fruits of action. This indicates the spiritual freedom of the enlightened, who are no longer bound by conventional duties or desires.

In contrast, the same Upanishad mentions, "Where there is an appearance of duality" (Br. IV. iv. 14), which refers to the unenlightened soul. Such individuals are trapped in the worldly state of duality, perceiving a distinction between self and other, subject and object. This leads to attachment to worldly objects, desires, and experiences, as the unenlightened soul is unable to perceive the oneness of all existence. The unenlightened are bound by the cycle of action and results, constantly seeking pleasures and avoiding pain, and are entangled in karma.

The Upanishads also address the idea that the attainment of absolute knowledge occurs within the context of the worldly state. The text suggests that the pursuit of knowledge of Brahman (the all-pervasive Reality) leads to immortality. However, this process first involves navigating the world of duality, where the soul interacts with the experiences of hunger, desire, and material attachments. This means that even though enlightenment is the ultimate goal, it arises from the empirical experiences and through the journey of the unenlightened state.

For the unenlightened individual, certain obligations, referred to as the three debts (debts to the gods, ancestors, and sages), act as impediments to higher spiritual progress. This reflects the traditional obligations the unenlightened must fulfill to progress spiritually.

On the other hand, for the enlightened individual who has realized the Self and Brahman, these debts are no longer relevant. The Upanishad states, "What shall we achieve through children" (Br. IV. iv. 22), indicating that for the enlightened, worldly concerns such as children and progeny are unnecessary.

Through Amma's teachings and these scriptural references, the difference between enlightened and unenlightened souls becomes clear. The unenlightened remain bound by duality, attachment, and worldly duties, while the enlightened transcend these limitations, resting in the infinite, unchanging reality of the Self.

Beyond Bondage and Liberation

"Bondage and liberation both arise within the illusion of ignorance, but the true Self remains ever-free, beyond duality. Through self-knowledge, we dissolve distinctions and realize the oneness that underlies all existence, untouched by the world's illusions." Amma

Both bondage and liberation arise within the framework of ignorance, as Amma points out. These experiences are tied to the misidentification with the body, mind, and ego. The deeper truth is that Paramatma, the Supreme Self, is ever-free, unchanging, and eternal. The world as we perceive it, through the lens of ignorance (avidya), is illusory—neither fully real nor completely non-existent. It can be compared to the perception of a second moon caused by an eye condition—a perceptual error. The world, though appearing real, is a projection of ignorance, and upon deeper inquiry, is understood as not being the ultimate reality.

Ajnanam, or ignorance, refers to the lack of knowledge of one's true nature as the Atma, which is eternal (nithya), pure (suddha), and ever-enlightened (Buddha). This ignorance leads to the false identification of the Self with the transient body, mind, and external objects. Such identification creates the perception of duality, which drives samsara—the cycle of birth, death, and suffering. Swaswarupa Jnanam, the knowledge of one's true Self, negates this ignorance and removes the false identification, helping one recognize the Atma as the pure, unchanging reality.

Atma Vidhya, or Self-knowledge, serves as the tool to dispel ignorance and dissolve the distinctions created by avidya. It reveals that all perceived divisions are simply illusions created by the mind. Through Atma Vidhya, the seeker realizes the Atma as beyond all limitations, recognizing that the dualities and multiplicities seen in the world are merely projections of ignorance.

However, as profound as Atma Vidhya is, it is not the ultimate goal (paramaardham). It is a means to an end, a process that clears away the illusions created by ignorance. But the knowledge itself is not the final state. The ultimate realization transcends even the need for knowledge, as the seeker directly experiences the Atma as one with Brahman, free from all distinctions, dualities, and even the concept of knowledge itself. This state is one of absolute unity, where the limitations of ignorance and knowledge dissolve into the boundless, non-dual Self.

In this highest state, the notions of bondage and liberation are revealed to be part of the same illusion. Both are constructs that exist only in the realm of ignorance, and once ignorance is dispelled, one realizes that the Atma was never bound nor in need of liberation. The true Self remains untouched by the world's illusions, ever-free, beyond all concepts of duality, bondage, or liberation.

Bliss

"Bliss and the Atma are not separate; they are one and the same. True bliss arises from the realization of oneness, where there is no duality—only the exclusive, infinite joy of the Self." Amma

Bliss and the Atma are intrinsically one, as Amma expresses, with true bliss arising from the realization of oneness, beyond all dualities. However, Anandam (bliss) as we experience it is often a reflection of virtuous actions or meditation practices (upasana) and should not be mistaken for the ultimate reality, which is Paramatma. Anandam is intuitively felt and does not generally cause doubts or uncertainties, but it remains a conditioned state, tied to external or internal factors.

The Anandamaya Kosha, one of the five sheaths (pancha koshas) that encase the Atma, represents this experience of bliss. While it is a sheath that covers the Self, it is not the Self itself. It is a reflection of the joy one feels due to accumulated punya (merit) from virtuous deeds and spiritual practices, but this bliss is still bound within the realm of conditioning and limitation. In this state, bliss is experienced, but it is still a layer that needs to be transcended in the pursuit of realizing the true nature of the Atma.

The Anandamaya Kosha is a modification (vikara) of Anandam and, while significant, does not represent the eternal, unchanging reality of Brahman. The bliss experienced in this kosha is temporary and conditional, based on merits and spiritual efforts. The ultimate goal, however, is to transcend all the koshas and realize the Atma, which exists beyond any such limitations or layers.

Atma, being the true substratum of all experiences, must be understood as distinct from Anandamaya Kosha. While bliss may be felt through this sheath, the Atma itself remains unaffected by these layers. Just as gold is the underlying reality of an ornament, the Atma is the unchanging essence, while Anandam remains an experience tied to external or internal conditions. The true realization comes when one goes beyond the experience of Anandamaya Kosha and understands the Atma as the only constant reality, unconditioned and free from limitations.

The koshas, particularly Anandamaya Kosha, are limiting adjuncts that shape the experience of Anandam. When an individual experiences joy or sorrow, it is the mind's engagement with these layers that determines the nature of the experience. The mind, influenced by thoughts and beliefs, creates transient experiences of joy or sorrow, but these are impermanent and not reflective of the pure, eternal Atma.

The practice of tapas, encompassing spiritual disciplines such as sathwika nishta (steadfast purity), brahmacharya (celibacy), and shraddha (faith), plays a vital role in purifying the inner instrument (anthakarna), including the mind and intellect. By purifying these faculties, tapas helps to reduce the influences of rajas (restlessness) and tamas (ignorance), allowing for anthakarna suddhi (purity of the inner self). As this purification deepens, the experience of Anandam becomes more aligned with vigjnanam (discriminative knowledge), enabling one to move beyond the fleeting joy and sorrow that arise from external stimuli.

Tapas, though challenging at times, brings about profound rewards in the form of phala purnatha (complete fulfillment of results). The experience of Anandam, when gained through the purification of the self, is lasting and more deeply rooted in one's essence, as opposed to the temporary pleasures derived from external events. This purified bliss, grounded in self-knowledge, leads to a deeper and more stable experience of joy.

In conclusion, while Anandam can be experienced through the koshas, the Atma is the true, unchanging source of bliss. True bliss, as Amma emphasizes, arises from the realization of oneness, where there is no separation between the experiencer and the experience—only the infinite joy of the Self.

Eclipse of Ignorance Fades Forever

"Ignorance is like a veil that clouds perception, but once the light of Self-knowledge dawns, the illusion dissolves completely. For the enlightened, ignorance can no longer return, just as clear vision is restored after a disease is cured." Amma

The profound distinction between the enlightened (jnani) and the unenlightened (ajnani) souls is central to Advaita Vedanta philosophy. This contrast is rooted in the transformative power of Brahmajnana (knowledge of Brahman) and the complete eradication of avidya (ignorance). Scriptural evidence and Vedantic teachings highlight how ignorance dissolves under the light of Self-knowledge, making its return impossible, much like Amma's statement of ignorance fading away forever.

Scriptures such as the Katha Upanishad (I. ii. 4) assert the inherent contradiction between knowledge (vidya) and ignorance (avidya). These two cannot coexist, just as contradictory qualities like heat and cold cannot be present in the same fire. This understanding aligns with Amma's analogy of clear vision being restored after the disease of ignorance is cured. Once the jnani realizes the truth, ignorance dissolves completely, and the illusion of duality vanishes forever.

The Kaivalya Upanishad emphasizes that immortality is not attained through karma, progeny, or wealth, but through renunciation. This renunciation reflects the shedding of attachments and the pursuit of Brahmajnana, much like the enlightened soul in Amma's teachings, whose vision is no longer clouded by worldly desires or misconceptions. The Svetāśvatara Upanishad further validates that those who transcend worldly duties are positioned to attain the supreme Reality.

The Chandogya Upanishad's declaration "Tat Tvam Asi" (Thou art That) underscores the non-dual nature of reality. This statement mirrors Amma's teaching on the dissolution of ignorance, as it reflects the jnani's realization of unity with Brahman. The separation caused by ignorance is erased, and the individual self merges with the universal.

The Upanishads often use analogies to explain the nature of knowledge and the Self. The Brihadaranyaka Upanishad compares the removal of ignorance to a fire that cannot hold both heat and cold, reinforcing the idea that once Self-knowledge is attained, ignorance cannot return. This metaphor aligns perfectly with Amma's analogy of cured vision after a disease, illustrating the permanence of enlightenment.

The Brihadaranyaka Upanishad highlights that knowledge leads to the realization of one's identity with Brahman, dissolving ignorance completely. This ties in with Amma's teaching that Self-knowledge is the ultimate remedy for ignorance. Once this realization occurs, the jnani is freed from the cycle of birth and death, achieving a state of permanent liberation.

The enlightened soul, as described in the Smriti texts, no longer fears death or worldly suffering. Amma's statement echoes this truth, as the dissolution of ignorance brings with it a complete eradication of fear. The jnani, fully immersed in the knowledge of their divine nature, remains unaffected by the trials of the world.

The realization of Brahman marks the final dissolution of ignorance. The Taittiriya Upanishad teaches that once the distinction between vidya and avidya is transcended, the jnani no longer oscillates between knowledge and ignorance. Through these scriptural references and Amma's profound analogy, we see how Brahmajnana brings an end to ignorance and leads to the permanent state of liberation, where the jnani lives in peace, free from the illusions of duality and fear.

Nowhere to Go, Everything Is That

"The ultimate goal is not to escape the world, but to transform our understanding of it. When we see all beings as one, the distinctions between knowledge and karma dissolve, and we enter the realm of non-duality." Amma

Amma's teaching emphasizes a profound realization: the ultimate goal of spiritual life is not to reject or escape the world, but to transform how we perceive it. This transformation arises from the understanding that all beings, actions, and experiences are united as expressions of the same underlying reality, Brahman. In this state of non-duality, the illusion of separation dissolves, and we come to see that everything is interconnected and one.

When we realize this oneness, the conventional distinctions between knowledge (jnana) and action (karma) begin to fade. In a dualistic mindset, knowledge and action appear to be separate, with knowledge representing contemplation and understanding, and karma representing engagement with the world. However, in the state of non-dual awareness, as Amma points out, these distinctions vanish. Every action is an expression of knowledge, and every moment of knowledge carries with it the essence of action.

The state of non-duality is a realization that all things—thoughts, actions, and experiences—are manifestations of the same universal Self (Atman). Liberation (moksha), therefore, is not about withdrawing from the world or abandoning one's duties. Amma's teachings remind us that the world is not something to escape from but to see clearly with new eyes.

In this state of clarity, the illusory barriers between self and others dissolve. No longer does one see themselves as separate from the rest of creation. Instead, they come to recognize that their true Self is the same Self that pervades all beings. It is this insight that allows for a deeper connection with the world and the realization that everything is a reflection of Brahman, the ultimate reality.

When distinctions such as those between the knower and the known, the doer and the deed, and action and inaction disappear, one transcends dualistic thinking. This transcendence leads to a state of freedom, not from the world, but within it. As Amma highlights, true freedom is the freedom from ignorance, fear, and desire, which are born of the illusion of separation. In the light of non-dual knowledge, one realizes that these forces no longer hold sway over them.

In this liberated state, an individual still exists in the world, continues to act, and engages in daily life. However, their perspective is fundamentally transformed. No longer bound by the cycles of karma, they see each action as part of a larger, divine whole. Even though they perform actions, they do so with the understanding that all is Brahman, and thus, they are no longer entangled by the results of those actions.

Amma's teaching encourages us to understand that liberation is not an otherworldly state achieved by withdrawing from life. Rather, it is a state of mind and heart where one sees the divine in all aspects of life. Every experience becomes an opportunity to witness the play of Brahman, and in this witnessing, one remains free from the attachments and desires that cause suffering.

In this state of non-dual awareness, even the play of the world—its challenges, joys, and sorrows—is seen as an expression of the divine. The individual recognizes that the world itself is not an obstacle to liberation but a means to realize it. The play of life is Brahman's manifestation, and through this realization, one can engage with the world while remaining free from its binding effects.

The Self is the essence of all existence, the unchanging reality that underlies the ever-shifting experiences of life. It is the source from which everything arises and to which everything returns. Recognizing the Self means understanding that we are not separate from the world or bound by the cycles of life. Instead, we realize that we are free—even as we live and engage in the activities of the world. This awareness liberates us from identifying with the fluctuations of life and allows us to rest in the essence of who we truly are.

This realization is not about escaping responsibilities or withdrawing from the world. Life continues, but the shift in perspective means that we are no longer driven by the illusion that we must achieve or acquire something to be whole. We live our daily lives, perform our duties, and even seek new experiences, but all from a place of rootedness in the Self. This change allows us to move through life without being attached to its outcomes.

Rooted in Self-awareness, we are no longer swayed by life's ups and downs. The repetitive nature of daily activities no longer feels tedious, and new experiences lose their compulsive allure. Instead, we engage fully with life, but with a detachment that gives us inner freedom. This detachment is not indifference but a form of freedom that comes from acting without attachment to results. We live in the world, but we are not weighed down by its constant demands and fluctuations.

In this state of Self-awareness, we see through the mirages of external experiences and relationships. We realize that while these are a part of life, they do not define our sense of self or happiness. Anchored in the deeper truth of our being, we understand that true contentment is found within, not in external achievements or possessions. This realization frees us from the endless cycle of striving for something outside ourselves and helps us see the unchanging reality of the Self.

At last, the shift from doing to being blossoms into peace and freedom. Life continues, yet it is lived with the quiet knowing that fulfillment has never been outside, but within. Amma reminds us that liberation is not a distant promise, but the very essence of this moment, here and now. In Self-realization we awaken to the truth that the Self has never been bound, that bondage was but a shadow cast by ignorance. With this recognition, fears and doubts fade like mist before the sun, leaving only the stillness of timeless awareness. Resting as Brahman, we abide in the unity of love and peace, as Amma gently guides us into the infinite embrace of our own true nature.

www.ingramcontent.com/pod-product-compliance
Ingram Content Group UK Ltd.
Pitfield, Milton Keynes, MK11 3LW, UK
UKHW041348190726
13845UKWH00026B/498

9 789363 782464